An INTRODUCTION TO CREATIVITY

*An anthology for college courses on creativity
which provides historical and current thinking
from interdisciplinary perspectives.*

Senior Editors

MICHAEL JOYCE, Professor, Department of Dramatic Arts and Dance,
Mary Washington College

SCOTT ISAKSEN, Professor, Center for Studies in Creativity,
Buffalo State College

Editors

FRED DAVIDSON, Professor, Department of Business Administration,
Mary Washington College

GERARD PUCCIO, Assistant Professor, Center for Studies in Creativity,
Buffalo State College

CAROL COPPAGE, Director, Dow Creativity Center,
Northwood University

Copley Publishing Group
Acton, Massachusetts 01720

Second Printing 1995

ISBN 0-87411-756-9

Cover design by Joyce Kemp

Acknowledgments:

pp. 4–17: From *American Psychologist*, Vol. 5, 1950 : 444-454. Copyright © 1950 by The American Psychological Association. Reprinted with permission.
pp. 18–25: From *Phi Delta Kappan*, Vol. 42, 1961. Copyright © 1961 by Phi Delta Kappan. Reprinted with permission.
pp. 26– 33: Copyright © 1991 by Stephan A. Schwartz. Reprinted with permission.
pp. 34–48: Reprinted from *Creative Approaches to Problem Solving* by Isaksen, Dorval and Treffinger, copyright © 1994 by Kendall/Hunt Publishing Company. Reprinted by permission of Kendall/Hunt Publishing Company.
pp. 49–56: "Why Study Creativity?" by Gerard J. Puccio. The first version of this article appeared in *Creativity & Innovation Yearbook*, Vol. 2, 1989, edited by Tudor Rickards and Susan Moger, published by Manchester Business School. Reprinted with permission.
pp. 60–63: "The Roots of Inspiration" by Neil McAleer, adapted from *Omni*, II (7) 1989, pp. 44-102. Copyright © 1989 by Neil McAleer, reprinted with the permission of General Media Publishing Group.
pp. 64–70: Reprinted from *Business Horizons*, 9 (1) 1986. Copyright © 1986 by the Foundation for the School of Business at Indiana University. Used with permission.
pp. 71–75: From *Brandeis Review*, 5 (1) 1985. Copyright © 1985 by Brandeis Review. Used with permission.
pp. 76–81: Reprinted from *Business Horizons*, 28 (5) 1985. Copyright © 1985 by the Foundation for the School of Business at Indiana University. Used with permission.
pp. 82–88: From *In Search of Human Effectiveness* by D. W. MacKinnon. Copyright © 1978 by the Creative Education Foundation and Bearly, Ltd. Used with permission.
pp. 91–97: From *The Journal of Creative Behavior*, 17 (2) 1983. Copyright © 1983 by The Creative Education Foundation. Used with permission.
pp. 98–104: From *The Journal of Educational Thought*, 21 (1) 1987. Copyright © 1987 by the Journal of Educational Thought. Reprinted with permission of the publisher and the author.
pp. 105–113: Chapter 6 from *The Creative College Student*, edited by Paul Heist. Copyright © 1968 by Jossey-Bass, Inc. Reprinted by permission of the publisher.
pp. 114–124: From *Problem Finding, Problem Solving and Creativity*, edited by Marc A. Runco, copyright © 1994. Reprinted with permission from Ablex Publishing Corporation.
pp. 125–134: From *The Journal of Creative Behavior*, 18 (3) 1984. Copyright © 1984 by The Creative Education Foundation. Used with permission.
pp. 137–145: From *GCT Magazine*, 7 (2), Issue 32, March/April 1984. Copyright © 1984 by GCT Inc. Used with permission.
pp. 146–148: From *In Search of Human Effectiveness* by D. W. MacKinnon. Copyright © 1978 by the Creative Education Foundation and Bearly, Ltd. Used with permission.
pp. 149–152: From *Management Review*, May 1990, copyright © 1990 by Barbara Block.

DEDICATIONS

Scott's: To Marves, Kristin, and Erik. To all those who share a serious interest in understanding and developing human creativity.

Gerard's: To Kristin, my creative spirit. To all students of creativity, may you reach your creative potential.

Carol's: To my iron John for his inspiration and support.

Michael's: To Courtney for her love and strength. To Bill for his guidance and energy.

Fred's: To Kiva, my creative partner.

CONTENTS

ACKNOWLEDGMENTS

We express our gratitude to our colleagues: Donald Treffinger, Sue Keller-Mathers, Mary Murdock, Brian Dorval, Roger Firestien, and William Kemp for their helpful feedback on the articles selected for inclusion in this book of readings.

Also, we wish to acknowledge the tremendous support Ken Lauer provided to this project by conducting literature searches, Debi Johnson through her adept handling of material, Susan Coppage and Patsy Conliffe for their research and typing, and Pat Ladd at Copley for her guidance, patience, and good humor.

INTRODUCTION
READ ME FIRST

This book has been primarily designed for students in an introductory course in creative studies. However, you may read it in a psychology class, an education class, or an arts class.

The format is straightforward. It begins with a general discussion on the definition of creativity and then follows with sections on the creative person, process, product, and press (environment, situation). There is no suggested order for assigning or reading the text. That is best decided by the instructor and the students.

This book will not make you more creative. This book is about ideas and research, not about process. It will acquaint you with the discipline of creative studies. Hopefully, it will ignite your interest in creativity and you will continue your study in both process and research.

Finally, the editors hope that you enjoy the readings and find them valuable. If you have any suggestions for the next edition of the book, please write to us.

SECTION ONE
WHAT IS CREATIVITY?

What is creativity? There are so many related words and ideas including: invention, innovation, creative thinking, intuition, insight, originality, and the list goes on. Some see creativity as a special talent reserved for great scientists or artists. Others argue that creativity belongs to every one of us.

Consider each of the following:

An inspired thought

An insight from a dream

A truly impressive musical or theatrical performance

An important scientific discovery

A breakthrough new product

A famous work of art

Inventions which provide a whole new lens on the world

A significant poem, sonnet, play or other masterpiece in literature

The renaissance or Elizabethan era

A new way of seeing or understanding an old problem or challenge

Generating many, varied and unusual ideas

Finding new ways to transform ideas into action

Are all these creative? Are you interested in what actually makes them creative? Could you be curious about how they came into being? Or are you more concerned with understanding the people who were responsible for them? Are some times or places more or less creative than others? Are all the great creative geniuses equally creative? Do they all create the same way? Can people learn to use more of their own creativity? All of these questions support the importance of having a definition of creativity that works for you.

The purpose of this section is to provide some insight into how creativity has been defined. Various approaches to understanding creativity will be presented through a series of readings. The variety of facets to this important area of human inquiry and application will be presented and summarized.

J.P. Guilford's article entitled "Creativity" is one of the most important contributions in the field of creativity and innovation. His presidential address before the American Psychological Association in 1950 is credited for boosting serious interest in work in this field. It is included in this section to provide a rich historical perspective on work done in this emerging field.

Only a decade or so after Guilford's address, well over a hundred different definitions were in the creativity literature. Mel Rhodes set out to analyze some of these and ended up developing four major strands of the creative person, the creative process, the creative product and the creative press (situation or place). These four strands provide the framework for this book of

1

readings. His piece is titled "An Analysis of Creativity" and provides a description and summary of the four strands of creativity definitions.

Schwartz's chapter deals with the relationship between "Creativity, Intuition and Innovation." He provides a summary of the five major components to the pattern of creative breakthroughs. Stephan Schwartz locates work on creativity, intuition and innovation within the broad area of the human potential movement and describes some of the critical reaction to this approach.

Creativity has been studied through a variety of approaches. In Scott Isaksen's chapter, you are given a comprehensive update from Rhode's earlier work on the four "P's" of creativity. He starts with some basic misconceptions, lays out some productive assumptions and then shares some current work from the perspective of each of the four major categories of work (person, process, product and press).

Gerard Puccio's chapter entitled "Why Study Creativity?" provides some general reasons for the importance and significance of understanding creativity. The twelve points Puccio points out are examples of the motivational force which has driven researchers to investigate creativity. (SI)

Of Additional Interest

Anderson, H.H. (Ed.). (1959). *Creativity and its cultivation.* New York: Harper.

Austin, J.A. (1978). *Chase, chance, & creativity: The lucky art of novelty.* New York: Columbia University Press. Balliner Publishing Company.

Coleman, D., Kaufman, P., & Ray, M. (1992). *The creative spirit.* New York, Penguin Books.

Colemont, P., Grøholt, P. T., & Smeekes, H. (Eds.). (1988). *Creativity and innovation: Towards a European network.* Dordrecht, Netherlands: Kluwer Academic Publishers.

Dacey, J. S. (1989). *Fundamentals of creative thinking.* Lexington, MA: Lexington Books.

Davis, G. A. (1991). *Creativity is forever (third edition).* Dubuque, IA: Kendall/Hunt.

de Bono, E. (1992). *Serious creativity: Using the power of lateral thinking to create new ideas.* New York: Harper Collins Publishers, Inc.

Drucker, P. F. (1985). *Innovation and entrepreneurship: Practice and principles.* New York: Harper & Row.

Fritz, R. (1991). *Creating.* New York: Fawcett Columbine.

Gamache, R. D., & Kuhn, R. L. (1989). *The creativity infusion: How managers can start and sustain creativity and innovation.* New York: Harper & Row Publishers.

Glover, J., Ronning, R. R., & Reynolds, C. R. (Eds.). (1989). *Handbook of creativity.* New York: Plenum Press.

Gowan, J. C., Khatena, J., & Torrance, E. P. (1981). *Creativity: Its educational implications.* Dubuque, IA: Kendall/Hunt Publishing Company.

Grøhaug, K., & Kaufmann, G. (Eds.). (1988). *Innovation: A cross disciplinary perspective.* London: Oxford University Press.

Gryskiewicz, S. S., & Hills, D. A. (1992). *Readings in innovation.* Greensboro, NC: Center for Creative Leadership.

Henry, J., & Walker, D. (Eds.). (1991). *Managing innovation.* Newbury Park: SAGE Publications.

Ijiri, Y., & Kuhn, R. L. (Eds.). (1988). *New Directions in creative and innovative management.* New York: McGraw-Hill.

Isaksen, S. G. (Ed.). (1987). *Frontiers in creativity research: Beyond the basics.* Buffalo, NY: Bearly Limited.

Isaksen, S. G., Murdock, M.C., Firestien, R. L., & Treffinger, D. J. (Eds.). (1993). *Nurturing and developing creativity: The emergence of a discipline.* Norwood, NJ: Ablex.

Isaksen, S. G., Murdock, M. C., Firestien, R. L., & Treffinger, D. J. (Eds.). (1993). *Understanding and recognizing creativity: The emergence of a discipline.* Norwood, NJ: Ablex.

Koestler, A. (1969). *The act of creation.* New York: MacMillan.

Parnes, S. J. (Ed.). (1992). *A Sourcebook for creative problem solving: A fifty year digest.* Buffalo, NY: Creative Education Foundation.

Ray, M., & Myers, R. (1986). *Creativity in business.* Garden City, NY: Doubleday.

Runco, M. A., & Albert, R. S. (Eds.). (1990). *Theories of creativity.* Newbury Park: Sage Publications.

Sternberg, R. J. (Ed.). (1988). *The nature of creativity: Contemporary psychological perspectives.* New York: Cambridge University Press.

Taylor, C. W., & Barron, F. (Eds.). (1963). *Scientific creativity. Its recognition and development.* New York: Wiley.

Torrance, E. P., & Myers, R. E. (1970). *Creative learning and teaching.* New York: Harper & Row.

CREATIVITY[1]

J. P. Guilford

I discuss the subject of creativity with considerable hesitation, for it represents an area in which psychologists generally, whether they be angels or not, have feared to tread. It has been one of my long-standing ambitions, however, to undertake an investigation of creativity. Circumstances have just recently made possible the realization of that ambition.[2] But the work has been started only within the past year. Consequently, if you are expecting answers based upon new empirical research you will be disappointed. What I can do at this time is to describe the plans for that research and to report the results of considerable thinking, including the hypotheses at which my students and I have arrived after a survey of the field and its problems. The research design, although not essentially new, should be of some interest. I will also point out some implications of the problems of creativity in vocational and educational practices.

Some Definitions and Questions

In its narrow sense, creativity refers to the abilities that are most characteristic of creative people. Creative abilities determine whether the individual has the power to exhibit creative behavior to a noteworthy degree. Whether or not the individual who has the requisite abilities will actually produce results of a creative nature will depend upon his motivational and temperamental traits. To the psychologist, the problem is as broad as the qualities that contribute significantly to creative productivity. In other words, the psychologist's problem is that of creative personality.

In defining personality, as well as other concepts preparatory to an investigation, definitions of an operational type are much to be preferred. I have often defined an individual's personality as his unique pattern of traits. A trait is any relatively enduring way in which persons differ from one another. The psychologist is particularly interested in those traits that are manifested in performance; in other words, in behavior traits. Behavior traits come under the broad categories of aptitudes, interests, attitudes, and temperamental qualities. By aptitude we ordinarily mean a person's readiness to learn to do certain types of things. There is no necessary implication in this statement as to the source of the degree of readiness. It could be brought about through hereditary determination or through environmental determination; usually, if not always, by an interaction of the two. By interest we usually mean the person's inclination or urge to engage in some type of activity. By attitude we mean his tendency to favor or not to favor (as shown objectively by approach-withdrawal behavior) some type of object or situation. Temperamental qualities describe a person's general emotional disposition: for example, his optimism, his moodiness, his self-confidence, or his nervousness.

Creative personality is then a matter of those patterns of traits that are characteristic of creative persons. A creative pattern is manifest in creative behavior, which includes such activities as inventing, designing, contriving, composing, and planning. People who exhibit these types of behavior to a marked degree are recognized as being creative.

There are certain aspects of creative genius that have aroused questions in the minds of those who have reflected much about the matter. Why is creative productivity a relatively infrequent phenomenon? Of all the people who have lived in historical times, it has been estimated that only about two in a million have become really distinguished. Why do so many geniuses spring from parents who are themselves very far from distinguished? Where is there so little apparent correlation between education and creative productiveness? Why do we not produce a larger number of creative geniuses than we do, under supposedly enlightened, modern educational practices? These are serious questions for thought and investigation. The more immediate and more explorable problem is a double one: (1) How can we discover creative promise in our children and our youth? and (2) How can we promote the development of creative personalities?

Neglect of the Study of Creativity

The neglect of this subject by psychologists is appalling. The evidences of neglect are so obvious that I need not give proof. But the extent of the neglect I had not realized until recently. To obtain a more tangible idea of the situation, I examined the index of the *Psychological Abstracts* for each year since its origin. Of approximately 121,000 titles listed in the past 23 years, only 186 were indexed as definitely bearing on the subject of creativity. The topics under which such references are listed include creativity, imagination, originality, thinking, and tests in these areas. In other words, less than two-tenths of one per cent of the books and articles indexed in the *Abstracts* for approximately the past quarter century bear directly on this subject. Few of these advance our understanding or control of creative activity very much. Of the large number of textbooks on general psychology, only two have devoted separate chapters to the subject during the same period.

Hutchinson, reviewing the publications on the process of creative thinking to the year 1931, concluded that the subject had hardly been touched by anyone. Markey, reviewing the subject of imagination four years later, reported very little more in the way of a fundamental contribution to the subject.

Some of you will undoubtedly feel that the subject of creative genius has not been as badly neglected as I have indicated, because of the common belief that genius is largely a matter of intelligence and the IQ. Certainly, that subject has not been neglected. But, for reasons which will be developed later, I believe that creativity and creative productivity extend well beyond the domain of intelligence.

Another important reason for the neglect, of course, is the difficulty of the problems themselves. A practical criterion of creativity is difficult to establish because creative acts of an unquestioned order of excellence are extremely rare. In this respect, the situation is much like that of a criterion of accident proneness which calls for the actual occurrence of accidents. The accidental nature of many discoveries and inventions is well recognized. This is partly due to the inequality of stimulus or opportunity, which is largely a function of the environment rather than of individuals. But if environmental occasions were equal, there would still be great differences in creative productivity among individuals.

There are, however, greater possibilities of observing individual differences in creative performance if we revise our standards, accepting examples of lower degrees of distinction. Such instances are more numerous. But even if we can detect and accept as creative certain acts of lower degrees of excellence, there are other difficulties. Creative people differ considerably in

5

performance from time to time. Some writers on the subject even speak of rhythms of creativity. This means that any criterion, and probably any tests of creativity as well, would show considerable error variance due to function fluctuation. Reliabilities of tests of creative abilities and of creative criteria will probably be generally low. There are ways of meeting such difficulties, however. We should not permit them to force us to keep foot outside the domain.

Another reason for the oversight of problems of creativity is a methodological one. Tests designed to measure intelligence have fallen into certain stereotyped patterns, under the demands for objectivity and for scoring convenience. I do not now see how *some* of the creative abilities, at least, can be measured by means of anything but completion tests of some kind. To provide the creator with the finished product, as in a multiple-choice item, may prevent him from showing precisely what we want him to show: his own creation. I am not opposed to the use of the multiple-choice or other objectively scorable types of test items in their proper places. What I am saying is that the quest for easily objectifiable testing and scoring has directed us away from the attempt to measure some of the most precious qualities of individuals and hence to ignore those qualities.

Still another reason for the neglect of the problems of creativity is to be found in certain emphases we have given to the investigations of learning. For one thing, much learning research has been done with lower animals in which signs of creativity are almost nonexistent. For another thing, learning theory has been generally formulated to cover those phenomena that are easiest to order in logical schema. Learning theorists have had considerable difficulty with the behavior known as insight, to which creative behavior shows much apparent relationship. It is proper to say that a creative act is an instance of learning, for it represents a change in behavior that is due to stimulation and/or response. A comprehensive learning theory must take into account both insight and creative activity.

The Social Importance of Creativity

There is general recognition, on the part of those outside the academic fold, at least, of the importance of the quest for knowledge about creative disposition. I can cite recent evidences of the general interest in discovery and development of creative talent. Large industries that employ many research scientists and engineers have held serious meetings and have had symposia written about the subject. There is much questioning into the reasons why graduates from the same institutions of higher learning, with high scholastic records and with strong recommendations, differ so widely in output of new ideas. The enormous economic value of new ideas is generally recognized. One scientist or engineer discovers a new principle or develops a new process that revolutionizes an industry, while dozens of others merely do a passable job on the routine tasks assigned to them.

Various branches of the government, as you all know, are now among the largest employers of scientific and technical personnel. These employers, also, are asking how to recognize the individuals who have inventive potentialities. The most common complaint I have heard concerning our college graduates in these positions is that while they can do assigned tasks with a show of mastery of the techniques they have learned, they are much too helpless when called upon to solve a problem where new paths are demanded.

Both industry and governmental agencies are also looking for leaders. Men of good judgment, planning ability, and inspiring vision are in great demand. How can leaders with imagination and vision be discovered? Can such qualities be developed? If those qualities can be promoted by educational procedures, what are those procedures?

We hear much these days about the remarkable new thinking machines. We are told that these machines can be made to take over much of men's thinking and that the routine thinking of many industries will eventually be done without the employment of human brains. We are told that this will entail an industrial revolution that will pale into insignificance the first industrial revolution. The first one made man's muscles relatively useless; the second one is expected to make man's brain also relatively useless. There are several implications in these possibilities that bear upon the importance of creative thinking. In the first place, it would be necessary to develop an economic order in which sufficient employment and wage earning would still be available. This would require creative thinking of an unusual order and speed. In the second place, eventually about the only economic value of brains left would be in the creative thinking of which they are capable. Presumably, there would still be need for human brains to operate the machines and to invent better ones.

Some General Theories of the Nature of Creativity

It is probably only a layman's idea that the creative person is peculiarly gifted with a certain quality that ordinary people do not have. This conception can be dismissed by psychologists, very likely by common consent. The general psychological conviction seems to be that all individuals possess to some degree all abilities, except for the occurrence of pathologies. Creative acts can therefore be expected, no matter how feeble or how infrequent, of almost all individuals. The important consideration here is the concept of continuity. Whatever the nature of creative talent may be, those persons who are recognized as creative merely have more of what all of us have. It is this principle of continuity that makes possible the investigation of creativity in people who are not necessarily distinguished.

The conception that creativity is bound up with intelligence has many followers among psychologists. Creative acts are expected from those of high IQ and not expected from those of low IQ. The term "genius," which was developed to describe people who distinguish themselves because of creative productivity, has been adopted to describe the child with exceptionally high IQ. Many regard this as unfortunate, but the custom seems to have prevailed.

There is much evidence of substantial, positive correlations between IQ as measured by an intelligence test and certain creative talents, but the extent of the correlations is unknown. The work of Terman and his associates is the best source of evidence of these correlations; and yet, this evidence is not decisive. Although it was found that distinguished men of history generally had high estimated IQ's, it is not certain that indicators in the form of creative behavior have not entered into those estimations. It would be much more crucial to know what the same individuals would have done on intelligence tests when they were children. Terman's study of the thousand children of exceptionally high IQ's who have now reached maturity does not throw much light on this theory. Among the group there is plenty of indication of superior educational attainment and of superior vocational and social adjustment. On the other hand, there seems to be as yet little promise of a Darwin, an Edison, or a Eugene O'Neill, although the members of the group have reached the age level that has come to be recognized as the "most creative years." The writers on that study recognize this fact and account for it on the basis of the extreme rarity of individuals of the caliber of those whom I have mentioned. It is hoped that further follow-up studies will give due attention to criteria of a more specifically creative character.

When we look into the nature of intelligence tests, we encounter many doubts concerning their coverage of creative abilities. It should be remembered that from the time of Binet to the present, the chief practical criterion used in the validation of tests of intellect has been achievement in school. For children, this has meant largely achievement in reading and arithmetic. This fact has generally determined the nature of our intelligence tests. Operationally, then, intelligence has been the ability (or complex of abilities) to master reading and arithmetic and similar subjects. These subjects are not conspicuously demanding of creative talent.

Examination of the content of intelligence tests reveals very little that is of an obviously creative nature. Binet did include a few items of this character in his scale because he regarded creative imagination as one of the important higher mental functions that should be included. Revisions of the Binet scale have retained such items, but they represent only a small minority. Group tests of intelligence have generally omitted such items entirely.

The third general theory about creativity is, in fact, a theory of the entire personality, *including* intelligence. I have defined personality as a unique pattern of traits, and traits as a matter of individual differences. There are thousands of observable traits. The scientific urge for rational order and for economy in the description of persons directs us to look for a small number of descriptive categories. In describing mental abilities, this economy drive has been grossly overdone when we limit ourselves to the single concept of intelligence. Furthermore, the term "intelligence" has by no means achieved logical or operational invariance and so does not satisfy the demand for rational order.

We do not need the thousands of descriptive terms because they are much interrelated, both positively and negatively. By intercorrelation procedures it is possible to determine the threads of consistency that run throughout the categories describing abilities, interests, and temperament variables. I am, of course, referring to the factorial conception of personality. From this point of view, personality is conceived geometrically as a hypersphere of n dimensions, each dimension being a dependable, convenient reference variable or concept. If the idea of applying this type of description to a living, breathing individual is distasteful, remember that this geometric picture is merely a conceptual model designed to encompass the multitude of observable facts, and to do it in a rational, communicable, and economical manner.

With this frame of reference, many of the findings and issues become clarified. The reason that different intelligence tests do not intercorrelate perfectly, even when errors of measurement have been taken into account, is that each test emphasizes a different pattern of primary abilities. If the correlations between intelligence-test scores and many types of creative performance are only moderate or low, and I predict that such correlations will be found, it is because the primary abilities represented in those tests are not all important for creative behavior. It is also because some of the primary abilities important for creative behavior are not represented in the test at all. It is probably safe to say that the typical intelligence test measures to a significant degree not more than a half-dozen of the intellectual factors. There are surely more intellectual factors than that. Some of the abilities contributing to creative success are probably non-intellectual; for example, some of them are perceptual. Probably, some of the factors must crucial to creative performance have not yet been discovered in any type of test. In other words, we must look well beyond the boundaries of the IQ if we are to fathom the domain of creativity.

Development of Creativity

Before referring to the experimental design and to more specific hypotheses concerning the nature of creativity, I will venture one or two opinions on the general problem of the development of creativity. For I believe that much can be done to encourage its development. This development might be in the nature of actual strengthening of the functions involved or it might mean the better utilization of what resources the individual possesses, or both. In any case, a knowledge of the functions is important.

We frequently hear the charge that under present-day mass-education methods, the development of creative personality is seriously discouraged. The child is under pressure to conform for the sake of economy and for the sake of satisfying prescribed standards. We are told by the philosophers who have given thought to the problem that the unfolding of a creative personality is a highly individual matter which stresses uniqueness and shuns conformity. Actually, the unfolding of the individual along the lines of his own inclinations is generally frowned upon. We are told, also, that the emphasis upon the memorizing of facts sets the wrong kind of goal for the student. How serious these charges are no one actually knows. We have very little experimental evidence that is decisive one way or the other and such evidence is hard to obtain.

Charles Kettering one time commented upon a survey in which it was found that a person with engineering or scientific training had only half the probability of making an invention compared with others. His comment was that an inventor should be defined as "a fellow who doesn't take his education too seriously." If the results of that survey represent the actual situation, either creative individuals do not seek higher education in engineering and science, or that kind of education has negative transfer effects with respect to inventiveness.

Many of us teachers assert that it is our main objective to teach students how to think, and this means also to think constructively. Certainly, if we succeeded in this objective, there should be much evidence of creativeness in the end product. I am convinced that we do teach some students to think, but I sometimes marvel that we do as well as we do. In the first place, we have only vague ideas as to the nature of thinking. We have little actual knowledge of what specific steps should be taken in order to teach students to think. Our methods are shotgun methods, just as our intelligence tests have been shotgun tests. It is time that we discarded shotguns in favor of rifles.

We all know teachers who pride themselves on teaching students to think and yet who give examinations that are almost entirely a matter of knowledge of facts. Please do not misunderstand me. I have a strong appreciation of knowledge of facts. No creative person can get along without previous experiences or facts; he never creates in a vacuum or with a vacuum. There is a definite place for the learning of facts in our educational system. But let us keep our educational objectives straight. Let us recognize where facts are important and where they are not. Let us remember, too, that the kinds of examinations we give really set the objectives for the students, no matter what objectives we may have stated.

The confusion of objectives is illustrated by the following incident. The story was told by a former dean of a leading Midwestern University. An old, experienced teacher and scholar said that he tried to encourage originality in his students. In a graduate course, he told the class that the term paper would be graded in terms of the amount of originality shown. One school teacher in the class was especially concerned about getting a high mark in the course. She took verbatim notes, continuously and assiduously, of what the learned professor said in class. Her term paper, the story goes, was essentially a stringing together of her transcribed lecture notes, in which the professor's pet ideas were given prominent place. It is reported that the professor read the term papers himself. When the school teacher's paper was returned, the professor's mark was an A, with the added comment, "This is one of the most original papers I have ever read."

Before we make substantial improvement in teaching students to think, in my opinion we will have to make some changes in our conceptions of the process of learning. The ancient faculty psychology taught that mental faculties grow strong by virtue of the exercise of those faculties. We all know from the many experiments on practice in memorizing that exercises in memorizing are not necessarily followed by improvement of memory in general. We all know that exercises in perceptual discriminations of certain kinds are not followed by improvement of perceptual discriminations in general. Thorndike and others concluded that the study of courses in high-school curricula did not necessarily result in a general improvement in intellect, but that the increases in test scores could be attributed to learning of a more specific nature. Following this series of experiments the conclusion has often been that learning consists of the development of specific habits and that only very similar skills will be affected favorably by the learning process.

In view of the newer findings concerning primary abilities, the problems of formal discipline take on new meaning, and many of the experiments on the transfer of training will have to be reexamined and perhaps repeated with revised conditions. The experiments just cited do justify the rejection of the concepts of a general memory power, a general perceptual-discrimination power, and perhaps, also, rejection of the concept of a single power called intellect. These findings are in harmony with factorial theory. But the other alternative to the idea of formal discipline is not necessarily a theory of specific learning from specific practice.

There is certainly enough evidence of transfer effects. Experiments should be aimed to determine whether the instances of positive, zero, and negative transfer effects conform in a meaningful way to the outlines of the primary abilities. The work of Thorndike and others that I have just cited does, in fact, actually throw some light on this question. Although this aspect of their findings is usually not mentioned, they reported that high-school students' experiences in numerical, verbal, and spatial types of courses—arithmetic and bookkeeping, Latin and French, and manual training—were associated with relatively greater gains in numerical, verbal, and spatial types of tests, respectively.

A general theory to be seriously tested is that some primary abilities can be improved with practice of various kinds and that positive transfer effects will be evident in tasks depending upon those abilities. At the present time some experiments of this type are going on in the Chicago schools under the direction of Thelma Gwinn Thurstone. In one sense, these investigations have returned to the idea of formal discipline. The new aspect of the disciplinary approach is that the presumed functions that are being "exercised" have been indicated by empirical research.

Factorial Research Design

The general outline of the design for a factor-analysis investigation is familiar to many of you. It has been described before but needs to be emphasized again. The complete design involves a number of steps, not all of which are essential but all of which are highly desirable if the investigator is to make the most efficient use of his time and to achieve results of maximum value. The major steps will be mentioned first, then more details concerning some of them.

One first chooses the domain of his investigation. It may be the domain of memory abilities, visual-perceptual abilities, reasoning abilities, or the domain of introversion-extraversion.

One next sets up hypotheses as to the factors he expects to find in that domain. His preparatory task of hypothesis formation goes further. It includes the framing of several alternative hypotheses as to the more precise nature of each factor. This is necessary as the basis for transforming each factor hypothesis into the operational terms of test ideas. He then constructs tests which he thinks will measure individual differences in the kind of ability, or other quality, he thinks the factor to be. He will want to include in the test battery some reference tests that measure already known factors. One reason for this is that the new tests will almost inevitably also measure to some extent factors that have previously been established, such as verbal comprehension, number facility, and visualization. If such variance is probably going to appear in more than one new test in the battery, it is best to have that variance clearly brought out and readily identifiable. Another reason is that it is possible, after all, that one or more of the hypothesized factors will turn out to be identifiable with one or more of the known factors. The possibility of this identification must be provided for by having the suspected, known factors represented in the battery.

The test battery is administered to a sample of adequate size from a population of appropriate qualifications. Certain kinds of populations are better for bringing out variances in some common factors and other kinds are more suitable for other purposes. There should be relative homogeneity in certain features that might be correlated with the factors, such as sex, age, education, and other conditions. Some thought should be given to whether tests should be speed tests or power tests or something between the two. Some consideration should also be given to the most appropriate type of score for each test.

Factors are extracted and their reference axes are rotated into positions that are compelling because of the nature of the configuration of test vectors in the hyperspace. The psychological nature of each factor is surmised by virtue of the kinds of tests that have substantial variance attributable to that factor in contrast to tests which lack that variance.

In many respects, the complete factor-analysis design has properties parallel to those of a good experiment. In both, we begin with hypotheses. In both, some conditions are held constant while other are varied. In both, the measured outcomes point toward or away from the hypotheses. One important difference is the possibility of a statistical test of significance of the measured result for the experiment but not for the factor analysis. Confidence in the latter case depends upon the compellingness of the factor structure and the repeated verification of a result.

As an illustration of this analogy to an experiment, I will cite the factorial study of the well-known figure-analogies test. In the Army Air Forces research results, the figure-analogies test exhibited variances in three factors denoted as reasoning I, II, and III. They were thus designated because they were peculiar to a number of reasoning tests, but their more precise natures were obscure. Examination of what one does in solving a figure-analogies item suggests several possible psychological functions or activities. First, one has to grasp correctly the relation between figure one and figure two. This suggests an ability to see a relationship between two objects. Second, one must observe the properties of the third figure. Then, one has to see what kind of a fourth figure it takes to satisfy the same relationship between figure three and figure four. Having decided upon the kind of figure needed, one has to find it among four or five that are supplied in the multiple-choice item. This is a kind of classifying act. There is still another possibility. The mislead responses may be so reasonable that considerable discrimination may be needed to select the best figure for the purpose. Considering the figure-analogies item from a more holistic point of view, there may be a primary ability involved in seeing that there is an identity of two relationships when the elements related are different. Or there may be a general reasoning-by-analogy ability. Transposability of relations may be a key function here. Thus, we have several hypotheses as to the functions involved. There could be others. For every one of them we also have the further question as to whether the ability implied is restricted to the visual perception of figures or whether it is more general, extending to work meanings, numbers, and sounds. And if it is general, what are its limits?

To seek answers by factorial methods, one would construct special tests, each limited, if possible, to one kind of act implied by each hypothesis. One would also vary the kind of material in each type of test to explore the scope of generality. The answers to the hypotheses (for each hypothesis is in reality a question) would be to find that the loading for each factor would rise with some of the variations and fall with others as compared to its loading in the traditional figure-analogies test. We would hope to find the changes in factor loadings so marked that we would not feel seriously the lack of t tests or F tests.

The question of the sources of factor hypotheses calls for some comment. In a domain in which there have already been factorial studies, the previous results are always suggestive. This makes it appear that the factorist merely moves from hypotheses to hypotheses. This is quite true. It is a fundamental truth of all scientists, no matter what their methods. Some hypotheses are merely better supported and more generally accepted than others at the time. There is enough uncertainty left in many a hypothesis to invite further investigation. That is what makes science interesting. That is what I think Kettering meant when he stated that the inventor is one who does not take his education (or knowledge) too seriously.

In a personality domain in which there has been little previous illumination of the underlying variables, other sources of hypotheses must be sought. The critical-incident technique of Flanagan would be one useful exploratory approach. Incidentally, one might say that this method has been used informally in connection with creative people from the "Eureka" episode of Archimedes down to modern times. The literature includes many descriptions of creative events. It would be more correct to refer to these historical reports as anecdotes, however, rather than critical incidents, since they suffer from most of the weaknesses of anecdotes. Where modern writers have attempted to interpret them psychologically, the interpretations have been quite superficial. They abound with vague concepts such as "genius," "intuition," "imagination," "reflection," and "inspiration," none of which leads univocally to test ideas. In the writings of those who have attempted to give a generalized picture of creative behavior, there is considerable agreement that the complete creative act involves four important steps.

According to this picture, the creator begins with a period of preparation, devoted to an inspection of his problem and a collection of information or material. There follows a period of incubation during which there seems to be little progress in the direction of fulfillment. But, we are told, there *is* activity, only it is mostly unconscious. There eventually comes the big moment of inspiration, with a final, or semi-final, solution, often accompanied by strong emotion. There usually follows a period of evaluation or verification, in which the creator tests the solution or examines the product for its fitness or value. Little or much "touching up" may be done to the product.

Such an analysis is very superficial from the psychological point of view. It is more dramatic than it is suggestive of testable hypotheses. It tells us almost nothing about the mental operations that actually occur. The concepts do not lead directly to test ideas. In attempting to distinguish between persons with different degrees of creative talent, shall we say, for example, that some individuals are better incubators than others? And how would one go about testing for incubating ability? The belief that the process of incubation is carried on in a region of the mind called the unconscious is of no help. It merely chases the problem out of sight and thereby the chaser feels excused from the necessity of continuing the chase further.

It is not incubation itself that we find of great interest. It is the nature of the processes that occur during the latent period of incubation, as well as before it and after it. It is individual differences in the efficiency of those processes that will be found important for identifying the potentially creative. The nature of those processes or functions will have to be inferred from performances of the individuals who have been presented with problems, even though the creator is largely unaware of them.

Specific Hypotheses Concerning Creative Abilities

The hypotheses that follow concerning the nature of creative thinking have been derived with certain types of creative people in mind: the scientist and the technologist, including the inventor. The consensus of the philosophers seems to have been that creativity is the same wherever you find it. To this idea I do not subscribe. Within the factorial frame of reference there is much room for different types of creative abilities. What it takes to make the inventor, the writer, the artist, and the composer creative may have some factors in common, but there is much room for variation of pattern of abilities. Some of the hypotheses mentioned here may apply also to areas of creative endeavor other than science, technology, and invention, but others may not. Included in the list of primary abilities that may contribute to creative efforts of these special groups are the reasoning factors, but I shall restrict mention here to other possible thinking factors that are more obviously creative in character.

First, there are probably individual differences in a variable that may be called *sensitivity to problems*. How this variation among individuals may come about will not concern us at this time. Whether it is best regarded as an ability or as a temperament trait will not concern us, either. The fact remains that in a certain situation one person will see that several problems exist while another will be oblivious to them.

Two scientists look over a research report. There are generally acceptable conclusions, but there is one minor discrepancy in the results. One scientist attributes the discrepancy to "experimental error." The other feels uneasy about the discrepancy; it piques his curiosity; it challenges him for an explanation. His further thinking about the matter develops into a new research project from which highly important findings result. Such an incident was reported by Flanagan; it could be found duplicated many times.

There are questions as to the generality of such a variable. Is the supposed sensitivity restricted to a certain kind of situation or problem? Is it a perceptual quality as well as a thought quality? Could it be a general impressionability to the environment? Is it our old friend "curiosity" under a new name? Is it an ability to ask questions? Is it a general inhibition against closure?

There may be other hypotheses just as pertinent. Each one suggests possible tests of individual differences.

Examples of possible tests follow. One might present the examinee with a short paragraph of expository material and instruct him to ask as many questions as he can that are suggested by the statements, with relatively liberal time allowed. A large part of the scientist's success depends upon his ability to ask questions, and, of course, to ask the right questions. In another test, one might name common household appliances, such as a toaster, or articles of clothing, such as trousers, and ask the examinee to list things that he thinks are wrong or could be improved. As a perceptual test, one might present pictures of objects or forms that are conventional and regular except for minor irregularities. Can the examinee detect the unusual features or will he overlook them? A third possibility is in the form of what we have called a "frustration test," merely because it is somewhat frustrating to many who have tried it. Contrary to the usual test practice, no task instruction is given: only items, and the very general instruction "do something with each item; whatever you think should be done." Each item is of a different type. One or two examinees have refused to do anything with the test.

There is very likely a *fluency* factor, or there are a number of fluency factors, in creative talent. Not that all creators must work under pressure of time and must produce rapidly or not at all. It is rather that the person who is capable of producing a large number of ideas per unit of time, other things being equal, has a greater chance of having significant ideas. There have been previous results yielding several verbal-fluency factors but I have insufficient time to acknowledge those studies properly here. It is probable that there are a number of fluency factors, nonverbal as well as verbal, yet undiscovered. There is a general problem to be investigated, apart from creativity, whether many of the primary thinking abilities have both a power and a speed aspect somewhat independent of each other. Some work of Davidson and Carroll suggests this in a result with regard to one of the reasoning factors.

One kind of fluency test would consist of asking the examinee to name as many objects as he can in a given time, the objects having some specified property; for example, things round, things red, or things to eat. In another test, the ideas might be more complex, as in naming a list of appropriate titles for a picture or for a short story. Still more demanding and also more restricting would be the task of naming exceptions to a given statement. Fluency of inferences may be tested by providing a hypothetical statement to which the examinee is to state as many consequences or implications as he can in a limited time. The statement might be: A new invention makes it unnecessary for people to eat; what will the consequences be? This type of test has been previously proposed by several investigators.

The creative person has *novel* ideas. The degree of novelty of which the person is capable, or which he habitually exhibits, is pertinent to our study. This can be tested in terms of the frequency of uncommon, yet acceptable, responses to items. The tendency to give remote verbal associations in a word-association test; to give remote similarities in a similies test; and to give connotative synonyms for words, are examples of indications of novelty of ideas in the category of verbal tests.

The individual's *flexibility* of mind, the ease with which he changes set, can possibly be indicated in several ways by means of tests. Although there have been disappointments in an attempt to establish a common factor of this type, the concept of flexibility and of its probable opposite, rigidity, will not be downed. In conjunction with some of the fluency tests, there may

14

be opportunities to obtain some indications concerning flexibility. Does the examinee tend to stay in a rut or does he branch out readily into new channels of thought? Tests whose items cannot be correctly answered by adhering to old methods but require new approaches, in opposition to old habits of thinking, would be pertinent here. Certain types of puzzles fit this requirement fairly well, for example, a problem in which the examinee cannot succeed without folding the paper on which he writes, and the idea of doing so must come from him.

Much creative thinking requires the organizing of ideas into larger, more inclusive patterns. For this reason, we have hypothesized a *synthesizing ability.* As a counterpart to this, one might well expect an *analyzing ability.* Symbolic structures must often be broken down before new ones can be built. It is desirable to explore many kinds of both synthesizing and analyzing activities, in both perceptual and conceptual problems, in order to determine the existence of such factors and their numbers and whether they cut across both perceptual and conceptual areas.

From Gestalt psychology comes the idea that there may be a factor involving *reorganization* or *redefinition* of organized wholes. Many inventions have been in the nature of a transformation of an existing object into one of different design, function, or use. It may be that this activity involves a combination of flexibility, analysis and synthesis, and that no additional hypothesis of redefinition is really needed, but the possibility must be investigated.

There is a possibility of a dimension of ability that has to do with the degree of *complexity* or of intricacy of conceptual structure of which the individual is capable. How many interrelated ideas can the person manipulate at the same time? The scientist must often keep in mind several variables, conditions, or relationships as he thinks out a problem. Some individuals become confused readily; they can keep only one or two items of structure delineated and properly related. Others have a higher resistance to confusion—a greater span of this type. Such an ability might be identifiable with the hypothesized synthesizing factor, but the study should make possible a separation of the two if the distinction is real.

Creative work that is to be realistic or accepted must be done under some degree of evaluative restraint. Too much restraint, of course, is fatal to the birth of new ideas. The selection of surviving ideas, however, requires some *evaluation.* In this direction there must be a factor or two. The evaluations are conceivably of different kinds, consequently the kinds of possible tests are numerous. In a paragraph of exposition, we may ask the examinee to say whether every underlined statement is best classified as a fact, a definition, or a hypothesis. He will, to be sure, need some preliminary instruction in these distinctions. In another test, we can present him with a stated problem, then ask him which of several items are relevant to its solution and which ones are not. In still another test, we can give a problem and several alternative solutions, all correct. The examinee is to rank the solution in the order of degree of excellence or fitness.

The hypotheses mentioned, as we stated earlier, refer more specifically to a limited domain of creative thinking more characteristic of the scientist and technologist. Even so, this entails a factorial study of substantial proportions. Similar studies will need to be made in the domains of planning abilities, in order to anticipate abilities more characteristic of the economic, the political, and the military leader. Still other restricted domains will need to be investigated to take care of the writer, the graphic artist, and the musical composer.

The question will inevitably arise, "How do you know your tests are valid?" There are two answers to this question. The first is that the factorial study of the tests is in itself one kind of validation. It will determine which tests measure each factor and to what extent. That is a matter of internal validity or factorial validity. It answers the question, "What does the test measure?" The second answer will be in terms of which factors are related to the creative productivity of people in everyday life. That calls for the correlation of the factor measures with practical criteria. I feel very strongly that only after we have determined the promising factors and how to measure them are we justified in taking up the time of creative people with tests. If a certain factor we discover turns out not to be related to creative production, we have made a bad guess, but we will have discovered a new factor that may have some other practical validity. If a certain factor is not related to the criteria of creative productivity, the tests which measure it uniquely will also prove to be invalid for predicting these criteria. It is better to fail in the validation of a single factor measure than to fail in the validation of a half-dozen tests. If we make a study of the practical validity of every creative test we can think of before it is analyzed, we are bound to exert considerable wasted effort of our own and of our examinees. This statement, incidentally, applies to the validation study of any test.

Creative productivity in everyday life is undoubtedly dependent upon primary traits other than abilities. Motivational factors (interests and attitudes) as well as temperament factors must be significant contributors. Hypotheses concerning these factors in connection with creative people might be fruitful starting points for factorial investigations. The design of the research would be much the same as that described for creative abilities.

Summary and Conclusions

By way of summary, it can be said that psychologists have seriously neglected the study of the creative aspects of personality. On the other hand, the social importance of the subject is very great. Many believe that creative talent is to be accounted for in terms of high intelligence or IQ. This conception is not only inadequate but has been largely responsible for the lack of progress in the understanding of creative people.

The factorial conception of personality leads to a new way of thinking about creativity and creative productivity. According to this point of view, creativity represents patterns of primary abilities, patterns which can vary with different spheres of creative activity. Each primary ability is a variable along which individuals differ in a continuous manner. Consequently, the nature of these abilities can be studied in people who are not necessarily distinguished for creative reasons. Productivity depends upon other primary traits, including interests, attitudes, and temperamental variables.

It is proposed that a fruitful exploratory approach to the domain of creativity is through a complete application of factor analysis, which would begin with carefully constructed hypotheses concerning the primary abilities and their properties. It is suggested that certain kinds of factors will be found, including sensitivity to problems, ideational fluency, flexibility of set, ideational novelty, synthesizing ability, analyzing ability, reorganizing or redefining ability, span of ideational structure, and evaluating ability. Each of these hypotheses may be found to refer to more than one factor. Some hypothesized abilities may prove to be identical with others, or accounted for in terms of others. At any rate, these hypotheses lead to the construction of tests of quite novel types, which is a promising condition for the discovery of new factors. The relation of such factors to practical criteria of creative performance will need to be established. It is likely that the tests have been aimed in the right direction.

Once the factors have been established as describing the domain of creativity, we have a basis for the means of selecting the individuals with creative potentialities. We also should know enough about the properties of the primary abilities to do something in the way of education to improve them and to increase their utilization. These ends certainly justify our best efforts.

Notes

[1] Address of the President of the American Psychological Association at Pennsylvania State College, September 5, 1950.

[2] A research project on the aptitudes of high-level personnel, supported by the Office of Naval Research.

References

1. Broyler, C. R., Thorndike, E. L., and Woodyard, E. A second study of mental discipline in high schools. *J. educ. Psychol.,* 1927, 18, 377-404.

2. Cox, C. M. *Genetic studies of genius,* Vol. II. Stanford, California: Stanford University Press, 1926.

3. Davidson, W. M., and Carroll, J. B. Speed and level components in time-limit scores. *Educ. & psychol. Meas.,* 1945, 5, 411-435.

4. Flanagan, J. C., et al. *Critical requirements for research personnel.* Pittsburgh: American Institute for Research, 1949.

5. Giddings, F. H. *Elements of sociology.* New York: Macmillan Co., 1907.

6. Guilford, J. P. (Ed.) *Printed classification tests,* Army Air Forces Aviation Psychology Research Program, Report No. 5. Washington, D.C.: Government Printing Office, 1947.

7. Hutchinson, E. D. Materials for the study of creative thinking. *Psychol. Bull.,* 1931, 28, 392-410.

8. Jones, L. V. A factor analysis of the Stanford-Binet at four age levels. *Psychom.,* 1949, 14, 299-331.

9. Kettering, C. F. How can we develop inventors? In a symposium on *Creative engineering.* New York: American Society of Mechanical Engineers, 1944.

10. Markey. F. V. Imagination. *Psychol. Bull.,* 1935, 32, 212-236.

11. Terman, L. M., and Oden, M. H. *The gifted child grows up.* Stanford, California: Stanford University Press, 1947.

12. Thorndike, E. L. Mental discipline in high school studies. *J. educ. Psychol.,* 1924, 15, 1-22, 83-98.

13. Thorndike, E. L., and Woodworth, R. S. The influence of improvement in one mental function upon the efficiency of other functions. *Psychol. Rev.,* 1901, 8, 247-261, 384-395, 553-564.

14. Thurstone, L. L. Implications of factor analysis. *Amer. Psychologist,* 1948, 3, 402-408.

15. Wertheimer, M. *Productive thinking.* New York: Harper & Bros., 1945.

Received July 17, 1950

AN ANALYSIS OF CREATIVITY

Mel Rhodes

The problems of modern life cry out for creative solutions. Hence the growing interest in creativity. But what is it? Can it be taught? Mr. Rhodes takes some of the fuzz off the concept of creativity and assures us that it can indeed be developed in children.

Just as I finished writing the first draft of this paper I had an irrepressible urge to start over. I knew suddenly that I could reorganize and rewrite my material for greater clarity. Then I thought to myself, isn't this experience an example of the creative process? Isn't creativity, in simple language, the process of reorganizing knowledge (general or specific knowledge), and of articulating that synthesis so that other people can understand the meaning. Also, I thought, haven't I in this instance visualized the key to the secret nature of creativity? That secret being that original ideas are the by-products of (1) a human mind grasping the elements of a subject, (2) of prolonged thinking about the parts and their relationships to each other and to the whole, and (3) of sustained effort in working over the synthesis so that it can be embodied or articulated competently.

The United States Supreme Court has ruled in numerous cases that an invention is an idea rather than an object. If a man can prove that an idea was his by demonstrating or providing evidence that only he had the knowledge from which it was synthesized, he can claim patent to the invention. Collaborators who might have helped to embody the idea into object, provided it can be proved that they lacked the basic knowledge components in the idea—even though they do all of the crafting—are classified as technicians or craftsmen.

Likewise with art. Art was defined, after lengthy trials in the highest courts of our land, as concept rather than object. The shipping charges for a piece of metal are based on weight. But in the now-famous court trial of 1927, Romanian-born Constantin Brancusi made art history when he contested the decision of United States customs officials concerning the proper charges for a curving brass column which he labeled *Bird in Space*. The customs officials contended the object was metal. Brancusi contended it was art. When sculptor Jacob Epstein was asked if a good mechanic could not polish up a brass rail and pass it off as art, he replied, "He can polish it up, but he cannot conceive of the object. That is the whole point." The court agreed. Its decision: "Objects which portray abstract ideas (in this case, "flight"), rather than imitate natural objects, may be classified as art."

My answer to the question, "What is creativity?", is this: The word creativity is a noun naming the phenomenon in which a person communicates a new concept (which is the product). Mental activity (or mental process) is implicit in the definition, and of course no one could conceive of a person living or operating in a vacuum, so the term *press* is also implicit. The definition begs the questions as to how new the concept must be and to whom it must be new.

Surge of Interest in Creativity

The big push of interest in the subject of creativity began in 1950 when J. P. Guilford of the University of Southern California was president of the American Psychological Association.

Guilford said in his presidential address to that organization that he found an appalling lack of research on creativity. He said he had searched *Psychological Abstracts* for a quarter of a century and found that only 186 out of 121,000 entries dealt in any way with creativity, imagination, or any topic closely related.

In the years since 1950 more than a dozen books have appeared on the subject, and I have approximately 300 reference cards to articles and monographs. The research undertaken since Guilford gave his speech has yielded results of basic significance to the field of education and to the archives of knowledge. These studies have rendered into baloney many former sacred cows. For instance, the idea that the IQ is a lump sum and that it is constant, the idea that "well-adjusted children" (often meaning conformers) will become the most useful citizens, the idea that people are born to be either creative or lacking in creative ability, the notion that creativity is more a way of feeling than a way of thinking, the idea that creativity is something mysterious, and the notion that the word creativity applies to a simple, uncomplicated mental process that operates in unrestraint.

It is now clear that, instead, intellect is complex, that divergent thinkers and people of complex temperament have more original ideas than conformers and people of placid temperament, that environmental factors at all times in life form a psychological press that may be either constructive or destructive to creativity, that the technique of getting ideas can be learned and can be taught. It is also clear that whatsoever factors of personality or of intellect, of learning process or thinking process, or of environment are congruent with creativity, the same are congruent also with the educative process in general.

It would be difficult to describe the scope of the contributions to knowledge and to the field of education rendered during the last ten years by scholars on the trail of creativity. This is why I was perturbed when I read in the October, 1960, issue of *Harper's* magazine what Jacques Barzun, provost and dean of faculties at Columbia University, had written about "The Cults of 'Research' and 'Creativity'." Here is a quotation from the article:

> What "creative" means in common usage is hardly clear—it seems to correspond to the idea of fullness, to the completion of effort, a synthesis of parts, while it also conveys, like "research," the notion of something new and unexpectedly good. . . . Use of the word creativity is a device by which we give ourselves easy satisfactions while avoiding necessary judgments. That the faculty of judgment is at stake can be shown from a simple enumeration:
>
> —Creative may mean the neglect of technical competence—witness a great deal of so-called new writing, new painting, and new art generally.
>
> —Creative may falsely dignify certain ordinary virtues—quickness of mind, sense of order and relevance and skill in using words—all of which can be subsumed under intelligence and intellectual training.
>
> —Creative may suggest modern, fresh, or unshackled by convention or tradition. In that sense it can be used to justify waste of time, as when students analyze contemporary writers and attribute to them as innovations literary devices that are found in Homer and Virgil.
>
> —Creative may also stand for a conscious or unconscious denial of the tremendous range of human ability. If a child in kindergarten is called creative for the finger-painting he produces, the distance between him and Rembrandt has somehow been short-

ened. Through a likening of potential and actual, a kind of democratic equality has been restored.

. . . If small talents are creative, then since everyone has them, everyone has a Leonardo-like mind.

I understand what Barzun is saying. Indeed, the words creative and creativity have been loosely used and overused. In many examples "creative" means or implies nothing more than emotional freedom, relaxing of tensions, disinhibition, or freedom from censorship. Examples of such usage occur in expressions like "creative dancing" (when the activity referred to is shimmying), "creative art" (when the activity referred to is finger-painting), and "creative writing" (when the activity is "kitsch"—i.e., stories that follow a formula and are essentially the same, even though slightly different in details, as in pulp magazine trash).

What is happening here is that a word which should be reserved to name a complex, multifaceted phenomenon is misused to name only one part of a phenomenon. It is like explaining a hurricane by describing wind or explaining a bird's flight by describing its perchings. But creativity cannot be explained alone in terms of the emotional component of the process or in terms of any other single component, no matter how vital that component may be.

About five years ago I set out to find a definition of the word creativity. I was interested also in imagination, originality, and ingenuity. In time I had collected forty definitions of creativity and sixteen of imagination. The profusion was enough to give one the impression that creativity is a province for pseudo-intellectuals.

But as I inspected my collection I observed that the definitions are not mutually exclusive. They overlap and intertwine. When analyzed, as through a prism, the content of the definitions form four strands. Each strand has unique identity academically, but only in unity do the four strands operate functionally. It is this very fact of synthesis that causes fog in talk about creativity and this may be the basis for the semblance of a "cult."

One of these strands pertains essentially to the person as a human being. Another strand pertains to the mental processes that are operative in creating ideas. A third strand pertains to the influence of the ecological press on the person and upon his mental processes. And the fourth strand pertains to ideas. Ideas are usually expressed in the form of either language or craft and this is what we call product. Hereafter, I shall refer to these strands as the four P's of creativity, i.e., (1) person, (2) process, (3) press, (4) products.

Persons

The term *person*, as used here, covers information about personality, intellect, temperament, physique, traits, habits, attitudes, self-concept, value systems, defense mechanisms, and behavior. Basic questions in this department are: What is the coefficient of correlation between intelligence test scores and creativity? Is everyone potentially creative, to some extent? Is creativity a function of temperament as well as intelligence? More than intelligence? Do physique or physiological factors have any bearing on creativity? How important are attitudes, habits, and value systems? And what kinds of habits, attitudes, and values? In what way are they significant? What about neurotic personality—is neuroticism essential or is it detrimental to creativity?

Lewis Terman of Stanford made extensive psychological studies of approximately 1,000 gifted children over a period exceeding thirty years. He observed a difference between high intelligence and high creativity and said in one of his last papers that not more than one-third of his people with IQ's over 140 showed a marked degree of creativity. On the East Coast, Leta Hollingworth observed essentially the same thing with children of 180 IQ or better. In Chicago, Thurstone studied the Quiz Kids and remarked afterwards that they had phenomenal memories for details but that they were noticeably lacking in creativity.

Guilford hypothesized that intelligence tests were not measuring creative factors. Now he hypothesizes, on the basis of factorial studies, that intelligence is made up of 120 or more kinds of abilities and has devised tests to measure approximately fifty factors. In the future he hopes to build instruments to measure additional factors of intellect. Guilford's studies indicate that people who stand out [from their fellows] as creative thinkers, are characterized by sensitivity to problems, fluency of ideas, mental flexibility, divergent thinking, and ability to redefine familiar objects and concepts.

Gertzel and Jackson note that children with quick humor are more creative.

Frank Barron found that people of complex temperament are more creative than people of simple temperament.

Mary Cover Jones submits the guess that late-maturers are more flexible thinkers than early-maturers, possibly because they have to be quick to keep up.

How Important Are Attitudes and Habits?

Eric Fromm observes that a creative person has the capacity to be puzzled, the ability to concentrate, a genuine sense of self and confidence in self, the ability to accept conflict and tension. Fromm accepts the concept that equality does not mean sameness. A person who is truly creative is one who is willing to be born everyday. He is willing to let go of all "certainties" and illusions.

Tuska, in his book *Inventors and Inventions*, says, "If you would invent, acquire the good habit of observing. Observe and question! Ask yourself questions: Why did that happen? Why did not something happen? What started that? What stopped that? For example, why can a spider walk on its own web without getting tangled? To what can I attribute the wonderful characteristics of a spider's thread? Where might I use such a thread to advantage? Could a spider's thread be synthesized? How? In brief, daydream with a purpose."

Thomas Edison said that invention is 1 per cent inspiration and 99 per cent perspiration.

Can a Creative Person Be Identified?

Almost any group of people, including school children, can name individuals among them who have off-beat ideas. Often the group will argue that so-and-so's ideas are crazy. But the question is, how crazy? Crazy enough to be useful? Crazy enough to change a trend? Crazy enough to revolutionize an industry—or a way of life?

Gilfillan, in his book *Sociology of Invention*, talks about the great lapses of time that have occurred between the time when ideas for great inventions were first merely mentioned and the development of the first working model or patent. Also, he discusses the time gap between patent and commercial use. The average time elapsed between first mention of the idea and commercial use of the same for nineteen inventions voted most useful (who voted was not stated) was 226 years. (These were inventions introduced between 1888 and 1913.) Studies regarding theories of government, philosophical insights, and scientific discoveries confirm the fact of time delay in communicating such ideas to the masses.

This fact of inability or reluctance on the part of the social group to accept new ideas, particularly unfamiliar concepts, complicates the task of identifying creative thinkers. But is not an individual who thinks differently from his associates and from sources of information doing his own thinking? And is he not the person who is likely to be creative?

Process

The term *process* applies to motivation, perception, learning, thinking, and communicating. Essential questions about process include: What causes some individuals to strive for original answers to questions while the majority are satisfied with conventional answers? What are the stages of the thinking process? Are the processes identical for problem solving and for creative thinking? If not, how do they differ? Can the creative thinking process be taught?

When the German physiologist and physicist Hermann Helmholtz was seventy years old, he was asked at his birthday party to analyze his thought processes. Later, Graham Wallas, in his book *The Art of Thought*, formulated Helmholtz's ideas into the familiar four stages: preparation, incubation, inspiration, and verification. The preparation step consists of observing, listening, asking, reading, collecting, comparing, contrasting, analyzing, and relating all kinds of objects and information. The incubation process is both conscious and unconscious. This step involves thinking about parts and relationships, reasoning, and often a fallow period. Inspirations very often appear during this fallow period. This probably accounts for the popular emphasis on releasing tensions in order to be creative. The step labeled verification is a period of hard work. This is the process of converting an idea into an object or into an articulated form.

In an address at M.I.T. in 1955, Alex Osborn, author of the popular book titled *Applied Imagination*, summed it up as follows: "I submit that creativity will never be a science—in fact, much of it will always remain a mystery—as much of a mystery as 'what makes our heart tick?' At the same time, I submit that creativity is an art—an applied art—a teachable art—a learnable art—an art in which all of us can make ourselves more and more proficient, if we will."

Yes, the creative process can be taught. It is being taught in hundreds of classes across the nation—in colleges, universities, business organizations, military schools, and industries. Osborn's book has gone into twelve printings and over 100,000 copies have been sold. There is considerable research evidence to support the statement that the creative process can be taught. And in 1954 the Creative Education Foundation was formed solely for the purpose of encouraging a more creative trend in American education.

Press

The term *press* refers to the relationship between human beings and their environment. Creative production is the outcome of certain kinds of forces playing upon certain kinds of individuals as they grow up and as they function. A person forms ideas in response to tissue needs, sensations, perceptions, and imagination. A person receives sensations and perceptions from both internal and external sources. A person possesses multi-factorial intellect, including ability to store memories, to recall and to synthesize ideas. Each idea that emerges reflects uniquely upon the originator's self, his sensory equipment, his mentality, his value systems, and his conditioning to the everyday experiences of life. Each person perceives his environment in a unique way: one man's meat is another man's poison and vice versa. Studies of press attempt to measure congruence and dissonance in a person's ecology. Stern and Pace have introduced instruments designed to take two temperatures—(1) the climate of a particular environment, and (2) the reaction of a person to his environment. If and when these two scores can be obtained they can be coordinated to show the congruence and dissonance between individuals and their environment.

Liphshitz, writing for the *Journal of the Patent Office Society*, opened fire, a few years ago, on the authors of most histories and of biographical studies of inventors for treating the inventor as something apart from the world in general. He said that an intensive study of the history of inventions makes clear that they originate in a response to social needs and that there must be a sufficiently advanced stage of culture and a proper technical heritage to foster or allow an invention to be made. History proves that great inventions are never, and great discoveries seldom, the work of any one mind. Every great invention is either an aggregate of minor inventions or the final step of the progression.

Gilfillan said, "Inventions are not just accidents, nor the inscrutable products of sporadic genius, but have abundant and clear causes in prior scientific and technological development. And they have social causes and retarding factors, both new and constant, of changed needs and opportunities, growth of technical education, of buying power, of capital, patent and commercial systems, corporation laboratories and what not. All such basic factors causing invention give means of predicting the same.

"The existing and overwhelming influence of causes for invention is proved by the frequency of duplicate invention, where the same idea is hatched by different minds independently about the same time."

Products

The word *idea* refers to a thought which has been communicated to other people in the form of words, paint, clay, metal, stone, fabric, or other material. When we speak of an original idea, we imply a degree of newness in the concept. When an idea becomes embodied into tangible form it is called a *product*. Each product of a man's mind or hands presents a record of his thinking at some point in time. Thus an idea for a new machine reflects the inventor's specific thoughts at the moment when the concept was born. And by probing backward from the moment of inspiration it may be possible to trace the thoughts and the events leading up to the idea. Products are artifacts of thoughts. Through the study of artifacts, archeologists reconstruct the way of life of extinct peoples, officers of the law reconstruct the events leading up to a crime, and psychologists reconstruct the mental processes of inventing. Objective investigation into the nature of the creative process can proceed in only one direction, i.e., from product to person and thence to process and to press.

A system is needed for classifying products according to the scope of newness. For example, theories such as relativity or electromagnetic waves or mechanical flight are of tremendous scope. From any one of these theories thousands of inventions may germinate. Therefore ideas in theory are of higher order in the scale of creativity than ideas for inventions. After inventions appear, numerous innovations or new twists in design or structure are suggested by users. Thus the idea for an invention is of higher order in the scale of creativity than an idea for an innovation to an existing invention. The significance of this suggestion to classify ideas by degree of newness is that it would place emphasis on higher mental processes rather than on dazzling objects.

In the history of the sciences, every branch floundered until facts were organized and classified. After a classification system was devised, the branch advanced rapidly. When astronomy grouped the heavenly bodies, outside of the sun and moon, into planets and fixed stars, it took a considerable step forward. When physics separated its phenomena into the broad categories of dynamics, sound, heat, light, electricity, and magnetism, the way was clear for more penetrating analyses. When Linnaeus devised the system of binomial nomenclature, biology became a science. This bit of history seems to suggest that the mystery surrounding creativity could be dissipated by organizing artifacts into categories, first by kinds and then within each kind by degrees of newness. If this were to be done, data could be collected concerning the person responsible for a given idea, concerning the circumstances leading up to the idea, and concerning the mental activity producing the idea.

Ideas have been described in various ways for different purposes. One system distinguishes ideas by media of expression: for instance, music, art, poetry, and invention. Another system recognizes mood: for example, pastoral, satiric, and didactic moods in poetry, and allegro, andante, and adagio moods in music. Still another system recognizes values: in art, pictures are classified according to their utility or their associative or esthetic value: while in the realm of mechanics, machines are recognized according to the use to which they are to be put. There are other classification systems based on form, as for example sonatas, concertos, and symphonies in music; and ballads, sonnets, odes, and elegies in poetry.

Notwithstanding these several ways of classifying products, there is no standard system for organizing artifacts according to idea value or degree of originality. Consequently, any artifact is called "a creation" and mystery surrounds them all.

Above the entrance to Washington Station these words are carved in stone, "Man's imagination has conceived all numbers and letters—all tools, vessels, and shelters—every art and trade—all philosophy and poetry—and all politics."

Ralph Waldo Emerson said, "Every reform was once a private opinion."

Within a year of our nation's founding, the U.S. Patent Office was established—on the concept that the country would profit by protecting the right of individuals to profit by their ideas and inventions. Between 1776 and 1960 more than 3,000,000 patents were granted.

In the last decade, as a direct response to Guilford's speech to the APA about the need for research in the area of creativity, new and tremendously significant knowledge has been collected and put to use—and this knowledge, as fast as it is being disseminated, is causing fundamental changes throughout Academe.

Granted, the word creativity has been overworked. And it is used loosely. Also, the formal study of creativity has not yet reached the stage of advancement which botany reached when Linneaus organized flora into phyla and into classes. Students of creativity have not yet taken the time to distinguish the strands of the phenomenon and then carefully to classify new knowledge according to the pertinence thereof to either person, process, press, or product. I submit that the time has come for more precision in definition and usage, that only when the field is analyzed and organized—when the listener can be sure he knows what the speaker is talking about—will the pseudo aspect of the subject of creativity disappear.

My appeal is that as educators we recognize the importance of continuing our interest in the nature of creativity, that we be appreciative of the spade work that has been done in the decade just past, that we continue to identify the factors associated with the creative process, and above all that we do not throw out the baby with the bath water just because the water is cloudy.

The subject of creativity has interdisciplinary appeal. This is true because the phenomenon to which the term creativity applies is the phenomenon of synthesizing knowledge. Hope for greater unification of knowledge lies in the continuance of studies of creativity. There are adventures ahead in researching the four P's of creativity, in learning to identify the creative person, in teaching the creative process, in learning how to take the temperatures of a person and of his environment under changing circumstances and of arranging for congruence between the two, in developing a scale for classifying products by degrees of newness within a scheme of like kinds of products. And ultimately there will be a new perspective of education with a backdrop of unified knowledge.

Now is the time for every teacher to become more creative!

Mr. Rhodes (Alpha Zeta 756) is an assistant professor of education at the College of Education, University of Arizona, Tucson. His Ph.D. dissertation (Arizona, 1957) was titled "The Dynamics of Creativity.

CREATIVITY, INTUITION, AND INNOVATION

Stephan A. Schwartz

They come in the night, or unexpectedly in a walk across the park, with friends playing games, or in the quiet of meditation. These are the provenances of creative breakthroughs that have changed the course of human history; the intuitive insights of single men or women. Nikola Tesla's invention of the electric motor, at the end of the 19th century, came in a vision as he walked across a city park.[1] Mozart and Copeland had music come to them in an instant.[2] Einstein "saw" Relativity as he idled away time in a canoe, after an illness. He later wrote: "I believe in intuition and inspiration. . . . Imagination is more important than knowledge. For knowledge is limited, whereas imagination embraces the entire world, stimulating progress, giving birth to evolution. It is, strictly speaking, a real factor in scientific research."[3]

Creativity concerns both the individual and society, and our survival as a species will be determined by our creative solution of problems so well-known their recitation has become a cliché. Our proficiency in understanding the creative process, and our values play in the world; whether our vision or another directs the course of future events. One does not need to be sophisticated in historical analysis to recognize the impact a single creative individual can have in a society supportive of breakthroughs, and how harmful suppression of creative initiative is to both individuals and the commonweal.

To cite but one example, one sufficiently removed in time for an objective analysis, consider the German chemist Paul Ehrlich. In addition to developing a long list of synthetic dies that transformed industries, and medical practices, this single man, and the teams he led, were responsible for a long list of pharmaceuticals, including the first synthesis of quinine substitute, a cure for sleeping sickness, and the most effective pre-antibiotic cure for syphilis.

Although he died in 1917 so great was the creative momentum produced by Ehrlich that, as historian Henry Hobhouse notes "In explosives, fertilizers, pharmaceuticals and synthetic substitutes of all kinds the German chemical industry was able to survive defeat in World War I, poor government and inflations in the 1920s, even the slump (depression, *ed.*), largely because of the technological lead derived from Ehrlich and his pupils."[4]

Information is available at a rate unimaginable 20 years ago; within another 20 it may be possible to buy everything that can be known in words or figures about a culture. And all manner of technological developments, help us to better understand or control physical reality. But information, and the power to manipulate it, are not creativity, although this difference is often missed.

As technology increases the role of creativity will increase, not lessen. When the power of technology ends, we must still confront that part of the problem-solving task which the machines can not emulate; the ineffable part, creativity. But what can we say about creativity, beyond the fact that it occurs? One useful perspective is to consider what people who have had creative breakthroughs—breakthroughs acknowledged by both their peers and history—say happened to them. Such as survey reveals that unnumbered major creative figures describe a link between creativity, intuition, and innovation.

And yet, although the critical triumvirate of creativity, intuition, and innovation are described over and over again, very little is known about the linkage of the parts. Psychologists and sociologists have studied the intellectual as well as some of the emotional and experimental aspects of creativity. Neurophysiologists and biologists probe the bio-chemical foundations of the brain, and its activity. Parapsychologists and physicists, as well as artists, have explored something of the process of intuition; and countless histories of innovation have been written. Each aspect, however, is usually treated as a separate subject. If we are to believe the words of Einstein, Mozart and others, however, it is the relationship amongst these parts, that holds the key.

Consider the description of Brahams describing the act of composition " . . . in this exalted state I see clearly what is obscure in my ordinary moods; then I feel capable of drawing inspiration from above as Beethoven did. . . . Those vibrations assume the form of distinct mental images. . . . Straightaway the ideas flow in upon me . . . and not only do I see distinct themes in the mind's eye, but they are clothed in the right forms, harmonies, and orchestration. Measure by measure the finished product is revealed to me when I am in those rare inspired moods. . . . I have to be in a semi-trance condition to get such results—a condition when the conscious mind is in temporary abeyance, and the subconscious is in control, for it is through the subconscious mind, which is part of the Omnipotence that the inspiration comes."[5]

Arthur Koestler coined the term *holons* to deal with this experience of comprehension[6] and even the most cursory analysis of either anecdotal or controlled intuitive experimentation produces numerous accounts from participants of this same wholistic experience. Typically researchers hear participants say "Images are all there . . . as if it were a hologram hanging in my mind."[7]

If we can say that creativity is something other than manipulating the known elements of a problem in some new and more elegant way, a leap into the unknown, as those accorded the title "creative genius" insist, then, perhaps research in parapsychology, the one discipline that studies rigorously controlled intuitive events may shed some insight. Studies at laboratories at Princeton, SRI and my own lab, Mobius, intriguingly, have indeed produced observations analogous to those reported by individuals making creative breakthroughs.

For example, when normal individuals are asked to carry out an intuitive task, known as Remote Viewing, which involves the ability to describe persons, places or events from which on is physically or temporally separated, and about which one could not know through normal sensory or intellectual channels, in debriefing sessions which follow and experiment participants frequently say, about their intuition that "it came in a flash." Our research suggests that both subjectively and objectively the statement is accurate. Studies have shown that there is a 10–20 second "window of intuition," which, then, closes as intellectual analysis of the images steps in.

The individual bits of information seem to come in a distinct pattern and we, and others have learned that there are also practical things to be done which can "fix" the image so that it remains available to memory—and does not vanish like a dream. One of the easiest, and best, is to make a simple drawing. This seems to allow a wide (and undefined) range of detailed information to be developed. These simple drawings look very much like the doodles made by many scientists, particularly physicists, as they attempt to translate their interior images into an expression they can share with colleagues. There are also suggestive connections between the description of such experiences and Jung's concept of the Collective Unconscious, the Morphogenetic Field Theory most recently espoused by Rupert Sheldrake, the ancient eastern concept of the akaskic record.[8,9]

Further, there is clear evidence of a direct correlation between intuitive functioning and creative decision making in business. Douglas Dean and John Mihalasky of Newark Institute of Technology carried out a series of experiments involving some 385 Chief Executive Officers of American Corporations.

The task required was to precognitively predict 100 randomly selected numbers. The results were then correlated with the financial report of the corporations. In every experiment a positive correlation was established between financial performance and high precognitive functioning—a correlation sufficiently strong that Dean was able to examine financial reports and predict how the CEO of that corporation would do in an experiment.[10]

For the past 10 years, we have been searching the biographies, and autobiographies of men and women to whom the title "creative genius" has been unequivocally awarded, the Einsteins, Mozarts, and Curries and, while we are only beginning to understand the creative "moment," there are five major components to the pattern of their creative breakthroughs:

1. **Intellectual Excellence:** Whether it is physics or sculpture, individuals of genius are masters in their field. Thinking visionaries, intellectually on the leading edge; it is their analytical prowess that gives them the power to define the problem to be addressed. This does not necessarily mean, however, that they are the smartest people. The late Nobel Laureate Richard Feynman, humorously recounts sneaking a look at his college file, and learning that his I.Q. was 124.[11] Superior, a level attained by less than 5 per cent of the population, but hardly an indicator of an internationally recognized and historically significant career in physics. Intelligence is needed, but creativity is more a function of working at full potential than having the highest I.Q.

   One correlation that does seem to hold was described to Dr. Mervin Freedman of San Francisco State College—a conclusion reached after studying the relationship between I.Q. and creative success. Dr. Freedman wrote, "Observations indicate that the more creative an individual students tend to be more troublesome to the average teacher than other students."[12] It is a finding which, by itself, urges better understanding of the creative dynamic, so that our educational system does not dismiss troublesome individuals who are simply bored. Or our businesses do not eliminate employees who present solutions that disturb the status quo.

   Edwin C. Land, the inventor of the Polaroid process, looked back on his work and the work of hundreds of scientists and engineers in his firm and concluded that the most significant discoveries are made, "by some individual who has freed himself from a way of thinking that is held by friends and associates who may be more intelligent, better educated, better disciplined, but who have not mastered the art of the fresh, clean look at the old, old knowledge."[13]

So strong is this iconoclastic factor, that we have developed a cultural stereo type image of the creative scientist and artist as a non-functional and not very stable individual. Like all such myths there is some truth in some cases. However, such an evaluation is too coarse to detect the central point. A considerable body of research exists suggesting that creativity is in some way a function of focus. Let me propose that this focus can be achieved either through neurosis (an obsessional focus) or a dedicated consciously-assumed focus (as in any of the martial arts). Because as a culture we do not provide effective and systematic training to achieve creative vision, when it does manifest it is often clouded by neurotic focus.

Nikola Tesla, for example was one of the towering figures of early 20th century science, yet his fear of germs led to his demand that everything on his table be sterilized, and that at least two dozen napkins be placed next to him when he sat down.[14] What produces these imbalances? Why do so many geniuses cling to debilitating hang-ups? Perhaps they are afraid that if they give up their obsessions they will lose their creative powers.

2. **The Deep Knowing That a Solution to the Challenge Does Exist:** Mastery of a field is also critical because it is a precursor to knowing (as opposed to believing) that a solution exists. As Einstein explained it, "I feel certain I am right while not knowing the reason."[15] This knowingness could be described as a "leap of faith."

3. **Strategies of Inward Looking:** It is essential to develop some technique of inward looking—some way of connecting with the factor that lies outside of the intellect. Here again the ability to focus is a central factor. Historical accounts and laboratory research suggest that meditation, gardening, even sports such as darts can help achieve this aim. Years ago, when I was covering the early years of the Space Program, I visited Cape Canaveral and while walking down the hall happened to see a group of engineers engaged in a dart game. Later that evening I happened to meet one of these engineers at dinner, and I teased him about spending the day at darts. He responded that it was his team's secret weapon. He told me, "When we get stuck and no intellectual solution suggests itself we begin playing. At first the conversation is about trivial things but, after a while someone is likely to offer a suggestion to the problem we face. A little while later someone else will add something and, suddenly, as if a spark caught fire we will all be talking about the problem again. I can't tell you how many insoluble problems we have solved this way." What all the techniques seem to have in common is the ability to allow the practitioner to enter into a relaxed, open-focus state. Clearly, understanding this process, holds substantial promise for learning how to create these states. Yet the idea of training students, or employees in techniques which would increase their ability to focus, are virtually unknown in the educational and business worlds.

4. **Surrender:** A surcease from intellectual struggle must occur in order for the breakthrough to take place. One must reach the eye of the intellectual hurricane, a place of peace and assuredness, in order for the moment of breakthrough to occur. Surrender leads to this kind of inner-listening to be effectively transformed into a socially useful contribution.

Darwin describes how, after years of collecting data, one relaxed and completely removed from his working place, the key issues of evolution fell into place in an instant.[16]

Alfred Wallace, who arrived at the same conclusions at almost the same time, has his experience of illumination when, after eight years of collecting specimens in the Malay Archipelago, he contracted a fever. After days of semi-delirium, like Einstein he experienced a breakthrough in which the basic principles of evolution's gradual change suddenly emerged in his rational mind.[17]

The French mathematician Jules Henri Poincare reported that on two occasions major breakthroughs seemed to come "from thin air."[18]

Frederick Nietzsche states that ALSO SPRACH ZORATHUSTRA came to him while he was walking through the woods beside Lake Silvaplana.[19] He "saw" the story in a moment, but took months to write out his vision.

Research since the mid-1970s, by teams of Harvard Medical School and Menninger Foundation, suggest a sound scientific basis for approaching this part of the process.[20] Visualization and stress-reduction strategies synthesizing Eastern and Western approaches provide detailed guidance on how to develop a personal inward looking discipline.[21,22]

Even the sleep state has its role to play in the creative process, as evidenced by both laboratory studies and auto-biographical accounts. Consider just one pattern apparent from our biographical study. Robert Lewis Stevenson recounts how he would go to sleep asking, "the gremlins of my mind to write a story while I slept."[23] Physician and researcher Dr. Jonas Salk, provides another account: "Intuition is something we don't understand the biology of yet," he says, "but it is always with excitement that I wake up in the morning wondering what my intuition will toss up to me, like gifts from the sea. I work with it, and rely upon it. It's my partner."[24] Salk is reported by Fortune Magazine editor Roy Rowan as crediting this technique in guiding him to make the correct leap that led the discovery of the polio vaccine.[25]

Perhaps the most ironic example, however is one given by Rene Descartes whose concept of science and its commitment to the primacy of the intellect has dominated how the technological cultures have thought about the world since the beginnings of the seventeenth century. The experience which led to what he called "a wonderful discovery," and "a marvelous science," was that most unintellectual of activities—a dream, which he had on Saint Martin's Eve (November 10th) 1619 in Neuberg, Germany.[26]

5. **Intellectual Explication and Verification:** Once the moment of illumination has taken place, the conscious, analytical, and synthesizing intellect comes back into play. Descartes gives a clear example of the process when he says that after his dream it took him the rest of his life to make that vision intelligible to others. There is also the necessity to winnow the valid inspirations from the erroneous ones. This, too, requires the special skills of the intellect.

These five steps, then, have a kind of natural rhythm, which suggests that different parts of the brain are used for different steps in the problem solving task. PET scans of brains, and other test procedures, suggest this as well. Clearly there is much fruit in the vineyards of the neurosciences. But neuroanatomy is not the main point here. The final point I would like to make is that the five steps can not be viewed in a vacuum. They will only take root in a climate that nourishes and sustains them.

For over thirty years a series of efforts that can loosely be called The Human Potential Movement have been developing. Millions of men and women have participated in these efforts, and report their lives deeply affected. An examination of their efforts reveal that all successful Human Potential schemes have a common thread: to make an individual more insightful, functional, and self-fulfilled. These goals seem noble and desirable, and fully consonant with The Declaration of Independence's call for " . . . the pursuit of happiness." Why, then, are they so controversial?

Why if millions have participated in the various aspects of the Human Potential Movement has the world view epoused by the movement had such a small acknowledged impact on American society has a whole? And, where there are exceptions to this, notably the physical fitness and nutrition movements, why have these programs been successful where others have failed? Also why, if these efforts have appealed so strongly to some sectors of our society, have they had virtually no appeal for other sectors? If this impact were extended what would be the consequences?

A survey of the criticism concerning the Human Potential Movement reveals that there is a marked discontinuity between the critics reality about these programs and the perceptions of those actually taking part in them. Critics charge that such activities are godless and in conflict with traditional church teachings, or at variance with standard American values. This is a valid perspective, and on which must be addressed.

When the criticism and the programs are compared it becomes obvious that most critics are actually ignorant of these developments, their goals and methods. It is also apparent that the difficulties are more a public relations problem than a difficulty of substance, and if proponents are to be effective in making their case, these insights about human functioning, particularly intuitive processes, must separate the practical aspects of the programs from their trappings, which are often seen as fringe at best and occult at the worst.

The way to do this is to base all such programs firmly in science; to separate the "movement" and "cult" aspects from what has actually been learned on the basis of appropriate research methodologies. Particularly for the business community it is the essence, the dynamic of the process that matters, not the scaffolding surrounding its implementation.

The conflict with traditional religious practices needs to be addressed by showing that mainstream Catholic, Jewish, and Protestant religious institutions already are making use of these dynamics in such programs as "Marriage Encounter Weekends," and visualization exercises for the seriously ill. It is important to realize that these inner processes do not conflict with religious views unless those views are extreme and fearful. Meditation, one of the most effective tools for relieving stress, and promoting intuitive functioning, to cite but one example, is not godless, or godful, although few who meditate fail to come to a deep appreciation of the importance of an inner spiritual life. Basically, meditation is a process that provides insight and empowerment to the mediator.

The quest for inner knowledge, of which intuitive decision making is but a single facet, is not a fringe activity. It is firmly rooted in one of the most significant historical dynamics of America. Far from being new or radical, it is the natural evolution of the vision—itself a statement of Human Potential—the lay at the core of the Founding Fathers' design for the United States. The United States was historically unique in its emphasis on human values, and the individual's free capacity to establish whatever form of inner life that met their needs. Proponents of human potential issues, are not secular humanists, unless they choose to be, and remarkably few do. And theirs is not the position of unproven belief. Unlike their critics, those advocating the agenda of enhancing human functioning are the ones with the "hard science." This conference is the direct descendent of the American Transcendental Movement which gave us Emerson, Thoreau, Melville, Holmes, the Chataqua Movement, and a host of other mainstream personalities and efforts. Such individuals are the progenitors of the issues of this conference.

Others who oppose this perspective argue that such things are expensive indulgences. In these hard times this is nothing for the strapped corporate manager to consider. In fact, such programs involve people and their intentionality, and the evidence is clear, in everything from health costs to productivity, that the human capacities agenda pays its way. Perhaps the best example of this is the integration of many human potential programs into the military beginning with the 1969–1975 period. Although some of the programs went too far, or were found to be unnecessary, in aggregate these efforts proved to be the most potent solution available to retention rates, racial conflict, minority rights, and high quality performance. It is very doubtful that the all-volunteer armed forces would have been possible without the human potential perspective. The performance of America's men and women in armed service in the Persian Gulf, provides the clearest most unequivocal proof of what happens when this agenda finds its way into the management practices of large organizations.

The Peace Corps is another example of human potential engineering that has never been truly acknowledged for its contribution to America. We tend to see the Peace Corps as helping others. In fact, it is the single largest education program ever undertaken by America in educating its own citizens as to what the rest of the world is like. Each volunteer was changed by their exchange with another culture and, in turn, changed hundreds of others. We can look to the Persian Gulf for another example. If policy makers had more fully understood the Arab mind and culture over the past two decades what other roads might have been taken?

When we seek to create and environment in which intuition and creative functioning works best we do not require complex technology, nor vast sums of money, nor a new bureaucracy. What is needed is the status of priority. Once that has been attained, small teams of professionals could fan out throughout a company working often within existing structures, including external activities such as church groups, and the hundreds of other activities maintained at the Regional, State, and local level. This cadre could train personnel in techniques that have proven worth, and involve more a change of perspective than anything else.

Ultimately, this is a grass-roots effort. It is not a turning away from traditional values, but a re-orientation to the historical mainstream values that were the central core of America. Up to the late 1940s, these were the values that most Americans supported and practiced in their own lives.

Notes

[1] Collected Papers on Nikola Tesla. (Tesla Institute: Yugaslovia, ND).

[2] Gail Delaney. Creativity in Music. *Proceedings*. Association for the Anthropological Study of Consciousness. Annual Meetings, 1984.

[3] Albert Einstein. Collected Papers. Princeton Center for Advanced Studies.

[4] Henry Hobhouse. *Seeds of Change: Five Plants That Transformed Mankind*. (Sidgwick & Jackson: London, 1985), pp. 24–25.

[5] A.M. Abell. *Talks with the Great Composers.* (G.E. Schroeder-Verlag: Garmisch-Parten-Kirchen, 1964), pp. 19–21.

[6] Arthur Koestler. *Janus.* (Random House: New York, 1978).

[7] Stephan A. Schwartz. *The Secret Vaults of Time.* (Grossett & Dunlap: New York, 1978).

[8] Carl Gustav Jung. *The Archetypes and the Collective Unconscious.* 2nd Ed. Trans. R.F.C. Hull. Vol 9. Part I. Bollingen Series XX. (Princeton: Princeton, 1968). pp. 42–53.

[9] Rupert Sheldrake. *A New Science of Life.* (Tarcher: Los Angeles, 1981).

[10] Douglas Dean, John Mihalasky, Sheila Ostrander, and Lynn Schroeder. *Executive Esp.* (Prentice-Hall: Englewood Cliffs, N.J., 1974).

[11] *People* Magazine. January 1986.

[12] Milton Freedman. *Scientific Creativity: Its Recognition and Development.* (New York: John Wiley & Sons, 1963).

[13] Edwin C. Land. Address to Polaroid Employees, 1963.

[14] *Reminiscences of Nikola Tesla.* (Tesla Institute: Jugaslavia, N.D.).

[15] Albert Einstein quoted in *Farady, Maxwell and Kelvin* by D.K.C. MacDonald (Doubleday: Garden City, N.J., 1964).

[16] W.I.B. Beneridge. *The Art of Scientific Investigation.* (New York: Vintage, 1957) 3rd ed.

[17] Ibid.

[18] Ibid.

[19] Ibid.

[20] Elmer and Alyce Green. *Beyond Biofeedback.* (Delacorte: New York, 1971).

[21] Herbert Benson. *Beyond the Relaxation Response.* (Times Books: New York, 1984).

[22] Robert Keith Wallace. The Physiological Effects of Transcendental Meditation. Doctoral Dissertation UCLA. Grant NIMH 2-TO1 MH 06515-12, 1971. See also Charles Tart. States of Consciousness and State-Specific Sciences. *Science.* 16 June 1972, vol. 176. pp. 1203–1210. and Ramakrishna Rao and H. Dukan. Meditation and ESP scoring. In W.G. Roll, R.L. Morris, and J.D. Morris (eds.). research in *Parapsychology* 1972. (Scarecrow: Meutchen, N.J., 1973). pp. 148–151.

[23] Lloyd Osborne. *An Intimate Portrait of R.L.S.* 1924.

[24] Roy Rowan. Those Business Hunches are More than Blind Faith. *Fortune.* 23 APRIL 1979. pp. 110–114.

[25] Ibid.

[26] C. Adams and P. Tannery. *Oeuvres De Descartes.* Vie de Descartes. vol. XII.

Correspondence: Stephan A. Schwartz • 520 Second Street, Manhattan Beach, California, 90254 • Voice: (310) 318-2188 • FAX: (310) 318-1728

Conceptions and Misconceptions of Creativity

Scott G. Isaksen

Overview

Many people hold strong personal views about creativity and how it can be used. In fact, there are many different views on creativity. Some are more fruitful than others. However, good communication about creativity requires a common language and framework. The purposes of this chapter are to examine some common misconceptions about creativity and share a productive framework for viewing creativity and its many applications. I hope to clearly demonstrate that creativity is not just one simple little thing. It is a challenging and useful concept which has at least a few productive meanings.

Some Creativity Mythology

Creativity can be a very confusing topic for many people who really want to understand what it is and how it can be learned and applied. It is often helpful to begin by clearing away some of the myths associated with creativity. In our work, we have identified at least three principal myths people hold about creativity. We call them the myths of mystery, magic and madness.

Some people believe that creativity is something so *mysterious* it cannot be studied productively. This belief is based on the observation that everyone seems to have their own definition of creativity. On the surface, these different perspectives seem to be "at odds" with each other. Given this state of confusion, people often think that the concept of creativity defies definition and is a topic that should be avoided. This becomes a problem when this belief inhibits or interferes with their desire or ability to make sense of their own creativity and how they might use it.

Other people believe that creativity is something that is *magical* which only a few gifted people *really* have. Those who hold this conviction suggest that creativity is a trick or gimmick that only certain people know. If you talk about how the

Figure 1. Some people are afraid of creativity.

34

trick is done or explain the gimmick, you will take away the "magic." If you hold this belief, you separate people into two groups: those lucky few who have it, and those who do not. This myth also discourages people from discussing how they use their creativity or how they can nurture it in others. This conception places the source of creativity onto something external, over which the individual has no control. When asked to explain the results of their creativity, people may indicate that they have no idea how it happened . . . "it just came to them like magic." Others who see creativity as magical believe that their source is a muse who will leave them if exposed or explained.

A third common myth is that creativity is linked with *madness*. Stories abound regarding highly creative people who have quirks in their personalities. Some cut off parts of their bodies, others took drugs, some committed suicide, still others did a range of very strange things. All in all, this notion of creativity provides an image which is not very inviting or positive. In other words, in order to be creative, you must be weird or abnormal. This suggests that creativity is unhealthy behavior which should be avoided.

These opinions about creativity promote a whole series of negative images and become the source of major challenge for those who want to understand or develop this important human resource. The myths by themselves actually offer intriguing ways to understand the source of the many misconceptions about creativity. For example, when you observe a particularly impressive performance or see a work of genius, you rightfully feel a sense of awe. This by itself may support the belief in magic as the source of creativity. The belief becomes a problem when it serves as a barrier to further understanding or use of your personal creativity or pursuing its deliberate development personally. It can also be a problem for using creativity in groups or even trying to establish ways to nurture it in organizations.

By the way, these are not all the myths associated with creativity. I have seen many others. While working in schools I observed the belief that creativity was equivalent with merrymaking. For a half-hour on some Fridays, students were often asked to take out their crayons and . . . "be creative." I have also seen some major organizations take on this belief. They ask for creativity consultants to . . . "do something creative for these people" . . . when they deserve a reward during a planning retreat. Just for fun, you may want to remember or observe how people around have treated (or are treating) the whole concept of creativity.

Some Productive Assumptions

In the face of so many common myths and misconceptions, it is a wonder that creativity has been studied seriously at all. However, there is an alternative set of assumptions and beliefs that allow us to be more productive in studying creativity. Creativity is complex but understandable, natural (present in everyone), healthy; enjoyable, and important.

Although creativity is a complex and challenging concept with no universally accepted definition, it is *understandable*. For more than forty years, people have been studying, reading and writing about, theorizing and researching creativity. Many theories have been developed to help us understand and organize the complex nature of creativity. Many research studies have established a body of evidence to guide us in understanding, recognizing and nurturing creativity. As Arieti (1976) indicated:

> "Whether it is considered from the viewpoint of its effects on society, or as one of the expressions of the human spirit, creativity stands out as an activity to be studied, cherished, and cultivated (p. IX)."

The importance of studying creativity is also supported by Rothenburg & Hausman (1976).

> "The investigation of creativity is at the forefront of contemporary inquiry because it potentially sheds light on crucial areas in the specific fields of behavioral science and philosophy and, more deeply, because it concerns an issue related to man's survival: his understanding and improvement of himself and the world at a time when conventional means of understanding and betterment seem outmoded and ineffective (p. 5)."

Creativity is a *natural* part of being human. It is not reserved only for those people with some sort of special gift. This suggests that creativity exists in all people. Certainly there are some who have an exceptional talent, gift or genius. I am not suggesting that we degrade their creativity or inflate others who lack their gifts. It is clearly appropriate to enjoy and appreciate the high level of creative talent existing in people. I am reminded of a particular performance of the Mozart Symphony in Vienna which was a special moment for everyone in attendance. Everyone seemed to

Figure 2. People have different beliefs about creativity.

know that they were moved and effected by a uniquely superior performance. Sometimes that high degree of creativity scares the rest of us away from believing that we also have some. If we see creativity as a natural human talent, then, even though people may have more of a particular kind, it is accessible to every one of us. People should naturally differ on how much of the creative talents they have, but also on how they prefer to use them. The challenge rightfully becomes learning how to understand and use the creativity you have. This belief is fundamental for those who are interested in identifying what creativity is and understanding how it can be developed.

Accessing and using creativity can release tension and help people lead *healthy* and more productive lives. Much of the popular creativity literature tends to focus on those stories of unusual artists or scientists who were highly creative and known for rather exotic or strange behavior. We often overlook creative individuals who lead "normal" lives. It can be easy to fall into the trap of believing that people need to display unusual behaviors in order to be creative. In the research conducted on creativity, there is no evidence to suggest that in order to be creative one *must* be sick, abnormal or unhealthy. To the contrary, there is some evidence to suggest that learning how to understand and use creativity can be mentally and physically healthy.

Creativity is *enjoyable* in that using it brings about a sense of satisfaction, accomplishment and reward. When you learn about and apply your creativity it can provide you with a sense of peacefulness and joy.

Creativity is also *important* in that the outcomes and consequences of using creativity have benefits for individuals, groups, and organizations. Creativity provides important benefits for all people in their personal life as well as in their work and enhances the quality of life for society as a whole.

The mythologies associated with creativity actually provide an opportunity to think through some alternative answers to questions about the source of human creativity. To move forward on recognizing and nurturing creativity, you will need to get around the barriers and find a more productive stance.

The Many Facets of Creativity

Once you commit to a more fruitful position regarding creativity and begin reading about the subject, you will discover it has quite a variety of definitions. In fact, this is one of the main reasons that there are so many misconceptions of creativity. It often seems that everyone who has ever written about creativity developed and shared a entirely new definition of the concept. Despite the fact that there is no consensus on a single definition, there does seem to be general agreement about several essential dimensions of a definition of creativity.

Figure 3. Noller's symbolic formula for understanding creativity.

For example, a study conducted by the Center for Creative Leadership in Greensboro, North Carolina (Gryskiewicz, 1987) found that when managers were asked to describe their understanding of creativity, two themes consistently emerged. Nearly all the managers identified "novelty" as central to their concept of creativity. Second, they suggested that the novelty must be "useful," meet a need, or be relevant to the issue at hand.

Ruth Noller, Distinguished Service Professor Emeritus of Creative Studies at Buffalo State College, developed a symbolic equation for creativity. She suggested that creativity is a function of an interpersonal attitude toward the beneficial and positive use of creativity in combination with three factors: Knowledge, Imagination and Evaluation (see Figure 3). Children are often viewed as naturally strong in imagination. They often need help in acquiring knowledge and expertise, as well as in understanding appropriate criteria for evaluating ideas or behavior. In comparison, practicing professionals often are seen as having a great deal of knowledge and evaluative strength but needing help with imagination.

There are a number of lessons from Noller's equation. One is that creativity is a dynamic concept. It changes through our experience. Also, creativity always occurs in some context or domain of knowledge. But, while expertise is important and necessary, it is not sufficient for determining creativity. Finally, creativity involves a dynamic balance between imagination and evaluation.

"The definitions of creativity are numerous, with variations not only in concept, but in the meaning of sub-concepts and of terminology referring to similar ideas. There appears to be, however, a significant level of agreement of key attributes among those persons most closely associated with work in this field . . . On the basis of the survey of the literature, the following definition is proposed: Creativity is the process of generating unique products by transformation of existing products. These products must be unique only to the creator, and must meet the criteria of purpose and value established by the creator (Welsch, 1980, p. 107)."

A Framework for Understanding Creativity

We can begin to deal with the very diverse concept of creativity by describing several important common dimensions among many definitions and theories. After collecting fifty-six definitions of creativity, Rhodes (1961) reported:

" . . . as I inspected my collection I observed that the definitions are not mutually exclusive. They overlap and intertwine. When analyzed, as through a prism, the content of the definitions form four strands. Each strand has unique identity academically, but only in unity do the four strands operate functionally (p. 11)."

The four strands of creativity, identified by Rhodes, are: understanding the traits, characteristics or attributes of creativity within people; describing the process, operations or stages of thinking they use; identifying the qualities of products or outcomes they produce; and examining the nature of the environment, context, or situation (press) in which they use creativity.

Figure 4 shows the four strands of creativity in a Venn diagram to emphasize the nature of their relationship (Isaksen, 1984, 1987). As Rhodes suggested, it is most beneficial to think of these four strands as operating together. For example, the most comprehensive picture of the creative person can be drawn by considering not only the characteristics or traits of the person, but also the kind of environment or context in which the person is working, the kinds of mental operations being used, as well as the nature of the desired outcomes or products.

You can attain a better understanding of the four major approaches (person, product, process and press) by examining each in more detail. Therefore, the remainder of the chapter will provide a brief overview of each of these four major aspects of creativity.

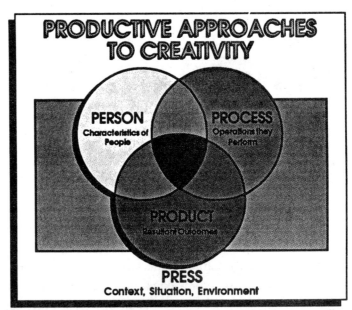

Figure 4. Isaksen's diagram of the relationship between the four approaches to understanding creativity.

The Creative Product

Creative products or outcomes come in a variety of sizes and shapes and from many different contexts. They are not limited to either the arts or the sciences. Many different areas and disciplines produce creative results and outcomes. Among these are: the fine arts, commercial and performing arts, sciences and technology, industrial design, architecture, and many more.

This aspect of creativity generally focuses on the characteristics of the outcomes or results rather than on the people or their environments. The major question is, "How do I know it's creative?" For many people, this area of study has been called "Innovation" rather than "Creativity" because of the focus on product rather than process (see Figure 5 for other distinctions). Creative products can be found in the arts, the sciences, the humanities, and in any discipline or domain of human endeavor. They can be the result of the efforts of individuals or groups. They may have varying degrees of novelty and usefulness.

Creative products can be both tangible and intangible. They may be concrete or "touchable" like an invention or marketable product. Other creative outcomes can be intangible such as learning and personal development, the development of a new service or improvement of an existing one, social technology, or the design of a new process or methodology.

There are many definitions of creative products. Rothenberg (1976) offered one which related to his general definition of creativity.

"Creations are products which are both new and valuable and creativity is the capacity or state which brings forth creations (p. 312)."

MacKinnon (1975) pointed out the importance of studying creative products. He stated:

"In a very real sense . . . the study of creative products is the basis

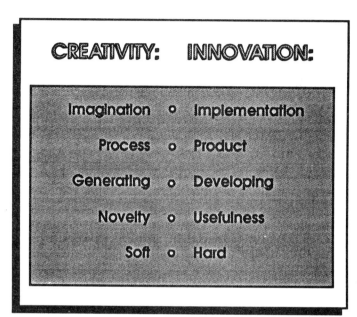

Figure 5. Some common distinctions between creativity and innovation.

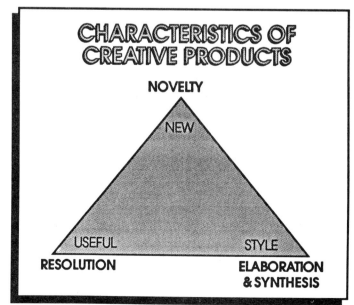

Figure 6. Characteristics of creative products and outcomes.

39

which all research on creativity rests and, until this foundation is more solidly built than it is at present, all creativity research will leave something to be desired . . . In short, it would appear that the explicit determination of the qualities which identify creative products has been largely neglected just because we implicitly know—or feel we know—a creative product when we see it (pp. 69-71)."

A relatively new approach to examining the characteristics of creative products or outcomes has been developed by Besemer and others (Besemer & Treffinger, 1981; Besemer & O'Quin, 1987). They developed ways to assess the creativity in a particular product or outcome, using a paper and pencil rating scale. Their assessment, initially called the Creative Product Analysis Matrix, and recently changed to the Creative Product Semantic Scale (O'Quin & Besemer, 1989), is based on asking people to identify the characteristics required in a product in order for it to be considered creative. As shown in Figure 6, creative products and outcomes can be evaluated on three dimensions: novelty; resolution; and elaboration and synthesis. The *Novelty* (originality, germinality, or transformality) dimension examines the amount of newness or originality contained in a product. The *Resolution* (useful, adequate, valuable) dimension examines how well the product solves the problem for which it is developed. The third dimension, *Elaboration and Synthesis* (attractiveness, well-craftedness, elegance, or expressiveness) focuses on the extent that a product extends beyond the basic requirements needed to solve a problem. It considers, for example, such factors as packaging and presentation.

Many organizations involved in new product development have a similar process for analyzing and developing new concepts. One of the Dun and Bradstreet Companies conducted a study of 51 US Companies. Figure 7 shows the results of the study. Note that it takes over 50 ideas to get one successful new product.

Current trends in many of the organizations with which we work point to some interesting implications for new concept and product development. Many organizations are trying to shorten the amount of time it takes to come up with the one successful new product. They are also trying to push more ideas through the entire process so that more than one successful new product would result.

This is having an effect on the kinds of new products being developed. Decreasing time, increasing throughput and other demands on the new product development process appears to be reducing the occurrence of highly novel products. Instead, this trend seems to promote an increase in the

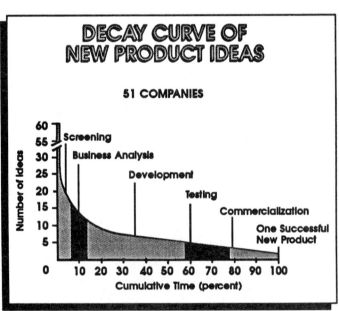

Figure 7. Creative product decay curve identified in Dun & Bradstreet study.

frequency of useful and stylistically modified products. For example, Tide™ was a very new product for Procter & Gamble when it was first produced. Tide with Bleach™ is a new product which is lower in novelty but emphasizes usefulness. The net result of the trends is that we are able to see more and more modifications and improvements on existing product lines (within many markets). Examining product and services lines, as well as examining customer demands can be fruitful applications of the Creative Product Semantic Scale. Inventors and companies can target the kind of new development they desire to meet market needs.

The development and nature of creative products and outcomes offers a fruitful and important aspect within various conceptions of creativity. Inventions, discoveries, innovations, and the development of new and improved services and products offer both tangible and intangible evidence of the significance and value of understanding creativity and its many applications. Recent developments in this area of creativity help to go beyond the traditional emphasis on new products being new and useful. The third dimension of stylistic elaboration and synthesis, made evident through recent research, expanded and extended our view of creative outcomes. The development of creative products and inventions is increasingly seen as a collaborative effort. Many organizations are attempting to shorten the product development cycle by involving all the relevant areas in cross-functional teams. This illustrates how creative people can wok together to create products or outcomes in particular places using a certain kind of creative methodology. This serves as just one example of how the four areas are related.

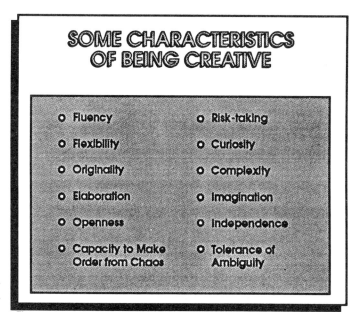

Figure 8. Characteristics of being creative.

Creativity in People

Much of the initial interest in creativity among psychologists and others working in applied settings started with curiosity about how highly creative people were able to demonstrate their creativity. Some of the initial approaches to understanding the characteristics of creativity in people involved finding and describing individuals who were generally agreed upon as being highly creative. The major challenge facing investigators who followed this approach was in determining how much creativity the individuals had. As a result of this approach, we had a great deal of information regarding the cognitive and affective characteristics of highly creative people. As indicated in Figure 8, these characteristics included attributes like: fluency, flexibility, originality, elaboration, curiosity, complexity, risk-taking, imagination and openness. Guilford (1950) indicated:

> "Creative personality is . . . a matter of those patterns of traits that are characteristic of creative persons. A creative pattern is manifest in creative behavior which includes such activities as inventing, designing, contriving, composing, and planning (p. 444)."

In addition to ability, however, several other factors need to be considered in order to obtain a more accurate and comprehensive picture of your creative strengths and potentials. For example, Torrance (1979) created a model for studying and predicting the occurrence of creative behavior in people. His model, represented in Figure 9, identified abilities, skills and motivations as important and interrelated factors in creative behavior. Torrance emphasized the need to consider more than simply ability when trying to understand and predict creative behavior. Skills involve knowing and using strategies for creating. Motivations involve your personal commitment of time, energy, effort, and enthusiasm to creative pursuits.

The majority of the work to understand creativity in people has focused on determining the level, capacity or degree of the characteristics highly creative people possess. A more recent approach to the study of creativity in people concerns how people show the creativity they have. Rather than asking the question "How creative are

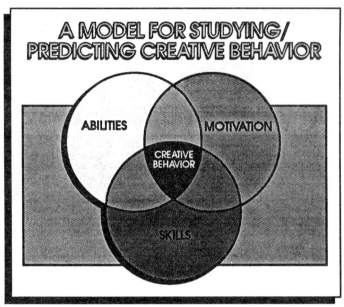

Figure 9. Torrance's model for studying and predicting creative behavior.

you? Those concerned with understanding style of creativity ask the question: "How are you creative?" This question deals more specifically with the form, kind or style of creativity, rather than the level, degree or amount and offers a new lens through which to search for and recognize creativity in people.

The Creative Environment

The creative environment concerns the context, place, situation or climate in which creativity takes place. It examines those factors which promote or inhibit creative behavior. Those conducting inquiry into the creative climate ask questions such as: What stops people from using their creativity? What is the environment, context or situation that is most conducive to creativity? How can someone establish a climate that encourages the release and development of creativity?

"Press" was the early word used to describe the broad area because it meant the interaction between the person and the situation. Factors in the environment pushed or pulled the person while factors, actions and qualities within the person pushed and pulled on the environment. The interaction between the person and environment will impact the appearance of creative behavior. This entire interaction was labeled press.

There are a number of different approaches to understanding the creative environment. For example, VanGundy

Figure 10. Describing obstacles that prevent ideas.

42

(1984) identified three categories of factors that help determine a group's creative climate: the external environment; the internal climate of the individuals within the group; and the quality of the interpersonal relationships among group members. In order to include the most important factors of the creative environment, we usually focus on the internal condition within the individuals as well as the external situation surrounding the person. Both "places" seem to be important in considering the most complete picture of the creative environment.

Internal Blocks to Creative Thinking

In order to understand and establish an environment conducive to using your creativity we have found it useful to examine the "internal" climate along with your perception of the external climate.

Figure 11. Characteristics that prevent creativity.

You may notice that in some situations you feel confident about yourself and your ability to succeed in a particular task, while in other situations you do not. One aspect of your approach or orientation to creativity is your awareness of blocks to creative thinking and behavior. It is only natural to have some resistance to novelty. Novelty requires you to change the approach, behavior, or way of thinking. It requires new learning and may increase the possibility of failure. Your internal climate is most likely formed as a result of some interaction between who you are and the environment or situation in which you operate. One of the ways to reduce the effects of blocks and barriers is to increase the likelihood of developing your strengths. Another way to overcome barriers is to know what they are and whether or not they are keeping you from productively making use of your strengths. You will overcome obstacles more effectively when you are conscious of their presence and impact.

We will examine three broad, overlapping categories of blocks: personal, problem-solving, and environmental (situational). Examples of personal blocks include: lack of self-confidence or self-image; a tendency to conform; a need for the familiar, habit-bound thinking; emotional numbness; saturation; excessive enthusiasm; various value and cultural influences; and lack of imaginative control.

As an example of personal blocks, Jones (1987) found four major categories. *Strategic barriers* relate to the inability to see and use a variety of possibilities for problem solving. Examples of strategic barriers include: resistance to using imagination; inability to tolerate uncertainty; or the inability to keep an open viewpoint to new ideas. *Value* barriers reflect the lack of flexibility displayed in applying personal values, beliefs and attitudes. Examples of this kind of barrier include: being rigidly custom bound; having a strong desire to conform to pre-existing patterns; or having dogmatically negative attitudes toward creative thinking. *Perceptual* barriers relate to seeing things in rigidly familiar ways and usually involve aspects of sensual acuity and awareness of the environment. Having difficulty in seeing a problem from a variety of view-

points, imposing unnecessary constraints, failing to use all the senses or stereotyping are examples of this kind of barrier. Finally, *self-image* barriers describe conditions where people do not assert themselves or make use of available resources. Sometimes, people have an extreme fear of failure, have a reluctance to exert influence or simply fail to take advantage of resources around them. These barriers are easily related to other problem-solving and situational blocks.

Problem-solving blocks are strategies, skills, or behaviors that inhibit your ability to focus and direct problem-solving activities, generate and identify options and alternatives, or turn

Figure 12. Barriers that kill creativity.

ideas into action. Some problem-solving blocks include: solution fixedness, premature judgments; habit transfer; using poor problem-solving approaches; lack of disciplined effort; poor language skills; various perceptual patterns which limit intake; and rigidity.

Environmental blocks are those factors in your context, situation or setting that interfere with your problem solving efforts. Environmental (situational) blocks to creativity include: the belief that only one type of thinking is required for innovative outcomes; resistance to new ideas; isolation; a negative attitude toward creative thinking; autocratic decision-making; reliance on

experts; various strategic blocks which limit the utilization of resources; and an over-emphasis on competition or cooperation.

These internal blocks and barriers often interact with your creativity strengths. They can often interfere with your ability, motivation and skill in being creative in a particular domain or activity. This level of interaction can also be effected by the external climate which exists or is perceived by the individual.

The External Climate for Creativity

What is the environment like in which creativity can flourish? Re-

Figure 13. Innovation often appears threatening

44

search on organizational obstacles to creativity done by the Center for Creative Leadership (Burnside, Amabile & Gryskiewicz, 1988) yielded a variety of barriers to innovation including: various organizational characteristics (inappropriate reward systems being overly bureaucratic, lack of cooperation across functions, etc.); lack of freedom in deciding what to do or how to approach a task or problem; perceived apathy toward task accomplishment; poor project management; perceived inappropriate evaluation systems, insufficient resources, insufficient time, and emphasis on the status quo.

The same research approach identified a variety of organizational stimulants to creativity including: freedom in deciding what to do or how to accomplish the task, good project management, sufficient resources, management exhibiting enthusiasm for ideas—creating a generally non-threatening and open environment, a collaborative atmosphere across levels and divisions, a general sense that creative work will receive appropriate feedback, recognition and reward, sufficient time, challenge due to the intriguing nature of the problem, its importance to the organization, or the context of the problem, and a sense of urgency which is internally generated.

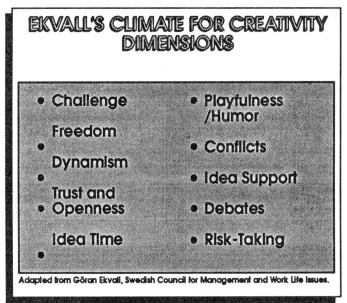

Figure 14. Ekvall's 10 Dimensions of the Climate for Creativity.

Our research uses the dimensions of the climate for innovation and creativity studied by Göran Ekvall of the Swedish Council for Management and Work Life Issues. The ten dimensions of this approach are identified in Figure 14. Ekvall suggested that all the dimensions are positively related to creative climate except one. The conflict dimension has a negative relationship to productive and creative climate (That is, the higher the conflict, the lower the level of creativity).

The Environment Conducive to Creativity

The following list of suggestions for creating or maintaining a climate for creativity draws upon the research of many scholars. It is not a totally comprehensive or conclusive list. In short, these suggestions provide recommendations to help you shape an atmosphere conducive to creativity and innovation. The items on this list are necessary for creativity to take place, although other factors may need to be present as well.

1. Provide freedom to try new ways of performing tasks; allow and encourage individuals to achieve success in an area and in a way possible for him/her; encourage divergent approaches by providing resources and room rather than controls and limitations.

2. Point out the value of individual differences, styles and points of view by permitting the activities, tasks or other means to be different for various individuals.

3. Establish an open, safe atmosphere by supporting and reinforcing unusual ideas and responses of individuals when engaged in both creative/exploratory and critical/developmental thinking.

4. Build a feeling of individual control over what is to be done and how it might best be done by encouraging individuals to have choices and involving them in goal-setting and decision-making processes.

5. Support the learning and application of specific creative problem solving techniques and skills in the workplace and on tasks which are appropriate.

6. Provide an appropriate amount of time for the accomplishment of tasks, provide the right amount of work in a realistic time-frame.

7. Provide a non-punitive environment by communicating that you have confidence in the individuals with whom you work. Reduce concern of failure by using mistakes as positives to help individuals realize errors and meet acceptable standards and provide affirmative feedback and judgment.

8. Recognize some previously unrecognized and unused potential. Challenge individuals to solve problems and work on new tasks in new ways. Ask provocative questions.

9. Respect an individual's need to work alone or in groups. Encourage self-initiated projects.

10. Tolerate complexity and disorder, at least for a period. Even the best organization and planning requires clear goals and some degree of flexibility.

11. Create a climate of mutual respect and acceptance among individuals so that they will share, develop, and learn cooperatively. Encourage a feeling of interpersonal trust and teamwork.

12. Encourage a high quality of interpersonal relationships and be aware of factors like: a spirit of cooperation, open confrontation and resolution of conflicts and the encouragement for expression of ideas.

The Creative Process

Creative process is also one of our four essential aspects of creativity. It is concerned with how creativity takes place. It examines the mental or cognitive processing, or the thinking that occurs as people use their creativity. Much of our early research on the creative process involved reports of how highly creative people described the processes they went through to develop their products. This type of investigation is based upon the assumption that we can " . . . take a single achievement or thought—the making of a new generalization or invention, or the potential expressions of a new idea—and ask how it was

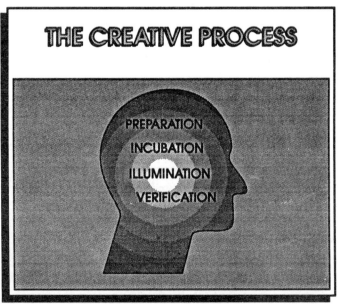

Figure 15. Wallas' Stages in creative process.

46

brought about. We can then roughly dissect out a continuous process, with a beginning and a middle and an end of its own (Wallas, 1926, p. 79)." Wallas developed one of the first descriptions of the creative process (see Figure 15). He suggested that it has four stages including: preparation (investigating the problem in all directions); incubation (thinking about the problem in a "not-conscious" manner); illumination (the appearance of the "happy idea"); and verification (validity-testing and reducing the idea to exact form).

One of the challenges to studying the creative process was in developing an accurate description of a person's thought processes. The goal was to help make the creative process more visible and understandable in order to improve creative thinking. This approach to understanding creativity has resulted in many different ways to nurture and develop creative skills. Literally, dozens of different techniques, approaches and methodologies have been developed over the years to help people strengthen their creative process (see Isaksen, Dorval and Treffinger, 1994; and VanGundy, 1988 & 1992 for further information).

Conclusion

This chapter has presented some major misconceptions and conceptions of creativity. Each of the four major facets of creativity; the creative product or outcome, creativity in people, the creative environment, and the creative process, were summarized.

Although the four facets were presented and described separately, the most complete picturing of creativity requires a look at all four. Imagine a stove with four burners. Each burner has one of the four "P's" of creativity boiling upon it. The steam above the stove containing a mix of all four facets describes creativity the best. Psychologists may have more of an interest in creativity in people, social psychologists and anthropologists may be more focused upon the culture, environment and situation which promotes creativity, educators and trainers may be more concerned with developing the creative process, and economists, managers and communication specialists may be more concerned with how new products are produced and marketed. All players can help bring some important learnings and insights to understanding this important human talent.

References

Arieti, S. (1976). *Creativity: The magic synthesis*. New York: Basic Books.

Besemer, S. P., & O'Quin, K. (1987). Creative product analysis: Testing a model by developing a judging instrument. In S. G. Isaksen (Ed.). *Frontiers of creativity research: Beyond the basics* (pp. 341-379). Buffalo, NY: Bearly Limited.

Besemer, S. P., & Treffinger, D. J. (1981). Analysis of creative products: Review and synthesis. *Journal of Creative Behavior*, 15 (3), pp. 158-178.

Burnside, R. M., Amabile, T. M., & Gryskiewicz, S. S. (1988). Assessing organizational climates for creativity and innovation: Methodological review of large company audits. In Y. Ijiri & R. L. Kuhn (Eds.). *New directions in creative and innovative management: Bridging theory and practice* (pp. 169-199). Cambridge, MA: Ballinger Publishing Company.

Gryskiewicz, S. S. (1987). Predictable creativity. In S. G. Isaksen (Ed.). *Frontiers of creativity research: Beyond the basics* (pp. 305-313). Buffalo, NY: Bearly Limited.

Guilford, J. P. (1950). Creativity. *American Psychologist*, 5, 444-454.

Isaksen, S. G. (1984). *Organizational and industrial innovation: Using critical and creative thinking*. A paper presented to the Conference on Critical Thinking: An Interdisciplinary Appraisal sponsored by Kingsborough Community College, New York.

Isaksen, S. G. (Ed.). (1987). *Frontiers of creativity research: Beyond the basics*. Buffalo, NY: Bearly Limited.

Isaksen, S. G., Dorval, K. B. & Treffinger, D. J. (1994). *Creative approaches to problem solving*. Dubuque, IA: Kendall-Hunt.

Jones, L. J. (1987). *The development and testing of a psychological instrument to measure barriers to effective problem solving*. Unpublished masters thesis. University of Manchester, UK.

MacKinnon, D. W. (1975). IPAR's contribution to the conceptualization and study of creativity. In I. A. Taylor & J. W. Getzels (Eds.). *Perspectives in creativity* (pp. 60-89), Chicago, IL: Aldine.

O'Quin, K., & Besemer, S. P. (1989). The development, reliability, and validity of the Revised Creative Product Semantic Scale, *Creativity Research Journal, 2*, 267-278.

Rhodes, M. (1961). An analysis of creativity. *Phi Delta Kappan, 42,* 305-310.

Rothenberg, A. (1976). The process of janusian thinking in creativity. In A. Rothenberg & C. R. Hausman (Eds.). *The creativity question* (pp. 311-327). Durham, NC: Duke University Press.

Rothenberg, A., & Hausman, C. R. (Eds.). (1976). *The creativity question*. Durham, NC: Duke University Press.

Torrance, E. P. (1979). *The search for satori and creativity*. Buffalo, NY: Creative Education Foundation & Creative Synergetic Associates.

VanGundy, A. (1984). *Managing group creativity: A modular approach to problem solving*. New York: American Management Association.

VanGundy, A. (1988). *Techniques of structured problem solving (second edition)*. New York: Van Nostrand Reinhold.

VanGundy, A. (1992). *Idea power: Techniques & resources to unleash the creativity in your organization*. New York: AMACOM.

Wallas, G. (1926). *The art of thought*. New York: Franklin Watts.

Welsch, P. K. (1980). *The nurturance of creative behavior in educational environments: A comprehensive curriculum approach*. Unpublished doctoral dissertation, University of Michigan.

WHY STUDY CREATIVITY?

Gerard J. Puccio

Introduction

The scientific investigation of creativity is a relatively recent phenomenon. In fact, the systematic study of creativity has been primarily limited to the 20th century, with a preponderance of inquiry occurring since the midpoint of this century. In comparison to other fields of study, such as philosophy, mathematics, and astronomy, it is easy to see that the investigation into the aspects of creativity has enjoyed a brief history.

The year 1950 is commonly cited as the birth of systematic research into the construct of creativity (e.g., Amabile, 1987; Barron, 1988; Helson, 1988; Isaksen, 1987; Rhodes, 1961). This was the year Guilford delivered his landmark inaugural address, simply entitled 'Creativity,' to the American Psychological Association. In his address, Guilford highlighted the paucity of research into this fundamental area of human functioning. He supported his assertion by citing the fact that of the 121,000 studies indexed in the *Psychological Abstracts* for the preceding 23 years, there were only 186 studies associated with creativity. However, for a variety of reasons, such as the post-war increase in scientific inventions (Getzels, 1987; Guilford, 1970; Helson, 1988), the launching of the space age (Helson, 1988; Talbot & Rickards, 1984), and the advent of a more humanistic approach in the field of psychology (Helson, 1988; MacKinnon, 1978), the study of creativity blossomed during the 1950s. In fact, according to Getzels (1987) during the years that followed Guilford's address there were almost as many studies of creativity occurring in any given year, as there were for the entire 23 years prior to his address. A recent search of the psychological literature from the year 1967 to 1994 (G. Wilson, personal communication, August 18, 1994) revealed more than 5,600 entries related to the topic of creativity and divergent thinking. Treffinger summarized the prevalence of creativity research since the 1950s when he stated, "Through more than thirty years of research and development, creativity has continued to be a topic of considerable interest and concern to educators as well as to social and behavioral scientists" (p. 19).

The purpose of this paper is to explore why there has been a tremendous increase in interest in the study of creativity. This paper summarizes the reasons why men and women in education, business, government, and other fields are interested in understanding, nurturing, and predicting creative performance. Few comprehensive reviews on this subject exist; most writers in the field of creativity appear to assume that the reader knows why the study of creativity is an important endeavor. As a result many writers in the field make ambiguous or general references to why the study of creativity is important and then quickly begin to describe their own study or theory. This approach fails to provide newcomers to the study of creativity with a sufficient understanding of the basic foundation to this field. Therefore, the purpose of this paper is to provide a summary of some of the more commonly cited reasons for the study of creativity.

Reasons for Studying Creativity

There are numerous factors which have served as catalysts to the growing interest in creativity and innovation. The following points have been identified by a number of authors as reasons behind the desire to understand better the concept of creativity. This list of reasons is not meant to be exhaustive, rather, it is a sampling of some of the reasons most often cited. In addition, these reasons are not mutually exclusive. Since creativity is considered to be a multifaceted phenomenon (MacKinnon, 1978) many of the reasons behind its study build on, and compliment, one another.

1. Develop human potential beyond IQ. One of the most commonly cited reasons for the investigation of creativity has been the desire to discover an area of human ability, beyond IQ, which would be useful in predicting performance (e.g., Getzels & Jackson, 1962; Guilford, 1986, 1987; Isaksen, 1987; Rhodes, 1961; Sternberg, 1988). A number of researchers (e.g., Guilford, 1950; Taylor, 1988; Torrance, 1972) have concluded that intelligence is a broad and complex concept which is not adequately explained by IQ alone. Taylor (1988) succinctly summed up IQ's inability to embody all of intelligence when he stated:

> IQ measures only small fish and has failed to catch and hold onto the truly big fish that the word "intelligence" signifies to most people. The general public has been misled and still readily believes that IQ is the "total intelligence" that encompasses all the dimensions of the mind, including all creative factors (and possibly all other dimensions not yet discovered and measured in the total mind-power) (p. 100).

Since there have been some reservations about IQ's ability to predict performance, especially creative performance, researchers have sought to go beyond this construct for predicting human ability. In 1950, Guilford stated that "probably, some of the factors most crucial to creative performance have not yet been discovered in any type of test. In other words, we must look well beyond the boundaries of the IQ if we are to fathom the domain of creativity" (p. 448). Guilford further criticized IQ enthusiasts when he argued that, "Many believe that creative talent is to be accounted for in terms of high intelligence or IQ. This conception is not only inadequate but has been largely responsible for the lack of progress in the understanding of creative people" (p. 454).

Since 1950, numerous researchers (e.g., Getzels & Jackson, 1962; Helson & Crutchfield, 1970; Milgram, Yitzhak, & Milgram, 1977; Torrance, 1972; Wallach & Wing, 1969) have examined the relationship between measures of general intelligence and creativity. In their review of these studies, Barron and Harrington (1981) concluded that the relationships between creative achievement and measured intelligence range from insignificant to small significant positive correlations. Wallach and Kogan (1965), who conducted one of the most elaborate studies on the relationship between general intelligence and creativity measures, asserted that individual differences in creativity are largely independent of the domain of general intelligence. In an examination of lay persons' implicit theories of intelligence, creativity, and wisdom, Sternberg (1985) found some degree of overlap among the constructs; however, they were not considered to be synonymous terms. Creativity proved to be the most distinct of the three constructs.

These studies have indicated that creativity is distinct from general intelligence, however, this is not to say that intelligence is completely unrelated to creative behavior. Most researchers agree that some degree of intelligence is a necessary, but not sufficient ingredient for creative performance. This finding has provided an important impetus to the study of creativity. It has prompted researchers to continue to examine factors, beyond intelligence, which may be useful in developing human potential.

2. Rapid growth of competition in business and industry. Another reason often cited (e.g., Ackoff & Vergara, 1988; Isaksen, 1987; Ray, 1987) as support for the increased interest in creativity is the growing competition in business and industry. The technological developments of this century are a tribute to man's ingenuity and creativity; however, it is these same technologies which have given rise to global competition. Technological developments in such areas as communication and transportation continue to draw the vast regions of the world closer together. Organizations no longer compete solely with other companies within their immediate region, but with competitors from around the world. Therefore, in order for today's organizations to remain competitive it is imperative that they incorporate creativity and innovation into all business functions. Creativity has become a central issue in the survival of a corporation. According to Geis (1988), "No longer is creativity seen as emanating from the fringe of corporate society. Generating new ideas and bringing them to market is now seen as a (if not the) central task of corporate management" (p. 25).

The rapid amount of change and growth which has occurred since the industrial revolution has brought much prosperity and wealth to a great number of industrial organizations. However, as this growth continues, industries, particularly older organizations, are experiencing a tremendous amount of pressure to continually improve on old systems and products. As Van Gundy (1987) noted, "Organizational growth and survival can be tied directly to an organization's ability to produce (or adopt) and implement new services, products, and processes" (p. 358). Tomorrow's successful businesses will be the ones which have effectively instilled creativity throughout the organization.

3. Effective use of human resources. One way for organizations to become more creative and innovative is to recognize, fertilize, and capitalize on the creative talents found within the organization. Barron (1988) has argued that, "Established organizations in government, industry, and education do not take creativity as a value and consequently do not make provisions for creative use of the creative individuals they employ" (p. 96). Creative contributions can be made from all levels of an organization, however, organizations must first establish an environment which explicitly nurtures and rewards creative efforts. As Ekvall (1991) has demonstrated, individuals who work in environments that support such factors as playfulness, idea support, trust, debates, risk taking, humor, and freedom are typically more productive than those who work in negative environments.

Creativity is a human resource (Barron, 1988). A resource which exists in all organizations—small and large, private and public. Organizations must endeavor to utilize this resource, wherever it exists, by designing environments which allow creative talent to flourish. The most important resource in any organization is its people; therefore, for organizations to thrive in today's economy it is imperative for them to nurture the creative potential of their human resources.

4. Contributes to effective leadership. Creativity is an essential skill for any person who is involved in some leadership role or capacity (Bennis & Nanus, 1985; Guilford, 1950). A creative leader can extend his or her influence well beyond that of a manager, who merely takes responsibility for guiding a group towards the stated objectives (Bennis & Nanus, 1985). Bennis and Nanus provided an excellent contrast between managers and leaders when they stated, "Managers are people who do things right and leaders are people who do the right things" (p. 21).

Creative leaders actively search for new problems; they can be considered to be problem finders. They are especially effective in handling novel challenges that require solutions outside of the routine or traditional strategies. They possess tremendous vision, and are capable of inspiring others with their vision. In short, it is the application of creativity skills that distinguishes a manager who maintains the status quo from a leader who supplies a new direction or vision.

5. Discover new and better ways to solve problems. Our society faces a diverse array of problems which require more and more creative solutions. This challenge was described by Ackoff and Vergara (1988):

> The accelerating rate of change is accompanied by a corresponding rate of obsolescence. An increasing number of problems have few or no precedents; hence, there is a decreasing number of opportunities to solve them effectively in familiar ways. The greater the need for new ways of doing things, the greater the need for creativity (p. 77).

To tackle world-wide challenges, such as pollution, starvation, terrorism, and the threat of nuclear war, more energy must be devoted to training in creative thinking and problem-solving skills. Guilford (1987) believed, "If by any approach we could lift the population's problem-solving skills by a small amount on the average, the summative effect would be incalculable" (p. 57). Future businessmen, scientists, educators, politicians, and others who will be involved in both professional and skilled positions will not only need to possess the knowledge associated with their specific field, but they will also need creative-thinking skills to solve problems in new ways. This necessary combination of skills will enable individuals to produce novel and useful solutions to challenges that appear to have no immediate solution. Knowledge about a particular domain is sufficient to solve problems that are straight forward; however, creative-thinking skills are required to solve more complex and open-ended problems.

6. Development of society. Another reason often given for the increased interest in creativity is its role in the preservation and growth of society (e.g., Helson, 1988; Isaksen, 1987; Taylor, 1987; Toynbee, 1964 & 1967). As Toynbee (1964) so aptly put it, "To give a fair chance to potential creativity is a matter of life and death for any society" (p. 4). Creativity is a central factor is our ability to continue to adapt to the changing environment (Rogers, 1959). Beyond the issue of survival, or the preservation of a society, Toynbee (1967) pointed out that if a nation actively seeks to nurture creativity it will play a part in making history. However, if a nation ignores the creative potential of its people, it will surely be surpassed by other nations.

7. Builds on all disciplines. A unique feature of the study of creativity is the fact that it is not confined to one particular discipline (Isaksen, 1987; MacKinnon, 1978). Creativity can be found in the sciences as well as the arts. Creativity-relevant skills can be applied to a myriad of fields (Amabile, 1988). The interdisciplinary nature of creativity is most evident in the diverse backgrounds represented by the researchers who are investigating this concept. Creativity researchers, for example, hail from such backgrounds as chemistry, engineering, psychology, sociology, education, philosophy, computer science, business, and economics.

8. Builds on the nature of knowledge. Creativity is a skill which can build upon or enhance general knowledge. As Isaksen (1987) indicated, "The increasing accumulation of factual information makes the comprehensive awareness of what is known more difficult, if not totally impossible. Developing awareness of creativity helps to examine the imaginative and productive applications of knowledge" (p. 4). Creative skills can assist in individual in enhancing his or her knowledge base. Without creative thinking an individual is condemned to stay within the knowledge base as it is given.

9. Natural human phenomenon. Creativity is like any other ability, everyone possesses it, but to varying levels and degrees (e.g., Guilford, 1986; Isaksen, 1987). This belief has provided much motivation for researchers and practitioners in the field of creativity. If creativity were considered to be a rare talent, possessed by only a few highly gifted individuals, then the knowledge gained from creativity research would be relevant and applicable only to these rare few. However, it is the belief that everyone is creative which impels the creativity researcher to continue to investigate this topic and to disseminate knowledge so others may live more creative and productive lives.

In addition to the varying levels of creativity, research carried out by Kirton (1976) has demonstrated that people also possess varying styles of creativity. Isaksen (1988) believed that "Everyone can use the level or style they have when provided with the appropriate opportunity" (p. 196).

10. Important aspect of mental health. Creative behavior is a necessary aspect of a mentally healthy life (Isaksen, 1987). Individuals who are able to incorporate creativity into their lives can enjoy the experience of discovering, developing, and utilizing their many talents. Conversely, individuals who find their creativity suppressed, for one reason or another, may experience frustration in attempting to maximize their abilities. Rogers (1959) has asserted that the primary motivation behind creativity is to enable oneself to fully actualize one's potential. Furthermore, skills relevant to creativity may also be useful in coping with life's challenges (Torrance, 1962). As Isaksen has so succinctly stated, "Releasing creativity is healthy" (p.5).

11. Enhance learning process. Finally, the nature of learning requires the use of skills associated with creativity (Barron, 1988; Bennis & Nanus, 1985; Guilford, 1950; Taylor, 1988). Several scholars (e.g., Barron, 1988; Guilford, 1987; Taylor, 1988) have argued that educational programs must provide instruction that explicitly encourages students to develop their creative-thinking skills. This encouragement will foster students who are more flexible in their thinking, and who become actively engaged in the material they are studying. The benefits of this form of instruction are applicable well beyond the school years.

12. Growing body of interest. As was discussed earlier, Guilford (1950) reported that in the 23 years preceding 1950, less than two tenths of one percent of the titles listed in *Psychological Abstracts* were directly related to the study of creativity. Since Guilford's address, there has been a substantial increase in the number of publications on the topic of creativity (e.g., Getzels, 1987; Isaksen, 1988; Stein, 1968). In fact, within the last 18 months, 176 publications can be found in the psychological literature alone (G. Wilson, personal communication, August 18, 1994). Furthermore, in recent years, a number of scholars have produced edited reviews of creativity research (e.g., Glover, Ronning, & Reynolds, 1989; Grønhaug & Kaufman, 1988; Isaksen, 1987; Isaksen, Murdock, Firestien, & Treffinger, 1993a; Isaksen, Murdock, Firestien, & Treffinger, 1993b; Sternberg, 1988). This growing body of literature represents the impressive progress which has been made in the understanding of the nature of creativity.

Beyond the documentation of interest in the aspects of creativity, there have been a large number of professional conferences on the topic. Perhaps the conference which has enjoyed the greatest longevity has been the Creative Problem-Solving Institute, sponsored by the Creative Education Foundation. The year 1994 marked the 40th anniversary of this annual summer conference held in Buffalo, New York. More recently, International Creativity and Innovation Networking Conferences have been initiated. Sites for these conferences alternate between North America and Europe. In addition to these international conferences, a series of conferences in the United States have focused on the connection between management practices and theories of creativity and innovation (Ijiry & Kuhn, 1988), as well as an annual conference on creativity in higher education hosted by the Dow Creativity Center at Norwood University in Midland, Michigan. If the number of publications and professional conferences can be considered a reliable indicator of intellectual inquiry, then it would appear that the study of creativity has certainly gained momentum throughout the years, and is currently an important issue for individuals from a number of different disciplines.

Summary

The various reasons discussed above provide a sampling of the underpinnings of creativity research. These twelve points serve as examples of the motivational factors that have impelled researchers to investigate this broad concept. They also highlight the critical value of creativity research for individuals, organizations, and societies. For other reviews of the rationale behind creativity research, see Isaksen (1987 & 1988) and Torrance (1962).

It is imperative for researchers and practitioners to understand the impetus behind their involvement in this particular area of study. This insight into one's personal motivation may provide the necessary vision to ensure the continuation of valuable contributions to the field of creativity. Moreover, it is essential for a professional in this field of inquiry to be familiar with the driving forces which sustain creativity research. This knowledge is particularly useful in combating the unproductive views many people have in regard to the field of creativity, such as the belief that only a handful of individuals are truly creative or that to be creative, one must be psychologically disturbed (Isaksen, 1987). If the study of creativity is to become a recognized discipline, then those involved must strive to clearly communicate the benefits this field has to offer. This should help to move creativity out of the realm of the mysterious and into more schools and organizations. Further, if researchers and practitioners can develop a common vision about the productive forces behind this area of study, then it will become much easier to forge a new discipline.

References

Ackoff, R. L., & Vergara, E. (1988). Creativity in problem-solving and planning. In R. L. Kuhn, ed., *Handbook for creative and innovative managers,* pp. 77–89. New York: McGraw Hill Book Company.

Amabile, T. M. (1987). The motivation to be creative. In S. G. Isaksen, (ed.), *Frontiers of creativity research: Beyond the basics,* pp. 222–254. Buffalo, New York: Bearly Limited.

Amabile, T. M. (1988). From individual creativity to organizational innovation. In K. Grønhaug & G. Kaufmann, eds., *Innovation: A cross-disciplinary perspective,* pp. 139–166. Oslo, Norway: Norwegian University Press.

Barron, F. (1988). Putting creativity to work. In R. J. Sternberg, (ed.), *The nature of creativity*, pp. 76–98. New York: Cambridge University Press.

Barron, F., & Harrington, D. M. (1981). Creativity, intelligence, and personality. *Annual Review of Psychology, 32*, pp. 439–476.

Bennis, W., & Nanus, B. (1985). *Leaders: The strategies for taking charge.* New York: Harper and Row.

Geis, C. T. (1988). Making companies creative: An organizational psychology of creativity. In R. L. Kuhn, (ed.), *Handbook for creative and innovative managers*, pp. 25–34. New York: McGraw-Hill Book Company.

Getzels, J. W. (1987). Creativity, intelligence, and problem-finding: Retrospect and prospect. In S. G. Isaksen, (ed.), *Frontiers of creativity research: Beyond the basics*, pp. 88–102. Buffalo, NY: Bearly Limited.

Getzels, J. W., & Jackson, P. W. (1962). *Creativity and Intelligence.* New York: Wiley.

Glover, J. A., Ronning, R. R., & Reynolds, C. R. (1989). *Handbook of creativity.* New York: Plenum.

Grønhaug, K., & Kaufman, G. (1988). *Innovation: Cross-disciplinary perspective.* Oslo, Norway: Norwegian Press.

Guilford, J. P. (1950). Creativity. *American Psychologist, 5*, pp. 444–454.

Guilford, J. P. (1970). Traits of Creativity. In P. E. Vernon, ed., *Creativity*, pp. 167–188. Middlesex, England: Penguin.

Guilford, J. P. (1986). *Creative Talents: Their nature, uses and development.* Buffalo, NY: Bearly Limited.

Guilford, J. P. (1987). A review of a quarter century of progress (1975). In S. G. Isaksen, (ed.), *Frontiers of creativity research: Beyond the basics*, pp. 45–61. Buffalo, NY: Bearly Limited.

Helson, R. (1988). The creative personality. In K. Grønhaug & G. Kaufmann, (eds.), *Innovation: A cross-disciplinary perspective*, pp. 29–64. Oslo, Norway: Norwegian University Press.

Helson, R., & Crutchfield, R. S. (1970). Mathematicians: The creative researcher and the average Ph.D., *Journal of Consulting and Clinical Psychology, 34*, pp. 250–257.

Hitt, M. A. (1975). The creative organization: Tomorrow's survivor. *Journal of Creative Behavior, 9*, pp. 283–290.

Ijiri, Y., & Kuhn, R. L. (1988). *New directions in creative and innovative management: Bridging theory and practice.* Cambridge, MA: Ballinger.

Isaksen, S. G. (1987). Introduction: An orientation to the frontiers of creativity research. In S. G. Isaksen, (ed.), *Frontiers of creativity research: Beyond the basics*, pp. 1–26. Buffalo, NY: Bearly Limited.

Isaksen, S. G. (1988). Educational implications of creativity research: An updated rationale for creativity learning. In K. Grønhaug & G. Kaufman, (eds.), *Innovation: A cross-disciplinary perspective*, pp. 167–203. Oslo, Norway: Norwegian University Press.

Isaksen, S. G., Murdock, M. C., Firestien, R. L., & Treffinger, D. J., (eds.), (1993a). *Nurturing and developing creativity: The emergence of a discipline.* Norwood, NJ: Ablex.

Isaksen, S. G., Murdock, M. C., Firestien, R. L. & Treffinger, D. J., (eds.), (1993b). *Understanding and recognizing creativity: The emergence of a discipline.* Norwood, NJ: Ablex.

Kirton, M. J. (1976). Adapters and innovators: A description and measure. *Journal of Applied Psychology, 61,* pp. 622–629.

MacKinnon, D. W. (1978). *In search of human effectiveness.* Buffalo, NY: Creative Education Foundation.

Milgram, R. M., Yitzhak, V., & Milgram, N. A. (1977). Creative activity and sex-role identity in elementary school children. *Perceptual and Motor Skills, 45,* pp. 371–376.

Ray, M. L. (1987). Strategies for stimulating personal creativity. *Human Resource Planning, 10,* pp. 185–193.

Rhodes, M. (1961). An analysis of creativity. *Phi Delta Kappan, 42,* pp. 305–310.

Rogers, C. (1959). Toward a theory of creativity. In H. H. Anderson, (ed.), *Creativity and its cultivation,* pp. 69–82. New York: Harper & Brothers.

Stein, M. I. (1968). Creativity. In E. F. Borgatta & W. W. Lambert, eds., *Handbook of personality theory and research,* pp. 900–942. Chicago, IL: Rand McNally.

Sternberg, R. J. (1988). Three-facet model of creativity. In R. J. Sternberg, (ed.), *The nature of creativity,* pp. 125–147. New York: Cambridge University Press.

Sternberg, R. J. (1985). Implicit theories of intelligence, creativity, and wisdom. *Journal of Personality and Social Psychology, 49,* pp. 607–627.

Talbot, R . J., & Rickards, T. (1984). Developing creativity. In C. Cox & J. Beck, (eds.), *Management development: Advances in theory and practice,* pp. 93–121. Chichester, England: Wiley.

Taylor, C. W. (1987). A high-tech high-touch concept of creativity—with its complexity made simple for wide adoptability. In S. G. Isaksen, (ed.), *Frontiers of creativity research: Beyond the basics,* pp. 131–155. Buffalo, NY: Bearly Limited.

Taylor, C. W. (1988). Various approaches and definitions of creativity. In R. J. Sternberg, (ed.), *The nature of creativity,* pp. 99–121. New York: Cambridge University Press.

Torrance, E. P. (1962). *Guiding creative talent.* Englewood Cliffs, NJ: Prentice-Hall.

Torrance, E. P. (1972). Predictive validity of the Torrance Tests of Creative Thinking. *Journal of Creative Behavior, 6,* pp. 236–252.

Toynbee, A. (1964). Is America neglecting her creative minority? In C. W. Taylor, (ed.), *Widening horizons in creativity,* pp. 3–9. New York: Wiley.

Toynbee, A. (1967). On the role of creativity in history. In C. W. Taylor, (ed.), *30 page booklet.* Salt Lake City, UT: University of Utah Press.

Treffinger, D. J. (1986). Research on creativity. *Gifted Child Quarterly, 30,* pp. 15–19.

Van Gundy, A. (1987). Organizational creativity and innovation. In S. G. Isaksen, (ed.), *Frontiers of creativity research: Beyond the basics,* pp. 358–379. Buffalo, NY: Bearly Limited.

Wallach, M. A., & Kogan, N. (1965). *Modes of thinking in young children.* New York Holt, Rinehart & Winston.

Wallach, M. A., & Wing, C. W., Jr. (1969). *The talented student: A validation of the creativity-intelligence distinction.* New York: Holt, Rinehart & Winston.

SECTION TWO
THE CREATIVE PERSON

Perhaps the topic that has received the greatest amount of attention within the field of creativity has been the examination of the creative person. For many, the search for the keys to creativity began with an exploration within people. To understand creativity it made sense to begin by investigating its source, the person. Researchers have investigated such questions as:

What traits distinguish highly creative individuals from those who are less creative?

Do highly creative people possess unique thinking skills?

To what degree does intelligence predict people's creativity?

To what extent do people show their creativity in different ways?

These and other questions about the nature of creativity in people have been the subject of scientific investigations for more than fifty years.

Although modern-day investigations of creativity are primarily limited to the last fifty years or so, there were a number of earlier works that helped to foster studies of the creative person. In particular, Galton (1869), Terman (1925) and others' work on genius acted as a forerunner to the direct study of creative people. Since Guilford's landmark speech to the American Psychological Association in 1950, the year often cited as the beginning of creativity research, countless studies have focused on identifying what makes certain people creative. Perhaps the most extensive study of creativity in people was carried out by MacKinnon (1978) and his colleagues at the Institute of Personality Assessment and Research. These investigators conducted intense investigations of creative people in such fields as architecture, mathematics, and science. Much of what we currently know about the personality traits of creative people is due to the work carried out by these researchers.

In a similar way, our current understanding of thinking-skills associated with highly creative people is due mainly to the investigations conducted by Guilford (1977) and Torrance (1979). The purpose of this section is to provide an introduction to what we know about creativity in people. The readings have been selected to provide some answers to the questions raised above. This section begins with a paper written by McAleer that summarizes some traits and thinking skills associated with creative people. Next, Agor and Amabile present detailed descriptions of two characteristics often associated with highly creative people, intuition and intrinsic motivation, respectively. Creative behavior can appear in many different forms.

The next two papers explore different ways in which people can show their creativity. Gold-smith and Matherly, for example, describe two different styles of creativity know as adaptive and innovative creativity. Armstrong's description of multiple intelligence explores seven different areas in which creative talent can emerge. Finally, this section closes with MacKinnon's overview of the well-known work carried out at the Institute of Personality Assessment and Research. (GP)

Of Additional Interest

Amabile, T. M. (1983). *The social psychology of creativity.* New York: Springer-Verlag.

Barron, F. (1969). *Creative person and creative process.* New York: Holt, Rinehart & Winston.

Barron, F. (1988). Putting creativity to work. In R. J. Sternberg (Ed.). *The nature of creativity: Contemporary psychological perspectives,* 76–98. New York: Cambridge University Press.

Boden. M. A. (1991). *The creative mind: Myths and mechanics.* New York: Basic Books.

Csikszentmihalyi, M. (1990). *Flow: The psychology of optimal experience.* New York: Harper & Row.

Dunn, R., Dunn, K., & Treffinger, D. J. (1992). *Bringing out the giftedness in your child.* New York: Wiley & Sons.

El Aasar, S. (1993). Human potential: An exploration of the role of creativity from an Arab perspective. In S. G. Isaksen, M. C. Murdock, R. L. Firestien, & D. J. Treffinger (Eds.). *Understanding and recognizing creativity: The emergence of a discipline,* 454–467. Norwood, NJ: Ablex.

Gardner, H. (1993). *Creating minds.* New York: Basic Books.

Getzels, J. W. (1987). Creativity, intelligence, and problem finding: Retrospect and prospect. In S. G. Isaksen (Ed.), *Frontiers of creativity research: Beyond the basics,* 88–102. Buffalo, NY: Bearly Limited.

Getzels, J. W., & Csikszentmihalya, M. (1976). *The creative vision: A longitudinal study of problem finding* . New York: Wiley.

Goleman, D., Kaufman, P., & Ray, M. (1992). *The creative spirit.* New York: Plume Books.

Guilford J. P. (1977). *Way beyond the IQ: Guide to improving intelligence and creativity.* Buffalo, NY: Creative Education Foundation.

Guilford J. P. (1986). *Creative talents: Their nature, uses and development.* Buffalo, NY: Bearly Limited.

Helson, R. (1988). The creativity personality. In K. Grøhaug & G. Kaufmann (Eds.). *Innovation: A cross disciplinary perspective,* 29–64. Oslo, Norway: Norwegian University Press.

Kirton, M. J. (1976). Adaptors and innovators: A description and measure. *Journal of Applied Psychology, 61,* 622–629.

Kirton, M. J. (Ed.). (1989). *Adaptors and innovators: Styles of creativity and problem-solving.* London: Routledge.

MacKinnon, D. W. (1967). Assessing creative persons. *Journal of Creative Behavior, 1,* 291–304.

MacKinnon, D. W. (1978). *In search of human effectiveness: Identifying and developing creativity.* Buffalo, NY: Creative Education Foundation & Creative Synergetic Associates.

Melrose, L. (1989). *The creative personality and the creative process: A phenomonological perspective.* Lanham, MD: University Press of America.

Simonton, D. K. (1984). *Genius, creativity and leadership.* Cambridge, MA: Harvard University Press.

Simonton, D. K. (1987). Genius: The lessons of historiometry. In S. G. Isaksen (Ed.), *Frontiers of creativity research: Beyond the basics* 66–87. Buffalo, NY: Bearly Limited.

Torrance, E. P. (1988). *The search for satori and creativity.* Buffalo, NY: Creative Education Foundation & Bearly Limited.

Torrance, E. P. (1988). The nature of creativity as manifest in its testing. In R. J. Sternberg (Ed.), *The nature of creativity: Contemporary psychological perspectives,* 43–75. New York: Cambridge University Press.

Wallace, D. B., & Gruber, H. E. (1989). *Creative people at work: Twelve cognitive case studies.* New York: Oxford University Press.

THE ROOTS OF INSPIRATION

Neil McAleer

Creativity is a passionate, exciting and challenging effort to make just the right connection amid the buffeting chaos of everyday reality. And in recent years the effort to understand humanity's imaginative quest has sprouted new wings. The reason for the renewed interest is the same today as it was 30 years ago: international competition.

Some scientists remain skeptical that we will ever fully understand the creative process. Nevertheless, many creativity researchers believe that a comprehensive psychology of creativity is within reach. And many hope to apply what we know about creativity to finding solutions to today's serious global problems. 'The idea that creativity spontaneously bubbles up from a magical well or gains a direct line to the Muses is just another myth among many about highly creative people and their work', says Harvard University psychologist David Perkins, co-director of Project Zero, a research project studying cognitive skills among scientists and artists. Momentary flashes of insight, often accompanied by images, make up only a small part of the creative continuum. At the heart of the process, personality and personal values shape an individual's intentional and sustained effort, often over a lifetime.

Creativity and genius have so often been considered bedfellows that creativity has been linked to intelligence. But intuition, much more than rational thought, appears to be vital to the creative thinking process. 'You don't have to have a high IQ to be intuitive,' says Frank Barron, a psychologist at the University of California at Santa Cruz who has measured and observed creativity for the last 40 years. 'Intuition depends less on reasoning and verbal comprehension [the main measure of IQ] than it does on feelings and metaphor.'

Scholastic skills do not predict whether a person can create something that will make a difference in society or even in his or her own life, Project Zero co-director Howard Gardner emphasizes. There are ample historical examples of creative individuals who had little interest in school or were poor students: Thomas Edison was at the bottom of his class; neither William Butler Yeats nor George Bernard Shaw was a very good speller; Benjamin Franklin was poor at maths.

Scrutinized and probed for some four decades, the creative personality has slowly revealed a number of common traits that are shared by artists and scientists—indeed, by all creative people. From the abundant laboratory data, as well as biographical evidence, Harvard's Perkins has developed what he calls the 'snowflake model of creativity.' Analogous to the six sides of the snowflake, each with its own complex structure, Perkins's model consists of six related but distinct psychological traits of the creative person. Creative people may not possess all six, Perkins points out, but the more they have the more creative they tend to be.

The first among the six traits is a strong commitment to a personal aesthetic, 'the drive to wrest order, simplicity, meaning, richness, or powerful expression from what is seemingly chaos,' Martindale says. Einstein's life, like his work, is full of examples of his powerful drive toward simplicity. Someone, for example, once asked him why he used hand soap for shaving instead of using shaving cream. 'Two soaps? That's too complicated,' Einstein replied.

As part of their personal aesthetic, creators have a high tolerance for complexity (some researchers call it ambiguity), disorganization, and asymmetry. They often enjoy the challenge of cutting through chaos and struggling toward a resolution and synthesis. 'In science very often the core challenge is to deal with a maze of ambiguities and forge a new identity,' Perkins says.

The second psychological trait, the ability to excel in finding problems, was demonstrated in studies involving art students. Through a battery of tests, University of Chicago researchers discovered that the students spent an unusual amount of time thinking about a problem and exploring all the options for solving it before they chose which solution to pursue.

Scientists value good questions because they lead to discoveries and creative solutions, to good answers. By asking the right questions and finding the right problem, creators can define and 'see' the boundaries of their fields that can be extended or broken. A student once asked Nobel laureate Linus Pauling, for example, how he found good ideas. Pauling replied that 'you have a lot of ideas and throw away the bad ones.' Such a winnowing out of ideas, however, depends on the ability to apply critical judgment to work that is often extremely personal and emotionally charged.

Mental mobility, the third trait, allows creative people to find new perspectives on and approaches to problems. One example of such mental gymnastics is so-called Janusian thinking. Remember the Roman god Janus, who had two faces, each looking in a different direction? Well, creative people have a strong tendency to think in terms of opposites and contraries metaphors and, as a matter of course, challenge assumptions. Pauling, for example, discovered the alpha helix (the most important way in which the polypeptide chains of proteins are folded) in large part because he questioned the assumption that all amino acids were not created equal. Pauling's idea, after years of frustrating work and dead ends, was that the amino acids are just one kind of unit, and, whatever their structures, they are equivalent to one another. By questioning the prevailing assumption he verified the helical structure in about two hours with a slide rule, a pencil, and a piece of paper. And he did it while in bed recuperating from a cold—before his vitamin C days.

The fourth psychological trait is the willingness to take risks. Psychologist Frank Farley has identified and studied risk takers and dubbed them Type T personalities for their thrill seeking. Creators as well as daredevils and criminals fit this criteria for Type T personalities, who, he says, constantly seek excitement and stimulation—physical thrills, mental thrills, or a mix of both. Farley explains that Type Ts may need more stimulation than other people because they have a low ability to become mentally aroused. In other words, they're not as responsive to stimuli as other personality types. The mental risk takers are the creators in whatever discipline or activity they pursue.

Along with risk taking, moreover, comes the acceptance of failure as part of the creative quest and the ability to learn from such failures. Many people believe that creative geniuses come up with ideas instantly, produce only masterpieces, never have any failures, and never take chances because they always know what they're doing. 'Such myths inhibit people from being as creative as they could be,' says psychologist Dean Simonton of the University of California at Davis. He argues that the odds of creative success depend on the number of attempts:

The more you produce, the higher your chances of creating something really important. 'Posterity tends to ignore the failures and praise the successes,' Simonton says. 'Picasso, for example, produced some 20,000 works of art, but much of it was mediocre.'

By working at the edge of their competence, where the possibility of failure lurks, mental risk takers are more likely to produce creative results. For some, taking risks in uncharted territory is exciting. Others may not relish the risk, but they accept it as part of the way to reach creative goals.

'When I'm in the middle of fieldwork, there's a sense of terra incognita, of really being out on a frontier discovering absolutely untried ground' says anthropologist Robert McCormick Adams, secretary of the Smithsonian Institution. 'You can also find terra incognita when you look into a microscope and other instrument-aided means of exploring the molecular or subatomic world or, for that matter, distant galaxies. Looking for new horizons is something that drives us. It's a particularly ingrained American trait because of the long influence of the frontier in the growth of the country.'

The popular image of creative individuals often highlights their subjectivity, personal insight, and commitment. But without objectivity, the fifth psychological trait, creative people simply construct a private world that has no reality. Creative people not only scrutinize and judge their ideas or projects, they also seek criticism. 'Contrary to the popular image, the creative person is not a self-absorbed loner,' said Perkins, who has studied professional and amateur poets. 'The poets who sought feedback produced poetry that a panel of experts judged to be better than the poetry of those who didn't seek criticism.' Objectivity, Perkins points out, involves more than luck or talent: it means putting aside your ego, seeking advice from trusted colleagues, and testing your ideas, as in scientific practice or marketplace settings.

The driving force behind creative efforts, however, is inner motivation, the sixth side of Perkin's snowflake model of creativity. Creators are involved in an enterprise for its own sake, not for school grades or paychecks. Their catalysts are the enjoyment, satisfaction, and challenge of the work itself. 'There are lots of people who have great potential for creativity,' says Brandeis University professor of psychology Teresa Amabile, who has conducted dozens of laboratory studies to verify the importance of intrinsic motivation in creativity. 'Many may have had some early success, but afterward they just dry up or are unable to produce, precisely because their work would or would not be evaluated. Amabile and her colleagues found ample evidence demonstrating that such factors as work evaluation, supervision, competition for prizes, and restricted choices in how to perform an activity undermine intrinsic motivation and inhibit creativity.

Words like love and passion frequently pop up when artists, scientists, and other creative people talk or write about their work. Such commitment is what motivates the scientist to discover, the artist to paint, or the writer to write. 'The emotional state which leads to such achievements resembles that of a worshipper or the lover,' Einstein wrote Max Planck in 1918. 'The daily struggle does not arise from a purpose or a program, but from an immediate need.'

As we delve deeper into the mysteries of creativity, learning more about its underlying nexus of biochemical, physiological, and psychological roots, we'll be able to increase creativity and instill more of it in more people. 'We are, in a perfectly real sense, creating creative thinking even as we study it,' Perkins says. And within the next 30 or 40 years, he believes, creative-thinking techniques will be used not just by artists, inventors, and scholars but by most of us.

The first step in that direction, University of California's Frank Barron suggests, is to think of creativity as the important human resource it really is. 'It is a unique force in the universe,' he says, 'a gift of life to the human species.'

References

Amabile, T. M. (1982) *The Social Psychology of Creativity*. New York: Springer Verlag.

Barron, F. (1968) *Creativity and Personal Freedom*. New York: Van Nostrand.

Gardner, H. (1983) *Frames of Mind: The Theory of Multiple Intelligences*. New York: Basic Books.

Perkins, D. (1981) *The Mind's Best Work*. Cambridge, MA: Havard University Press.

Simonton, D. K. (1984) *Genius, Creativity and Leadership*. Cambridge, MA: Havard University Press.

How Top Executives Use Their Intuition to Make Important Decisions

Weston H. Agor

The decade of the 1980s may well become known as that period in management history when intuition finally gained acceptance as a powerful brain skill for guiding executive decision making. Until recently, most organizations in America relied predominantly on left-brain analytical techniques such as MBO, PERT, and economic forecasting models to chart their future courses. But top executives have learned through painful experience that analysis by itself is often both inappropriate and inadequate.

Why is this so? Today, and increasingly in the future, top executives need to make major decisions in a climate characterized by rapid change and in times laden with crises. All too often, emerging new trends make linear projection models based on past trends either inaccurate or misleading. Decisions frequently must be made under circumstances where complete data bases necessary for "left-brain" (linear, deductive) processing will not be available or adequate—or where it will be too costly to gather such data in a timely fashion.

Intuition is a brain skill that is particularly useful for making major decisions in a management climate where:

- There is a high level of uncertainty;
- There is little precedent;
- Variables are often not scientifically predictable;
- "Facts" are limited;
- Facts don't make clear which way to go;
- Time is limited and there is pressure to be right; and
- It is necessary to choose from several plausible alternatives.

What Is Intuition?

Just what is intuition anyway? Psychologist Frances E. Vaughan defines it as a "way of knowing . . . recognizing the possibilities in any situation."[1] Webster's defines intuition as "the power of knowing . . . a quick or ready apprehension." Laurence R. Sprecher, senior associate with Public Management Associates in Oregon, argues that intuition is really a subspecies of logical thinking, one in which the steps of the process are hidden in the subconscious portion of the brain."[2] In research that more recently has been corroborated by others, Carl Jung, the famous psychologist, found that managers skilled in the use of intuition tend to possess particular decision-making skill most people lack.[3]

These managers have a sense or vision of what is coming—and how to move their organization in response to that vision. They are particularly adept at generating new ideas and in providing ingenious solutions to old problems. They also function best in crises or situations of rapid change.

Both practicing managers and students of the field of management alike now recognize that intuition is, and increasingly will become, a critical brain skill necessary for the successful company executive in the "megatrend," "future shock" environment we now face.

Studies of Intuitive Decision Making

For this reason, in 1981 I began a series of studies concerning executives' *ability to use* intuition—and their *actual use* of this skill—in making management decisions. By now I have tested several thousand executives from a wide range of different organizations and settings all over the country. These executives include private sector chief executive officer (CEOs), emergency preparedness military personnel, community college presidents, state health and rehabilitative services managers, city managers, state legislators and staff, and professional civil servants.

The results of these studies are reported in detail in two books: *Intuitive Management: Integrating Left and Right Brain Management Skills* and *The Logic of Intuition: A Research-Based Approach for Top Management.*

My findings are dramatic. Without exception, top managers in every organization differ significantly from middle and lower level managers in their ability to use intuition to make decisions on the job. Furthermore, women consistently score higher than men in their ability to use intuition, as do managers with Asian backgrounds. This finding may suggest that both women and persons with Asian backgrounds who have high levels of intuitive ability should consider marketing and developing their intuitive skills more actively as one effective vehicle for career advancement in the organizations of tomorrow.

According to test results, managers with higher levels of intuitive ability are likely to be particularly effective in such key occupations as marketing, personnel/organizational development, and sales, where imagination, creativity, and other "right brain" skills are demanded (see **Table 1**).

I also conducted extensive interviews with those executives who scored in the top ten percent on the intuition test nationally. I wanted to determine how they actually use their intuitive ability to help make major decisions. Executives in this group include top executives at General Motors and at Dow Chemical Company's worldwide headquarters and board members of Chrysler Corp., Burroughs, and the Ford Foundation.

As a group, these highly intuitive executives readily acknowledge that they use their intuitive ability to guide their most important decisions. They are quick to point out that they are not advocating the use of intuition exclusively nor the abandonment of traditional "left-brain" management practices. These executives believe, however, that *intuition itself* is a key management resource that should be neither ignored nor abandoned. Many top executives stress that good intuitive decisions are based in part on input from facts and experience gained over the years, combined and integrated with a well-honed sensitivity and openness to other, right-brain cues.

Table 1

Practical Use of Intuition in Organizations

Skills possessed by an intuitive executive

Sees possibilities
Supplies ingenuity to problems
Can deal with and solve complex issues
where data are incomplete
Furnishes new ideas
Sees the future
Motivates people to do the impossible

Some occupations where these skills are useful

Marketing/advertising
Specialty buyer
Communications (writing)
Sales
Nursing
Personnel/organizational development
Counseling
Intelligence
Investments
Real estate development

For example, Victor A. Casebolt, a top executive at International Paper Company in New York City, says that the MBAs he has worked with are often "overcautious and slow to act, a tendency I have ascribed to fear of making a mistake and/or 'analysis paralysis'." He wonders if the cause is "lack of experience on which to base self-confident, intuitive judgment."[4]

William G. McGinnis, a city manager in California, offers this definition of an intuitive decision:

> I believe that good intuitive decisions are directly proportional to one's years of challenging experience, plus the number of related and worthwhile years of training and education, all divided by lack of confidence or the fear of being replaced.[5]

Intuitive Cues

If we accept at face value that the intuition-guided decisions are in fact successful ones, one question remains: How do these executives know which course to take when they are faced with the options in front of them?

Highly intuitive managers describe the "feeling cues" they experience at the point of decision: "A sense of excitement—almost euphoric"; "a growing excitement in the pit of my stomach"; "a total sense of commitment"; "a feeling of total harmony"; "warm, and confident"; and "a burst of enthusiasm, energy." One manager muses, "It feels like a bolt of lightning or sudden flash that this is the solution."

These executives also seem to share a common set of feelings when they sense that an impending decision may be incorrect, that a particular option is inappropriate, or that they need to take more time to process the cues they are receiving in order to arrive at the best possible decision. At these times, managers speak of feeling a sense of anxiety, discomfort or an upset stomach, receiving mixed signals, and having sleepless nights.[6]

Factors That Impede the Use of Intuition

If highly intuitive executives receive clear signals that act as guideposts—telling them when they have chosen a workable option, when they have not, and when they need to take more time before reaching a final decision, why aren't these executives always correct?

Table 2
Keys to Developing and Using Your Intuition in Management

Intent	Value intuition and set about developing it.
Time	Take time and create a space in your life for developing intuition.
Relaxation	Let go of physical and emotional tension.
Silence	Learn to quiet the mind through such techniques as meditation.
Honesty	Face your own self-deception; be honest with yourself and others.
Receptivity	Be open to new and different ways of doing and seeing things.
Sensitivity	Tune into both your inner and outer cues.
Trust	Trust yourself.
Openness	Be open to experiences, both inner and outer.
Courage	Be willing to experience your fears and confront them.
Acceptance	Adopt a nonjudgmental attitude toward things as they are.
Nonattachment	Be willing to let things be as they are.
Practice	Practice using your intuition daily.
Support Group	Find friends and colleagues with whom you can share your intuitive experiences without their judging you.
Journal Keeping	Keep a record of your intuitive insights.
Love	Practice love and compassion.
Non-verbal Play	Practice nonverbal expression (for example, music, drawing) without a specific goal in mind.
Enjoyment	Find peace and satisfaction from expanding your consciousness through all these steps.

What emerges from my interviews is the following pattern: Top managers do indeed make errors in their decisions, but these errors do not appear to be caused by following their intuition. Rather, faulty decisions often appear instead to be caused by *failing to follow their intuition.* That is, when these top executives make errors in judgment, it is at least in part because they have violated one or more of the basic principles of intuition. As **Table 2** shows, psychologists working in this field for many years have identified the principles that are most effective for using intuition to guide major decisions.

Common errors that executives make involve *failing to be honest* (using self-deception and pretense) and *attachment* (failure to let things be as they are rather than trying to make them the way they would like them to be). This self-deception and this attachment apply both to themselves and to the decision they are about to make. Put another way, they engage in what psychologists commonly refer to as *projection*.

Projection is the process whereby our own ego clouds the intuitive cues we are able to receive as to *what is in fact true*. Hence, we transform reality into *what we would like to be true*.

For example, in some cases executives may become personally involved with people about whom they have to make management decisions. They fail then to see these people objectively, as these people are versus how they would like them to be.

Or they may not be receptive and open to the intuitive cues they are fully capable of receiving because they are afraid that the intuitive picture accurately projected will not fit well with their own preconceived notion or preference for reality.

A highly placed executive vice-president of one of the largest corporations in America tells how the president of that same organization sometimes lets his own ego involvement cloud his normal ability to make sound decisions:

> Sometimes he just gets too ego involved. He wants 100% on an issue when he could get 95% with a lot less grief. I've often had conflicts with him about his tendency to be this way.

Techniques to Activate Intuition for Decision Making

Intuitive executives have a clear set of techniques that they use in bringing their brain skill "on line" to help guide their most important decisions. These techniques are summarized in **Table 3**. What is worthy of note here is that this list coincides well with many of the techniques recommended by experts in the field of intuitional development.

For example, in his recent book, *The Intuitive Edge*, Philip Goldberg recommends "adopting a certain playfulness and an appreciation of whimsy" and "brainstorming with yourself."[7] These recommendations are similar to the actual practice of top executives who "play freely with ideas without a specific goal in mind."

The Secret Use of Intuition

Expert psychologists working in this field generally agree that one important vehicle for using and strengthening one's intuitive ability is to develop a support group. Such a group is composed of friends and colleagues with whom an executive can share the experience of using intuitive skills.

However, executives are in large measure reluctant to engage in such practices. Management training across the country has heavily emphasized in recent years the use of left-brain techniques almost to the total exclusion of other potentially useful skills and methods. Because organizational and community culture has tended to reinforce this tendency, it is not surprising to find that nearly half of the highly intuitive executives tested indicate they "keep it a secret" that they use intuition to make major decisions.

One top female executive explains that revealing this fact would tend to undermine her effectiveness:

> At work, I work with men; men who tend to regard the use of intuition as suspect, female, and unscientific. If I revealed my "secret," I'd have an even harder time persuading them to accept my suggestions.

Because intuitive executives often feel that their colleagues do not or will not understand that intuition can be a reliable basis on which to make important decisions, they often engage in elaborate games to legitimate the direction they propose taking.

Table 3

Techniques and Exercises Executives Use
to Activate Their Intuition

Relaxation Techniques
Clear mind mentally.
Seek quiet times.
Seek solitude.
Listen to classical music.
Sleep on problem.
Fast.
Meditate.
Pray.
Drop problem and return
    to it later.
Exercise.
Joke.

Mental Exercises
Play freely with ideas without a
    specific goal in mind.
Practice guided imagery.
Practice tolerating ambguity and
    accepting lack of control.
Practic flexibility, openness to
    unknowns as they appear.
Practice concentration.
Try to think of unique solution.
Be willing to follow up on points
    that have no factual justification.

Analytical Exercises

Discuss the problem with colleagues who have different perspectives as well as with
    respected friends.

Concentrate on listening to not only *what* but also *how* people express themselves.

Immerse yourself totally in the issue at hand.

Identify pros and cons; then assess your feelings about each option.

Consider the problem only when you are most alert.

Tune into your reactions to outside stimuli.

Analyze dreams.

Insist on a creative pause before reaching a decision.

Ask "What do I want to do?" and "What is right to do?"

A top executive at one of the largest and most successful corporations in America put it this way: "Sometimes one must dress up an intuitive decision in data clothes to make it acceptable/palatable."

Another typical response is this one:

> I share this fact easily with other friendly intuitives, but try to disguise it as careful planning, research, or an intellectual effort around others. This is not a matter of adopting a cunning strategy: those without the willingness or ability to use their own intuition are often frightened by intuitive demonstrations or reject any evidence not fitting their current paradigm.

Steps to Take

There is no question that the effective use of intuition in management can be a significant resource for increasing management productivity in the decade ahead. For example, John Naisbitt and Patricia Aburdene, in their new book *Re-inventing the Corporation,* note that intuition is gaining new respectability in corporate boardrooms as a decision-making skill.[8] The key step for executives to take now is to accept this fact and to practice techniques for bringing their own skills "on line" for more effective decision making.

Specifically, executives should focus their creative energy in a new and more innovative direction by adopting a more positive attitude about their own intuitive ability. They might also want to implement programs that quantify objectively intuitive decision-making processes and establish success records for intuition.

Sharing these findings could facilitate our understanding of how intuition might best be developed and used in the applied organizational settings that are likely to emerge in the decades ahead.

Notes

[1] Frances E. Vaughan. *Awakening Intuition* (Garden City, N.Y.: Anchor, 1979): 3.

[2] Laurence R. Sprecher, "Intuition Anyone?" *Public Management,* February 1983: 18.

[3] For corroboration of Jung's research, see, for example, Isabel Briggs Myers, *Introduction to Type* (Palo Alto: Consulting Psychologists Press, 1980) and Gordon Lawrence, *People Types and Tiger Stripes: Guide to Learning Styles,* 2nd ed. (Gainesville, Fla.: Center for Psychological Type, Inc., 1982).

[4] Victor A. Casebolt, "How Managers Think," *Harvard Business Review,* January 1985: 184.

[5] William G. McGinnis, Decision-Making Process," *Public Management*, February 1983: 17.

[6] It is important to note that this description of the specific cues that intuitive executives receive to guide their decisions is consistent with the experiences described by the famous personalities interviewed by Marilee Zdenek for her recent book, *The Right-Brain Experience* (New York: McGraw-Hill, 1983).

[7] Philip Goldberg, *The Intuitive Edge* (Los Angeles: J. P. Tarcher, Inc., 1983): 157.

[8] John Naisbitt and Patricia Aburdene, *Re-inventing the Corporation* (New York: Warner, 1985): 31–33.

Weston H. Agor is professor and director of the Masters in Public Administration Program at the University of Texas at El Paso. He is also president of ENFP Enterprises, a management consulting firm that specializes in the use of intuition in decision making. Agor is the author of Intuitive Management *(Englewood Cliffs, N.J.: Prentice-Hall, 1984), which has been adopted for use by many of the leading management schools in the country, including Harvard, Yale, Indiana, and Stanford. His article "Using Intuition to Manage Organizations in the Future" appeared in the July-August 1984 issue of* Business Horizons. *Agor has developed the AIM Survey, an instrument for measuring and developing intuitive management skills.*

A more detailed treatment of this topic will appear in Agor's forthcoming book, The Logic of Intuition: A Research-Based Approach for Top Management, *to be published later this year by Greenwood Press.*

The author thanks the Alden B. Dow Creativity Center in Midland, Michigan, for providing a resident fellowship and staff support to complete this research.

THE PERSONALITY OF CREATIVITY

Teresa M. Amabile

The chemist who had just arrived for his appointment looked no different from the others I'd been interviewing all day at this major R&D laboratory in a large chemical company. Over two dozen scientists had already answered my standard question: "Can you tell me about an example of high creativity from your work experience, as well as an example of low creativity?" I'd asked them to discuss any features of these events—the persons involved, the work environments—that seemed distinctive. The stories I'd been hearing were full of rich, intriguing detail. But I was completely unprepared for this man's startling remarks.

"One thing I've done to stay creative is to cut my salary down, so management doesn't worry about what I'm doing every moment. Once a salary gets up there, management is forced to get involved in everything you do, because every moment of your time costs the company money. So I avoid this by turning down the raises. I'm here to have a good time. I have the joy of thinking . . . I love just thinking things over, just circling a problem. I am interested in things that don't work, and I even seek them out. When I see conceptual contradictions, I go get them. Just let me play. Give me a big enough playpen, and I'll go from there."

Not surprisingly, I would later learn that this man's colleagues and supervisors considered him to be eccentric and difficult to manage. At the same time, though, they agreed that he consistently produced the laboratory's most creative work.

Although, of the 120 scientists my colleagues and I interviewed, he was the only one to say he refused salary increases, this man merely presents an extreme form of an attitude that we found quite prevalent among the most creative participants: they are in it for the fun and the personal sense of satisfaction they get from meeting an intriguing challenge. If anything gets in the way of that fun and satisfaction—particularly constraints placed on them by their work environment—their level of creative productivity suffers.

We can ask two questions about this revelation. What does it tell us about the special characteristics of creative people—"the creative personality"? What does it tell us about the special characteristics of creative thinking—"the personality of creativity"? When psychologists first started studying creativity about 35 years ago, they tackled the first question. In 1950, in his presidential address to the American Psychological Association, J. P. Guilford urged personality researchers to describe fully the special traits and talents that distinguish outstandingly creative people. Throughout the 1950s and 1960s, this work proceeded apace. Don MacKinnon and Frank Barron at the Institute for Personality Assessment and Research in Berkeley identified a number of traits that described their creative subjects (architects, mathematicians, and writers). Among those traits were independence, nonconformity, and a propensity toward risk-taking. During these same decades, two pioneers in creativity training began their work: Alex Osborn was devising his "brainstorming" training procedures, and W. J. J. Gordon was developing "synectics," on the basis of findings about the cognitive styles of very creative people.

And all researchers during this time acknowledged the importance of special talents in the highest levels of creative work.

But still, extraordinary talent and personality and cognitive ability seem not to be enough. Arthur Schawlow, the Nobel laureate in physics, said this about his own creativity and that of his colleagues: "The labor of love aspect is important. The successful scientists often are not the most talented, but the ones who are just impelled by curiosity. . . . They've got to know what the answer is." That extra something that determines creativity, that "labor of love aspect," is what my students, my colleagues, and I have studied over the past ten years. Our research can be summarized in the Intrinsic Motivation Principle of Creativity: people will be most creative when they feel motivated primarily by the interest, enjoyment, satisfaction, and challenge of the work itself—and not by external pressures. In other words, people will be most creative when they are intrinsically motivated (motivated primarily by intrinsically interesting aspects of the work itself) and not extrinsically motivated (motivated primarily by goals outside of the work itself, such as supervisory restrictions, deadlines, or reward structures).

We are not alone in this belief. Albert Einstein saw intrinsic motivation as conducive to creativity and extrinsic motivation as detrimental. As he said, "It is a very grave mistake to think that the enjoyment of seeing and searching can be promoted by means of coercion and a sense of duty." The observations of outstandingly creative people such as Einstein, Schawlow, and other scientists, writers, artists, and musicians constitute our first source of evidence on the Intrinsic Motivation Principle of Creativity. The second source of evidence comes from controlled experiments that we have conducted in our laboratory with young children, college students, creative writers, and business managers. By systematically varying the presence or absence of extrinsic constraints in the work environment (factors such as restricted choice, expected evaluation, competition, or surveillance of work), we have examined the effects of each of these factors on artistic, verbal, and problem-solving creativity. The third source of evidence comes from the interview study of R&D scientists, which I conducted with Dr. Stan Gryskiewicz of the Center for Creative Leadership. Through a detailed content analysis of our scientists' descriptions of creative and uncreative events, we found that this nonexperimental study provided striking confirmation of the laboratory experiments.

In short, we have discovered six methods for killing creativity—six factors that, when imposed on someone who is doing an interesting and potentially creative task, can undermine both the interest and the creativity. (1) Expected evaluation; people who are concentrating on how their work will be evaluated are less creative than people who are not made to worry about evaluation. (2) Surveillance; people who are conscious of being watched as they are working will be less creative than people who are not conscious of being watched. (3) Reward; people who see themselves as doing something primarily in order to gain a tangible reward will be less creative than those who are not working primarily for reward. (4) Competition; people who feel themselves in direct, threatening competition with others in their work will be less creative than those not focusing on competition. (5) Restricted choice; people who have their choice in how to do a task restricted will be less creative than people given a freer choice. This factor seems to be especially important for creativity in the scientists we studied. In the R&D interviews, freedom of choice in how to do one's work was the single most potent feature of environments supporting high creativity. Conversely, constraint of choice was the single most potent feature of environment in the low creativity examples. (6) Extrinsic orientation; people who are led to think about all the extrinsic reasons for doing what they are doing will be less creative than people who are thinking about all the intrinsic reasons.

This is not to suggest that extrinsic motivation is all bad. Indeed, in routine tasks that do not require any creativity, extrinsic motivation may be absolutely essential. Most of us don't want our bookkeepers to dream up new ways of playing with the accounts; in jobs such as this, motivation by rewards, evaluation expectation, surveillance, and so on may be perfectly appropriate for getting the work done, getting it done on time, and getting it done accurately. But if we are trying to get our scientists to produce innovative ideas, our advertisers to dream up novel campaigns, our graduate students to formulate elegant new hypotheses, and our children to exercise their growing creative talents, then we had best find ways for supporting intrinsic motivation.

How is it that intrinsic motivation stimulates creativity and extrinsic motivation undermines creativity? Although much more work on this complex question is needed, we now use a metaphor to guide our thinking on the issue. Imagine that a task is like a maze that you must get through. Say, for simplicity's sake, that there is only one entrance to the maze. Say also that there is one very straightforward, well-worn, familiar pathway out of the maze—a straight line that you have followed a hundred times, and that you could practically follow in your sleep. You can consider this path to be an algorithm you have learned for doing this task or similar tasks; it is a series of steps that you follow by rote. And it does lead you out of the maze. By getting out, you have fulfilled the basic requirements of the task. You have found a solution that is adequate. It is also quite uncreative. There are, of course, other exits from the maze—and these solutions might well be creative, elegant, and exciting. The problem is that none of these exits can be reached from the familiar, straightforward pathway. Some deviation is required, some exploration through the maze. Moreover, *risk-taking* is required; in any maze, there are more dead ends than there are exits. The explorer must have the flexibility to recover from getting stuck in a dead end, to back up and intelligently try something else.

If you are extrinsically motivated, you are motivated primarily by something *outside* of the maze—something outside of the task itself, such as a promised reward for finishing. The most reasonable thing for you to do under these circumstances is to take the simplest, safest path— to follow the familiar routine, the conservative method. That way, you run no risks and the extrinsic goal is surely achieved. If, however, you are intrinsically motivated to do the task, you *enjoy being in the maze.* (This is not to say that you want never to get out. Certainly, the whole point of being there is the challenge of finding a new way out.) You enjoy the activity itself. You *want* to explore in the maze, and you will be able to take those dead ends in stride. It is only when you start out intrinsically motivated, *and* only when your work environment allows you to retain that intrinsic focus, that you will be likely to discover a creative exit.

Intrinsic motivation is necessary for creativity, but it is by no means all that you need. The theory of creativity that I have been developing these last few years proposes *three* components that are necessary for creativity. (1) *Domain-relevant skills;* these are skills in the specific domain (for example, mathematics, music, or literature)—a combination of talents and skills learned through formal education and experience. (2) *Creativity-relevant skills;* these are ways of thinking and working that are conducive to creativity in any domain—for example, an independent, nonconforming personality, a high energy level, and a way of taking new perspectives on problems. (3) *Task motivation;* an intrinsic motivation to do a particular task is more conducive to creativity on that task than an extrinsic motivation. This, of course, is the point that my own work has highlighted. Some people may naturally be more intrinsically oriented toward their work, and others may be more extrinsically oriented. In fact, my students and I have developed a brief test called the Work Preference inventory that measures general intrinsic and extrinsic motivation. But our research shows that whatever a person's basic motivational orientation, social factors in the work environment (such as evaluation, surveillance, reward, and so on) can often undermine whatever intrinsic motivation is there.

So what's the good news? We know that the "personality of creativity" is such that it can be severely hindered by extrinsic motivators. We know six reliable ways to kill creativity—and so, apparently, do many teachers, business managers, and parents. How can we keep creativity alive? At this point, we can suggest three possibilities. First, it is important to have a high level of knowledge and experience—in other words, to have a high level of domain-relevant skills and creativity-relevant skills. According to our theory, the overall level of creativity in an idea or a product is determined jointly by a person's level of domain-relevant skills, creativity-relevant skills, and task motivation. If task motivation is somewhat low on the intrinsic dimension, that might be partially compensated for by high levels of skill. In other words, a person might be able to produce moderately creative work, even if somewhat more extrinsically than intrinsically motivated, if he or she is extremely skilled in the domain and experienced in thinking up new ideas.

The second method for keeping creativity alive is to take the focus off extrinsic goals and constraints. Ideally, we should be able to maintain our intrinsic motivation (and our creativity) by somehow shrugging off the strong extrinsic pressures under which we must work. But since this is difficult to do, it would help if our work environments did not impose unnecessarily strong systems of evaluation, reward, competition, and other forms of extrinsic motivators.

Third, it should help if we can concentrate on intrinsic motives. This suggestion is a companion to the previous one. If we can somehow be really aware of our sense of interest, enjoyment, personal challenge, and internal satisfaction in our work, then we might be less subject to the ill effects of extrinsic constraints on our motivation and creativity.

We have just gathered some exciting new data on these last two points. Beth Hennessey (a Ph.D. candidate in Psychology at Brandeis), Barbara Grossman '83 (a research assistant on this work), and I tried to train children to focus on their intrinsic motives for doing various types of schoolwork and to minimize the importance of extrinsic constraints. We used a simple modeling procedure. The children in the study watched videotapes in which other children served as models of intrinsically motivated individuals. When the adult on the videotape asked the child-models what they liked to do in school and why, the models replied (according to a script we had written) with statements of interest, excitement, and deep involvement in some aspect of their studies. When the adult asked how they felt about teacher approval and getting high marks, the models said that, although such things were nice, they were not as important as really trying to enjoy your work. There was one dominant message throughout the training videotape and the accompanying discussion we had with the children in this study: it's nice to get rewards, approval, and so on, but the most important factor is to be aware of the intrinsically interesting, satisfying, and challenging aspects of whatever you are doing.

The training succeeded: those children who had been trained showed higher levels of intrinsic motivation than children who had not gone through the training. More importantly, the trained children showed no decrement of creativity under extrinsic constraint. In effect, what we have done is to show that children—and, we hypothesize, adults, too—can be *immunized* against the negative effects of extrinsic constraints on their intrinsic motivation and creativity.

If we can continue with this work, finding new ways to accommodate both persons and environments to the special "personality of creativity," we will have come a long way toward promoting what Einstein called "the enjoyment of seeing and searching." The result will surely be *more* searching, *better* seeing—in short, greater creativity.

Teresa M. Amabile, associate professor of psychology, has conducted extensive research on the psychology of creativity. Her findings have been published in numerous professional journals. She has received research grants from the National Institute of Child Health and Human Development, the Brandeis University Mazer Fund, the Foundation for Child Development, the National Institute of Mental Health, and the National Institutes of Health. She is a member of the International Advisory Board of the Center for Studies in Creativity, and a research associate of the Center for Creative Leadership. Her book, The Social Psychology of Creativity, *was published in 1983.*

THE TWO FACES OF CREATIVITY

Timothy A. Matherly and Ronald E. Goldsmith

Whenever academics or managers discuss the characteristics which they feel are essential for the long-term success of business organizations, they are certain to put creativity near the top of the list. Creative individuals assume almost mythical status in the corporate world, as tales of an Edison or a Steinmetz transmit the culture of the organization to new members. An organization with a reputation for creativity inevitably is considered a good place to work.

Nothing testifies quite so well to the corporate concern with creativity as the plethora of techniques designed and sold to enhance creativity in the decision-making process. From the Madison Avenue razzle-dazzle of brainstorming to the sedately systematic Nominal Group Technique, there has been neither a supply shortage of tips, techniques, and systems to enhance creativity nor a lack of demand for these products.

While creativity long has been assumed to be of value in such areas as marketing and product development, there is a growing feeling that its impact on the strategic planning process makes creativity desirable at the highest level of the firm. The strategic decision process within the firm may be inhibited or blocked because of an absence of the ability or inclination to engage in the necessary creative process. One leading textbook, in discussing reasons why the strategic planning process often fails to come to fruition, notes:

> Strategic decision making is fundamentally a creative process that is difficult. It demands a type of thinking and breadth of knowledge that many executives who have arrived at top management levels have neglected as they rose in the ranks because they devoted themselves to solving short-range problems in their narrow functional areas of expertise.[1]

Traditional efforts at enhancing creativity, whether from the perspective of a firm desiring improvement or the individual offering techniques, tend to suffer from at least two basic deficiencies. First, they tend to be vague and imprecise in defining creativity. Post hoc judgments decree that those actions which subsequently result in radical improvements in organizational performance must have been creative. Secondly, they tend to emphasize creative *processes* to the neglect of creative *persons*. The first deficiency is not significant if one is in the business of creating legends. However, it provides little help for the manager concerned with identifying and nurturing creativity in its embryonic stages. The second deficiency stems, perhaps, from a democratic (or perhaps self-aggrandizing) belief that we all possess great stores of creative potential just waiting to be released. However, it ignores the readily observable fact that the majority of creative ideas in any organization are generated by a handful of people.

Another puzzle emerges when creative behavior is examined from the perspective of the organization. There is often a significant difference between what organizations *say* they value and what their common *practice* indicates.[2] Although organizations persistently endorse open communication, flexibility, risk-taking, trust, and innovation, standard practice often seems to discourage these behaviors and to reinforce evasion, rigidity, caution, suspicion, and stability.

The Nature of Creativity

A portion of the difficulty in identifying and encouraging creative management can be traced to unclear, imprecise, or inadequate conceptualizations of the nature of creativity. Too often, creativity is seen as the generation of unique solutions to problems through the discovery of previously unobserved relationships between known factors or the insightful revelation of solutions to previously unsolvable problems. While the activities in this definition certainly may be desirable, by themselves they fail to identify the total scope of an organization's demands for creativity or even the role of creativity in the functioning of the organization.

This view of creativity, from a practical perspective, is by no means guaranteed to pay off in any way that substantively benefits the organization, its members, or its constituents. As Theodore Leavitt observed, "A powerful new idea can kick around unused in a company for years, not because its merits are not recognized, but because nobody has assumed the responsibility for converting it from words into actions. What is often lacking is not creativity in the idea-creating sense, but innovation in the action-producing sense, i.e., putting ideas to work."[3]

A further inadequacy of the traditional notion of creativity is that it places a premium on revolutionary change precipitated by identifiable discontinuities in the operations of the firm. There are certainly situations where this sort of turnaround is probable—and, indeed, some situations in which it is absolutely necessary. Most firms, however, are rather competent at what they do, having invested considerable effort, experience, and intelligence in mastering their respective crafts. Managers in these firms may recognize the desirability of radically improving the organization's performance. They also understand that the probability of winning this sort of creative lottery is quite low and that the best odds for enhancing the company's fortunes lie in small increments of improvement, arduously obtained.

A more useful definition of creativity is **the generation of ideas that result in the improvement of the efficiency or effectiveness of a system.** The advantages of this conceptualization of creativity are that (1) it is *results*-oriented, thus establishing some objective criteria for the evaluation of creative input; and (2) it opens the door to a proper valuation of creative activities that may be overlooked because they are not spectacular.

Adaptors and Innovators: Two Problem-Solving Styles

Insight into the influence of personal characteristics on creativity comes from Michael Kirton's research into the nature of the creative process.[4] Basically, Kirton posits a continuum of decision-making styles. Where individuals are located on the continuum depends on whether they tend to be adaptors or innovators. Adaptors are those who seek to solve problems by "doing things better." They prefer to resolve difficulties or make decisions in such a way as to have the least impact upon the assumptions, procedures, and values of the organization; they seek to improve the existing framework and do not "rock the boat." Innovators, on the other hand, are inclined to "do things differently." They are likely to see the solution to problems in the alteration of the basic approaches and framework of the organization; a certain amount of disruption may contribute positively to the achievement of the organization's goals.

Individuals differ, then, not only in their *levels* of creativity but also in the *form* that creative expression takes. Thus there are both qualitative and quantitative differences in individual styles and levels of creativity. The **Table** summarizes some of the characteristics of adaptors and innovators.

Adaptor	Innovator
Employs disciplined, precise, methodical approach	Approaches task from unusual angles
Is concerned with solving, rather than findin, problems	Discovers problems and discovers avenues of solutions
Attempts to refine current practices	Questions basic assumptions related to current practice
Tends to be means-oriented	Has little regards to means
Is capable of extended detail work	Has little tolerance for routine work
Is sensitive to group cohesion and cooperation	Has little or no need for consensus; often insensitive to others

Adapted from Micheal Kirton, "Adaptors and Innovators: A Description and Measure," *Journal of Applied Psychology, 61,* No. 5 (1976): 623.

In reality, of course, most people do not fall strictly and exclusively into one of these two personality types. Rather, this typology represents opposite ends of a continuum, with most people representing some combination of these two extremes and incorporating elements of both styles in their approaches to problem solving. Individual problem-solving styles normally are distributed across almost the entire range of possibilities, with women tending to be more adaptor-inclined than men and with younger adults tending to be somewhat more innovative than older adults.[5] Interestingly, neither intelligence, level of education, nor occupational status appears to be significantly related to adaptation/innovation style.

Each of these basic problem-solving styles has its own strengths and weaknesses and makes its own contribution to the function of the organization. For some problems the methodical, detailed application of the existing organizational methods yields the most effective result. Some problems, on the other hand, cry out for the original, innovative solution that gives the organization a totally new direction. The presence of different approaches to problem solving within a single organization or operating unit may lead to disagreement over the desirability of solutions, disagreement that ranges beyond simple discussion of technical merits. Adaptors and innovators may not see eye to eye and may not understand that their differences lie at a fundamental psychological level. Thus, the potential for considerable interpersonal conflict arises, with both individuals and organizations paying the price.

To adaptors, innovators may seem to be neurotics, grandstanders, and misfits, bent on upheaval and destruction within the organization. Innovators, on the other hand, may view adaptors as dogmatic and inflexible "organization types" who serve as insurmountable obstacles to fundamental change in the organization. Although objectively inaccurate, such pejorative stereotypes tend to polarize decision makers and prevent objective evaluation of the merits of individual ideas.

A Place for Everyone

In their own ways, adaptors and innovators may be equally creative. Each cognitive style may lead to solutions that increase organizational effectiveness. Adaptation/innovation is a distinction between *styles* of creativity, not *levels* of creativity. Although most theory, research, and discussion of creativity stress the generation of novel ideas, adaptive solutions may cope well with new situations, new information, or new problems while preserving the essential values, assumptions, and equilibrium of the organization. The opposite of creativity is not the generation of conventional ideas, but rather the failure to generate ideas at all.

Indeed, there are often sound reasons for an organizational bias toward adaptive solutions to problems. Not only do adaptors tend to be better suited for the prolonged, routine activities involved in implementing a decision, but the fact that adaptive solutions tend to minimize institutional disruption also makes them more palatable to most organizations.

Innovators, too, have their place in the organizational process. The importance of their contribution may be illustrated by an analogy to Kuhn's model of the progress of science.[6] According to this model, the development of scientific theory tends to be organized around and directed by a dominant paradigm or conceptual model. However, when a mass of evidence accumulates that is inconsistent with this model, a "paradigm switch" occurs, in which the old model is precipitously abandoned in favor of a new paradigm that better accommodates existing data and impels productive inquiry.

In a similar sense, innovators are inclined to challenge the prevailing view of how the organization operates and how it defines its mission. For the organization that is functioning well under its existing paradigm, this may be neither necessary nor desirable. For the organization in which the paradigm is being invalidated by contradictory data—declining profits or market share, loss of technological leadership, or other deteriorating performance criteria—or for those aspects of operations in which a successful mode of performance is not established, innovation may range anywhere from being valuable to being critical for the survival of the firm.

Managing for Creative Results

Concern for creativity in management is perhaps well founded. However, with an awareness of the alternative forms that creativity can take, management can target specific areas for improvement. Some specific suggestions are offered here.

Matching Creative Style to Organizational Needs. As previously noted, there are some situations in which stability is highly valued, and others in which flexibility is essential. For example, six categories of managerial personalities (management archetypes) have been identified for six basic strategic directions.[7] For three of these directions—Explosive Growth, Expansion, and Retreat-Reposition—a flexible, divergent individual with an innovative bent is desired. For the other three—Continuous Growth, Consolidation, and Harvest—a stable, adaptive personality is more appropriate. Similarly, the stage of the company's life cycle may influence the requisite capabilities of a management team, with entrepreneurial (that is, innovative) skills and administrative and integrative (that is, adaptive) abilities shifting in importance at various stages.[8]

Matching Creative Style to Job Requirements. One of the most critical tasks for any organization is that of matching the skills of people to the demands of the jobs they are to perform. Considerable attention is devoted, therefore, to screening, testing, interviewing, and evaluating both potential and current employees to select those whose aptitudes best suit them to the requirements of particular jobs. This matching process is no less important in the case of managers, whose skills, especially in communication and problem solving, are deemed of critical importance. It is no easy matter, however, to identify the salient characteristics of managers or potential managers.

Creative style may prove to be especially important to certain positions; for example, in product development. There is increasing evidence that firms must be able to develop and market new products or services in order to ensure long-term survival. Innovative problem-solvers may be ideally suited to the task of creating and developing new products, where the emphasis is upon novel solutions or ideas. Adaptors may be better suited to administering existing product lines, where the usual demands involve maintenance, administration, and improvement of existing systems.

Training. An awareness of the Adaptation/Innovation continuum may benefit organizational training programs in three areas. First of all, judgmental barriers need to be overcome. If managers are to interact on a more objective, less psycho-emotional plane, they need to put aside the pejorative stereotypes adaptors apply to innovators and vice versa. A second possibility lies in the potential for expanding individual creative repertoires. Adaptors can be encouraged to introduce greater novelty in their problem solving; innovators, on the other hand, can be encouraged to develop more systematic ways of approaching problems and implementing solutions. Finally, knowledge of their own creative styles can help individual managers adapt to specific problems and situations and adopt appropriate problem-solving behavior.[9]

The ability of a firm to generate internal changes in procedures, to produce new products, or to react to new competitive situations is often essential to its long-term survival. Change may take the form of radical departure from the organization's established operations, or it may involve less sweeping modifications in behavior of and in the organization. Though they differ in style, both the innovative and the adaptive contributions are creative. The truly creative firm is one where both types of creative input are recognized and valued for what they can offer, and where each is encouraged in those situations in which it is appropriate. By recognizing the potential contributions of both of these creative personality styles, organizations can build balanced, creative management teams and enhance organizational effectiveness.

Notes

[1] George A. Steiner, John B. Miner, and Edmund R. Gray, *Management Policy and Strategy: Text, Readings, and Cases,* 2nd ed. (New York: Macmillan, 1982).

[2] Chris Argyris, "Interpersonal Barriers to Decision Making," *Harvard Business Review,* March-April 1966: 84–97.

[3] Theodore Leavitt, "Creativity Is Not Enough," *Harvard Business Review*, May-June 1963: 72–83.

[4] Michael Kirton, "Adaptors and Innovators: A Description and Measure," *Journal of Applied Psychology,* October 1976: 622-629.

[5] Ibid.

[6] Thomas S. Kuhn, *The Structure of Scientific Revolutions,* 2nd ed. (Chicago: University of Chicago Press, 1970).

[7] J. G. Wissema, H. W. VanderPol, and H. Messer, "Strategic Managment Archetypes," *Strategic Management Journal,* January 1980: 43.

[8] Ichak Adizes, "Organizational Passages—Diagnosing and Treating Lifecycle Problems of Organizations," *Organizational Dynamics,* Summer 1979: 3–25.

[9] Stanley S. Gryskiewicz. "Creative Leadership Development and the Kirton Adaptation-Innovation Inventory" (Greensboro, N. Car.: Center for Creative Leadership, 1982).

Timothy A. Matherly and Ronald E. Goldsmith are assistant professors in the departments of management and marketing respectively at The Florida State University.

RECAPITULATION:
WHAT MAKES A PERSON CREATIVE?

D. W. MacKinnon

In 1956, a group of psychologists began a nationwide study of human creativity. They wanted the scientific answers to the mystery of human personality, biology, intelligence, and intuition that makes some persons more creative than others.

Investigating Stereotypes

Working under a grant by the Carnegie Corporation of New York, the researchers were faced with the usual stereotypes that picture the highly creative person as a genius with an I. Q. far above average, an eccentric not only in thinking but in appearance, dress, and behavior, a bohemian, an egghead, a longhair. According to these unproved stereotypes, he was not only introverted but a true neurotic, withdrawn from society, inept in his relations with others, totally unable to carry on a conversation with others less gifted than himself. Still others held that the creative person might be profound but that his intelligence was highly one-sided, in a rather narrow channel, and that he was emotionally unstable. Indeed, one of the most commonly held of these images was that he lived just this side of madness.

The Actual Study

The psychological researchers who sought a more precise picture of the creative person conducted their investigations on the Berkeley campus of the University of California in the Institute of Personality Assessment and Research. At the Institute, the persons to be studied have been brought together, usually ten at a time, for several days, most often a three-day weekend. There they have been examined by a variety of means—by the broad problem posed by the assessment situation itself, by problem-solving experiments, by tests designed to discover what a person does not know or is unable to reveal about himself, by tests and questionnaires that permit a person to manifest various aspects of his personality and to express his attitudes, interests, and values, by searching interviews.

The professional groups whose creative members were chosen for study were writers, architects, research workers in the physical sciences and engineering, and mathematicians. In no instance did the psychological assessors decide which highly creative persons should be studied. Rather, they were nominated by experts in their own fields; and to insure that the traits found to characterize the highly creative were related to their creativity rather than indigenous to all members of the profession, a wider, more representative sample of persons in each of the professional groups was also chosen, though for somewhat less intensive study. All told, some 600 persons participated.

As the study has progressed it has become abundantly clear that creative persons seldom represent fully any of the common stereotypes, and yet in some respects and to some degree there are likenesses. It is not that such images of the creative person are fantastic but that they

82

are caricatures rather than characterizations, heightening and sharpening traits and dispositions so as to yield a picture recognizable, yet still out of accord with reality. There are, of course, some stereotypes that reflect only error, but more often the distortion of the reality would seem to be less complete.

Intelligence

As for intellectual capacity, it will come as no surprise that highly creative persons have been found to be, in the main, well above average. But the relation between intelligence and creativity is not as clear-cut as this would suggest, if for no other reason than that intelligence is a many-faceted thing. There is no single psychological process to which the term "intelligence" applies; rather, there are many types of intellective functioning. There is verbal intelligence, and on a well-known test of this factor creative writers, on the average, score higher than any of the other groups. But there is also spatial intelligence—the capacity to perceive and to deal with spatial arrangements—and on a test of this aspect of intelligence creative writers as a group earn the lowest average score, while creative architects as a group are the star performers. There are, of course, many elements of intelligence in addition to these two.

Alert and Adaptive in Response

If for a moment we ignore those patterns of intellective functioning which clearly and most interestingly differentiate one creative group from another, there are some more general observations that may be noted. It is quite apparent that creative persons have an unusual capacity to record, retain, and have readily available the experiences of their life history. They are discerning, which is to say that they are observant in a differentiated fashion; they are alert, capable of concentrating attention readily and shifting it appropriately; they are fluent in scanning thoughts and producing those that serve to solve the problems they undertake; and, characteristically, they have a wide range of information at their command. As in the case of any intelligent person, the items of information which creative persons possess may readily enter into combinations, and the number of possible combinations is increased for such persons because of both a greater range of information and a greater fluency of combination. Since true creativity is defined by the adaptiveness of a response as well as its unusualness, it is apparent that intelligence alone will tend to produce creativity. The more combinations that are found, the more likely it is on purely statistical grounds that some of them will be creative.

Relation of Intelligence and Creativity

Yet intelligence alone does not guarantee creativity. On a difficult, high-level test of the more general aspects of intelligence, creative persons score well above average, but their individual scores range widely, and in several of the creative groups the correlation of intelligence as measured by this test and creativity as rated by the experts is essentially zero.

Certainly this does not mean that over the whole range of creative endeavor there is no relation between general intelligence and creativity. No feeble-minded persons appeared in any of the creative groups. Clearly a certain degree of intelligence, in general a rather high degree, is required for creativity, but above that point the degree of intelligence does not seem to determine the level of one's creativeness. In some fields of endeavor, mathematics and theoretical physics for example, the requisite intelligence for highly creative achievement is obviously high. But it does not follow that the theoretical physicist of very superior I. Q. will necessarily be creative, and, in many fields of significant creative endeavor, it is not necessary that a person be outstanding in intelligence to be recognized as highly creative, at least as intelligence is measured by intelligence tests.

Absence of Repression and Suppression

Regardless of the level of his measured intelligence, what seems to characterize the creative person and this is especially so for the artistically creative is a relative absence of repression and suppression as mechanisms for the control of impulse and imagery. Repression operates against creativity, regardless of how intelligent a person may be, because it makes unavailable to the individual large aspects of his own experience, particularly the life of impulse and experience which gets assimilated to the symbols of aggression and sexuality. Dissociated items of experience cannot combine with one another; there are barriers to communication among different systems of experience. The creative person, given to expression rather than suppression or repression, thus has fuller access to his own experience, both conscious and unconscious. Furthermore, because the unconscious operates more by symbols than by logic, the creative person is more open to the perception of complex equivalencies in experience, facility in metaphor being one specific consequence of the creative person's greater openness to his own depths.

Masculine/Feminine Interests

This openness to experience is one of the most striking characteristics of the highly creative person, and it reveals itself in many forms. It may be observed, for example, in the realm of sexual identifications and interests, where creative males give more expression to the feminine side of their nature than do less creative men. On a number of tests of masculinity-femininity, creative men score relatively high on femininity, and this despite the fact that, as a group, they do not present an effeminate appearance or give evidence of increased homosexual interests or experiences. Their elevated scores on femininity indicate rather an openness to their feelings and emotions, a sensitive intellect and understanding self-awareness, and wide-ranging interests including many which in the American culture are thought of as more feminine, and these traits are observed and confirmed by other techniques of assessment. If one were to use the language of the Swiss psychiatrist C. G. Jung, it might be said that creative persons are not so completely identified with their masculine *persona* roles as to blind themselves to or deny expression to the more feminine traits of the *anima*. For some, of course, the balance between masculine and feminine traits, interests, and identifications is a precarious one, and for several it would appear that their presently achieved reconciliation of these opposites of their nature has been barely achieved and only after considerable psychic stress and turmoil.

Childhood and Family

It is the creative person's openness to experience and his relative lack of self-defensiveness that make it possible for him to speak frankly and critically about his childhood and family, and equally openly about himself and his problems as an adult.

One gets the impression that by and large those persons who as adults are widely recognized for their creative achievements have had rather favorable early life circumstances, and yet they often recall their childhood as not having been especially happy.

In studying adult creative persons, one is dependent upon their own reports for the picture they give of their early years. Although they may often describe their early family life as less harmonious and happy than that of their peers, one cannot know for certain what the true state of affairs was. In reality the situation in their homes may not have been appreciably different from that of their peers. The differences may reside mainly in their perceptions and memories of childhood experiences, and it seems the more likely since one of the most striking things to be noted about creative persons is their unwillingness to deny or repress things that are unpleasant or troubling.

The theme of remembered unhappiness in childhood is so recurrent that one is led to speculate about its role in fostering creative potential. In the absence of a sensitive awareness of one's own experience and of the world around one, without considerable development of and attention to one's own inner life, and lacking an interest in ideational, imaginal, and symbolic processes, highly creative responses can hardly be expected to occur. Something less than complete satisfaction with oneself and one's situation in childhood, if not a prerequisite for the development of a rich inner life and a concern for things of the mind and spirit, may nevertheless play an important contributory role.

There is no doubt, too, that some of the highly creative persons had, as children, endured rather cruel treatment at the hands of their fathers. These, to be sure, constitute the minority, but they appear today to be no less creative than those who could more easily identify with their fathers. There is some evidence, however, that those who were harshly treated in childhood have not been so effective or so successful in the financial and business (masculine) aspects of their professions as the others. There is in these persons more than a hint that they have had some difficulty in assuming an aggressive professional role because, through fear of their fathers, their masculine identifications were inhibited.

Psychology of the Creative Person

Both in psychiatric interviews that survey the individual's history and present psychological status, and in clinical tests of personality, creative persons tend to reveal a considerable amount of psychic turbulence. By and large they freely admit the existence of psychological problems and they speak frankly about their symptoms and complaints. But the manner in which they describe their problems is less suggestive of disabling psychopathology than of good intellect, richness and complexity of personality, and a general candor in self-description. They reveal clearly what clinical psychologists have long contended: that personal soundness is not an absence of problems but a way of reacting to them.

We may resort again to Jung's theory of the psychological functions and types of personality as an aid in depicting the psychology of the creative person. According to this view it might be said that whenever a person uses his mind for any purpose he either perceives (becomes aware of something) or he judges (comes to a conclusion about something). Everyone perceives and judges, but the creative person tends to prefer perceiving to judging. Where a judging person emphasizes the control and regulation of experience, the perceptive person is inclined to be more interested and curious, more open and receptive, seeking to experience life to the full. Indeed, the more perceptive a person is, the more creative he tends to be.

In his perceptions, both of the outer world and of inner experience, one may focus upon what is presented to his senses, upon the facts as they are, or he may seek to see, through intuition, their deeper meanings and possibilities. One would not expect creative persons in their perceptions to be bound to the presented stimulus or object but rather to be intuitively alert to that which is capable of occurring, to that which is not yet realized; this capacity is, in fact, especially characteristic of the creative person.

One judges or evaluates experience with thought or with feeling, thinking being a logical process aimed at an impersonal analysis of the facts; feeling, on the other hand, being a process of appreciation and evaluation of things which gives them a personal and subjective value. The creative person's preference for thinking or for feeling in his making of judgments is less related to his creativeness as such than it is to the type of material or concepts with which he deals. Artists, in general, show a preference for feeling, scientists and engineers a preference of thinking, while architects are more divided in their preference for one or the other of these two functions.

Everyone, of course, perceives and judges, senses and intuits, thinks and feels. It is not a matter of using one of the opposed functions to the exclusion of the other. It is rather a question of which of them is preferred, which gets emphasized, and which is most often used. So also is it with introversion and extraversion of interest, but two-thirds or more of each of the creative groups which have participated in the study have shown a rather clear tendency toward introversion. Yet, interestingly enough, extraverts, though they are in the minority in our samples, are rated as high on creativity as the introverts.

Whether introvert or extravert, the creative individual is an impressive person, and he is so because he has to such a large degree realized his potentialities. He has become in great measure the person he was capable of becoming. Since he is not preoccupied with the impression he makes on others, and is not overconcerned with their opinion of him, he is freer than most to be himself. To say that he is relatively free from conventional restraints and inhibitions might seem to suggest that he is to some degree socially irresponsible. He may seem to be, and in some instances he doubtless is if judged by the conventional standards of society, since his behavior is dictated more by his own set of values and by ethical standards that may not be precisely those of others around him.

The highly creative are not conformists in their ideas, but on the other hand they are not deliberate nonconformists, either. Instead, they are genuinely independent. They are often, in fact, quite conventional in matters and in actions that are not central to their areas of creative endeavor. It is in their creative striving that their independence of thought and autonomy of action are revealed. Indeed, it is characteristic of the highly creative person that he is strongly motivated to achieve in situations in which independence in thought and action are called for, but much less inclined to strive for achievement in situations where conforming behavior is expected or required. Flexibility with respect to means and goals is a striking characteristic of the groups we have studied.

Interests

On a test that measures the similarity of a person's expressed interests with the known interests of individuals successful in a variety of occupations and professions, creative persons reveal themselves as having interests similar to those of psychologists, architects, artists, writers, physicists, and musicians, and quite unlike those of purchasing agents, office men, bankers, farmers, carpenters, policemen, and morticians. These similarities and dissimilarities of interest are in themselves less significant than the abstractions and inferences that may be drawn from them. They suggest strongly that creative persons are relatively less interested in small details, in facts as such, and more concerned with their meanings and implications, possessed of considerable cognitive flexibility, verbally skillful, eager to communicate with others with nicety and precision, open to experience, and relatively uninterested in policing either their own impulses and images or those of others.

Philosophical Values

With respect to philosophical values—the theoretical, economic, esthetic, social, political, and religious as measured on one of our tests—there are two values most emphasized by all the creative groups. They are the theoretical and esthetic. One might think that there is some incompatibility and conflict between a cognitive and rational concern with truth and an emotional concern with form and beauty. If this is so, it would appear that the creative person has the capacity to tolerate the tension created in him by opposing strong values, and in his life and work he effects some reconciliation of them. Perhaps a less dramatic and more cautious interpretation of the simultaneous high valuing of the theoretical and the esthetic would be that for the truly creative person the solution of a problem is not sufficient; there is the further demand that it be elegant. The esthetic viewpoint permeates all of a creative person's work. He seeks not only truth but also beauty.

Closely allied to his strong theoretical and esthetic values is another pervasive trait of the creative, his preference for complexity, his delight in the challenging and unfinished, which evoke in him an urge, indeed a need to discover unifying principles for ordering and integrating multiplicity.

Summary

In so brief a report, emphasis has had to be placed upon the generality of research findings. What needs to be equally emphasized is that there are many paths along which persons travel toward the full development and expression of their creative potential, and that there is no single mold into which all who are creative will fit. The full and complete picturing of the creative person will require many images. But if, despite this caution, one still insists on asking what most generally characterizes the creative individual as he has revealed himself in the Berkeley studies, it is his high level of effective intelligence, his openness to experience, his freedom from crippling restraints and impoverishing inhibitions, his esthetic sensitivity, his cognitive flexibility, his independence in thought and action, his unquestioning commitment to creative endeavor, and his unceasing striving for solutions to the ever more difficult problems that he constantly sets for himself.

SECTION THREE
THE CREATIVE PROCESS

The creative process has always been something of a mystery. Why is it that two people of equal intelligence can perform the same tasks with desire and diligence and yet one's result is considered "more creative" than the other's? In the movie *Amadeus,* court composer Antonio Salieri curses God for granting the frivolous Mozart greater musical genius. Is creativity a mystical gift or is it a working process that we can all master if we can only discover the formula? Can we learn to be more creative?

C.W. Kaha believes that an "individual must shift, alter or expand already existing boundaries" in order to do creative work. Kaha examines Freud's ideas about primary and secondary processes of the mind to determine how individuals recognize and utilize knowledge in performing creative tasks.

Musicians and artists often receive their training informally. They follow the centuries old tradition of apprenticeship. Ralph J. Gleason discusses the role of formal education in the development of jazz musicians. More importantly, however, he illustrates how musicians were forced to "break away from tradition" to develop innovative styles and become virtuoso performers and composers.

Some educators have maintained that an emphasis on creativity in the classroom diminishes the quality of student work. Sharon Bailin addresses this dichotomy in "Creativity or Quality: A Deceptive Choice." She examines a creative process model and makes a stand that runs contrary to what many believe. Not only is process important, but so is the end product which should be of significant achievement. Bailin also emphasizes that creative thinking is a discipline and as such should encourage the development of strong cognitive skills.

Although advertising professionals are labeled "creative," Moriarty and Vandenbergh found that there was little emphasis on creative process in advertising courses. Through an open-ended questionnaire Moriarty and Vandenbergh asked American Advertising Federation award winners how they got their ideas, what methods they used, and how they broke through mental blocks. They have some interesting conclusions concerning pressure, tension and deadlines .

Finally, Treffinger, Isaksen and Dorval tackle the process of Creative Problem Solving. Their approach is a specific method which is the result of four decades of research and has been applied in various situations successfully. A descriptive framework and a step-by-step process is clearly articulated. This method was the obvious choice for this text because each of the editors has training in CPS. It is not presented as the only approach, but we believe that it offers a firm foundation for anyone beginning serious study in creative thinking. (MJ)

Of Additional Interest

Adams, J. L. (1984). *Conceptual blockbusting: A guide to better ideas.* New York: Random House.

Adams, J. L. (1986). *The care and feeding of ideas: A guide to encouraging creativity.* New York: W. W. Norton.

Anderson, J. V. (1993). Mind mapping: A tool for creative thinking. *Business Horizons, 36* (1), 41–46.

Albrecht, T. W. (1984). *Brain building: Easy games to develop your problem solving skills.* Englewood Cliffs, NJ: Prentice-Hall

Aristotle. (1976). Creation as making. In A. Rothenberg & C. R. Hausman (Eds.), *The creativity question,* 33–37. Durham, NC: Duke University Press.

Armstrong, T. (1993). *Seven kinds of smart: Identifying and developing your many intelligences.* New York: Plume.

Barron, F. (1969). *Perspectives in creativity.* New York: Holt, Rinehart & Winston.

Behrens, P. R. (1977). Camouflage. cubism, and creativity: The dissolution of boundaries. *Journal of Creative Behavior, 11* (2), 91–97.

Biondi, A. M. (Ed.). (1972). *The creative process.* New York: D.O.K. Publishers

Bohm, D., & Peat, F. D. (1991). Science, order and creativity. In J. Henry (Ed.), *Creative management,* 24-33. London: Sage Publications.

Bransford, J. D., & Stein, B.S. (1984) *The ideal problem solver.* New York: Freeman.

Caine, R. N., & Caine, G. (1991). *Making connections: Teaching and the human brain.* Alexandria, VA: Association for Supervision and Curriculum Development.

Chance, P. (1985). *Learning to think.* New York: Teachers College Press.

deBono, E. (1970) *Lateral thinking: Creativity step by step.* New York: Harper & Row.

Edwards, B. (1989). *Drawing on the right side of the brain.* Los Angeles, CA: Tarcher.

Edwards, B. (1986). *Drawing on the artist within.* New York: Simon & Schuster.

Fritz, R. (1991). *Creating.* New York: Fawcett Columbine.

Gardner, H. (1983). *Frames of mind: The theory of multiple intelligences.* New York: Basic Books.

Goldberg. P. (1983). *The intuitive edge.* Los Angeles, CA: Tarcher.

Grudin, R. (1990). *The grace of great things: Creativity and innovation.* New York: Ticknor & Fields.

Howard, P. J. (1994). *The owner's manual for the brain.* Austin, TX: Leornian Press.

Jung, C. G. (l966). *The spirit in men, art and literature.* New York: Bolligen Foundations.

Michalko, M. (1991) *Thinkertoys.* Berkeley. CA: Ten Speed Press.

Minninger, J. (1984). *Total recall: How to boost your memory power.* Emmaus, PA: Rodale.

Nadler. G., & Hibino, S. (1990). *Breakthrough thinking.* Rocklin, CA: Prima.

Nierenberg, G. I. (1985). *The idea generator.* Berkeley, CA: Experience in Software.

Restak, R. M. (1991). *The brain has a mind of its own.* New York: Harmony.

Wallas, G. (1926). *The art of thought.* London: J. Cape.

THE CREATIVE MIND:
FORM AND PROCESS

C. W. Kaha

Creativity is predicated on a system of rules and forms, in part determined by intrinsic human capabilities. Without such constraints we have arbitrary and random behavior, not creative acts. (Chomsky, 1975)

"In Switzerland there once lived an old count who had only one son, but he was stupid and couldn't learn anything. So the father said, 'Listen my son, I can't get anything into your head, as hard as I try. You've got to get away from here. I'll turn you over to a famous master; he shall have a try with you. The son studied with this master for a year. When he returned, the father was disgusted to hear that all he had learned was 'what the dogs bark.' Sent out for another year of study with a different master, the son returned to tell that he had learned 'what the birds speak.' Furious that his son had again wasted his time, the father threatened, 'I'll send you to a third master, but if again you learn nothing, I shall no longer be your father.' When the year was over, the son's reply to the question of what he had learned was 'what the frogs croak.' In great rage, the father cast his son out, ordering his servants to take the son into the forest and do away with him. But the servants had pity on the son, and simply left him in the forest.

"So the hero of 'The Three Languages' goes off into the world. On his wanderings he comes first to a land in deep trouble because the furious bark of wild dogs permits nobody to rest; and worse, at certain hours a man must be handed over to the dogs to be devoured. Since the hero can understand the dog's language, the dogs talk to him, tell him why they are so ferocious and what must be done to pacify them. When this is done, they leave the country in peace, and the hero stays there awhile. After some years the hero, who has grown older, decides to travel to Rome. On his way, croaking frogs reveal his future to him, and this gives him much to think about. Arriving in Rome, he finds that the Pope has just died and the Cardinals cannot make up their minds whom to elect as the new Pope. Just as the cardinals decide that some miraculous token should designate the future Pope, two snow-white doves settle on the hero's shoulders. Asked whether he would be Pope, the hero does not know if he is worthy; but the doves counsel him to accept. Thus he is consecrated, as the frogs had prophesied. When the hero has to sing Mass and does not know the words, the doves, which continually sit upon his shoulders, tell him all the words in his ears" (Bettelheim, 1975).

This is the story of a child who is not wise in the world's ways, who is stupid according to his own father. And yet, learning the languages of an inner life, he is able to integrate that knowledge to achieve mastery over the world. The dogs, birds and frogs are symbols of those elements of mind which are usually inaccessible, but the integration of those elements, of the three languages, results in worldly transformations. The dog, bird and frog point symbolically to different elements of inner life. While frogs "symbolize the most ancient part of man's self," the birds "which can fly high into the sky symbolize a very different freedom—that of the soul to soar." "The ferocious dogs. . . symbolize the violent, aggressive, and destructive drives in man" (Bettelheim, 1975). Fairy tales describe inner states by means of images and actions. "There is general agreement that myths and fairy tales speak to us in the language of symbols representing unconscious content. There appeal is simultaneously to our conscious and unconscious mind. . ." (Bettelheim, 1975). It is these elements of inner life, of the conscious and unconscious, that are central to the creative process. In this paper I will attempt to convey an understanding of how inner languages transform the outer world.

In order to explore those conscious and unconscious elements of the creative process, I will be forced to use a multitudinous array of terms: primary process, preconscious, extraconscious, incubation, secondary thinking. It is important to realize that these terms are descriptions of theoretical constructs rather than description of the actual brain. The human brain does not contain small white picket fences with one kind of thinking on each side. No one understands the actual structure of the brain well enough to pinpoint any of these theoretical terms in any exclusive area. It is also important to realize that we direct our thoughts on this subject by the use of such terms, and yet these terms often come to direct our thinking. For example, how can anyone explore the unconscious if it is believed, as Freud stated, that the unconscious is repressed and uncontrollable? To the extent that we place implicit faith in any theoretical terms we limit and restrict the field of inquiry. It is better to proceed with a strong sense of curiosity.

I would define creativity as a process which results in innovation. In order to characterize creative innovation, I will contrast cultural breakthrough as opposed to fads:

> Fads generate initial excitement by using a particular mode of inquiry in a fresh way. Usually, however, they do not reexamine the assumptions of 'normal culture,' but rather shift attention within the already accepted framework. Consequently, their repetition over time eventually loses its impact. *In contrast, a cultural breakthrough changes some aspect of the framework that is used to experience reality and understand it.* Extensions of that outlook, as a consequence, continue to generate excitement for long periods of time and can eventually redefine 'normal culture' as the perspective becomes widely shared (Heinrich, 1976).

I perceive the creative process as an activity of mind characterized by an optimum level of unity, health, and awareness. Creative innovation is a measure of health insofar as "the measure of health is flexibility, the freedom to learn through experience" (Rothenberg, Hausman 1976). To explore how innovation originates, to explore the creative process or to explore those states of mind evidenced in the creative process is to explore a way of thinking which is available potentially to every individual.

In order to "change some aspect of the framework that is used to experience reality," the individual must shift, alter or expand already existing boundaries. "Any creative search, whither for a new image or idea, involves the scrutiny of an often astronomical number of possibilities" (Rothenberg, Hausman,1976). In exploring those states of mind or the inner language of creativity, two principal questions seem evident. First, how does the mind seek out answers among "an often astronomical number of possibilities," and secondly, once the right answer is found, how does an individual *know* it as the right answer. Discussion in this article will move tangentially around these two questions. While direct answers are at this point impossible, it is possible to allow these questions to exist in a wider field.

The major historical distinction placed upon the functions of mind has been that of conscious vs. unconscious. The unconscious within the Freudian tradition was considered inaccessible. Freud later postulated the primary process and secondary process as being two distinct modes of thinking available to every individual. "The secondary process is conceptually organized" and referred to as "reality oriented thinking" (Wason & Laird, 1968). The primary process is much more interesting. Primary process, referred to by Arieti as primordial " . . . have little to do with content. . . . They deal with processes and forms" (Arieti, 1976). Freud placed the primary process within the unconscious. The logic of the primary process is not the logic of secondary processes. First, there is identification based on similarity which is "characterized by metamorphoses, the equivalence of part and whole, and the interchangeability of objects" (Arieti, 1976). There is an altered relation of word and meaning. "At times a word evokes images. . . acquires a quasiperceptual quality and an emotional tone" (Arieti,1976).

Terms like linear, rational and discursive do not apply to primary process. Terms like metaphorical thinking, day dreaming, and intuitive or imagistic thinking refer to primary processes. At best, there is a radical discontinuity between primary and secondary processes. Maslow (1957) suggests that creative thinking results from suitable cooperation between primary and secondary processes.

The primary process model has been challenged by Kubie. He proposes a trichotomy to explain mental processes: "The communicable processes of consciousness, the quick and flexible thinking that results in creativity (the preconscious) and the deep unconscious restraints of anxiety and neurosis" (Wason & Laird, 1968). "Preconscious activity is fast, complex, and prolific. It has the functional properties that other theorists ascribe to the primary process" (Wason & Laird, 1968). The preconscious is hedged on both sides by the conscious and unconscious. The Preconscious, as with primary process, speaks a different language than conscious reason. There is a large "inadequacy of the cognitive (conscious) functions—of 'knowing' sign and symbol—to communicate the unified precognitive experience" (Burrow, 1964). Not the word "unified" in the above quote. Both primary process and preconscious partake of a kind of unity: " . . . continuity with all things is the essence of this mood" (Burrow, 1964). Kubie places creativity essentially within the realm of the preconscious. He states that "the preconscious system is the essential implement of all creative activity; and that unless preconscious processes can flow freely there can be no true creativity" (Rothenberg & Hausman, 1976).

The preconscious is also strongly indicated in the phenomena of incubation. Wallas in his article on "Stages in the Creative Process" states that "during incubation we do not voluntarily or consciously think on a particular problem and . . . a series of unconscious and involuntary mental events may take place during that period" (Rothenberg & Hausman, 1976). It might be plausible to remove the word unconscious from the previous quote and replace it with the word preconscious. Kris in his article on "Preconscious Mental Processes" states: "Similarly, the shift from consciousness to preconsciousness may account for the experience of clarification that occurs when after intense concentration the solution to an insoluble problem suddenly presents itself following a period of rest" (Rothenberg & Hausman,1976). The central feature of incubation is that we are simply unaware of it. Incubation can be posited as a theoretical construct only because of the resulting illumination or insight which seems to come from nowhere. We posit incubation to explain that 'nowhere'. Some persons attempt to speak of incubation in terms of hemispheric functions. They refer to incubation as "any technique of relaxation of the conscious cognition (left cerebral hemisphere function) . . . which allows subliminal processes (right hemisphere function) to operate" (Gowan, 1979). Right hemispheric function is regarded in this sense as imagistic thinking. While there is an important idea embedded within this notion of hemispheric function which I will refer to later, I doubt if it is as simple as left and right.

Incubation is again referred to as a hunch by Cannon. In an attempt to explain such hunches he posits the idea of extraconscious processes. "By using the term 'extraconscious processes' to define unrecognized operations which occur during attention to urgent affairs or during sleep, the notion of a subconscious mind can be avoided" (Rothenberg & Hausman, 1976). Extraconscious is an important term because it presents an alternative to Freud's notion of unconscious. "Evidence appears to be strong that mind or consciousness is associated with a limited but shifting area of integrated activity in the cortex of the brain. . . . Such activities could go on, however, in other parts of the cortex and at the time be unrelated to conscious states" (Rothenberg & Hausman, 1976). Such a theory indicates that the very fact of consciousness as we know it is but one component of the mind, and perhaps a component that developed as a result of earlier extraconscious activities.

Another construct is posited by Ehrenzweig which supports, in some ways the notion of the extraconscious. He suggests "a new principle of dedifferentiation, a form of unconscious functioning that is more basic that any particular formal operation such as the mechanisms of primary process thinking" (Rothenberg & Hausman, 1976). "Undifferentiated perception can grasp in a single undivided act of comprehension data that to conscious perception would be incompatible" (Rothenberg & Hausman, 1976). Dedifferentiation points to, or indicates, an area of functioning arising from the extraconscious. Though dedifferentiation is referred to as unconscious scanning, it is a form of vision which is not totally unconscious. It is also characteristic of the primary process in that it "registers details irrespective of whether they belong to the figure or the ground" (Rothenberg & Hausman, 1976). Dedifferentiation is, I suspect, just another way of becoming aware of processes which are not under the strict control of the more rational secondary processes.

Each of these theories, notions, or ideas attempts to explain how the individual recognizes and integrates innovative knowledge. "As it is, the creative thinker has to make a decision about his route without having the full information needed for his choice. This dilemma belongs to the essence of creativity" (Rothenberg & Hausman, 1976). But obviously the information is there in some form. Whether through primary thinking, or the preconscious, or incubation, or the extraconscious, access is gained to information that is not, at some point, fully conscious. There are two things to consider in this process. First, the information, in the form of insight or image or knowing, becomes conscious; and second, the way in which that information becomes conscious, or is given access, remains steadfastly unconscious, or at best, subliminal. "When we picture the solution of a problem as the sudden combination and organization of elements, it is not at all surprising to find that the very thing which sets off this combination is unexperienced" (Wason & Laird, 1968). Most of the terms referred to above attempt a description of mental processes, but the terms are in no sense explanatory. Though they are useful in constructing a possible focus or location for such activity, the terms do not explain how that activity occurs.

It must be apparent to anyone who has thought about it that there is a kind of experience available to the individual which resembles the primary process. Given the great similarity between the preconscious and primary processes, it is possible to link these two elements as form and function: preconscious being the form or structure giving rise to a function of thinking called primary process. Both these terms are marked by a sense of emotional unity and an

94

absence of rationality, characterized more by the metamorphosis of a prelogical or "paleologic (from the Greek paleo, meaning old)" (Arieti, 1976) form of thinking. This kind of thinking is characteristic of the language of fairy tales. Also, like fairy tales, it is not always available to the adult, appearing, at inopportune times, to be as confusing as the language of the dogs and birds mentioned at the beginning of this paper. For the adult, stuck firmly in a reasonable world, stories and poems incorporating the primary process simply don't make sense. "This form of thinking is not illogical or alogical, but it does follow a logic different from that . . . " of the mature secondary process (Arieti, 1976).

While the preconscious and primary process do not explain creativity, they do, as conceptual terms, present a valuable focus for exploration. "Many psychologists and others have speculated that the primary process is the source of creativity" (Wason & Laird, 1968). The dominant, and most important feature is a sense of unity. Boundaries do not remain fixed within the preconscious. Objects, ideas and form blend one into another, marked more by similarity than by any sense of difference. "In this earlier mode of being, differentiation and cognition play little part. The sense of inner completeness and the feeling—continuity with all things is the essence of this mood" (Burrow, 1964). To the extent that the preconscious or primary process is central to the creative process it is because of the lack of boundaries, of differentiation. The lack of boundaries and recognition of similarities would allow for the emergence of new perceptual forms. "In the creative process there is an incessant dialectic and an essential tension between two seemingly opposed dispositional tendencies: the tendency towards structuring and integration and the tendency towards disruption of structure and diffusion and energy and attention" (Barron, 1969). The primary process provides such a disruption of structure; dream, metamorphosis and metaphor are its characteristic forms. In this sense the primary process serves a special function.

One might ask why, if we have this special and creative source of knowledge, do we not have an easier more conscious access to it? Why does it appear, as if with a will of its own, as illumination, insight, dream, imagination, bringing its own images and logic? Because it is not logical in a reasonable way, could it be that the primary process is set apart, or separated from the secondary processes in order to preserve its very unique characteristics? Given conscious access, we might wish to label, classify and organize that which, by its very nature, cannot be known in those terms. The real fascination concerning primary and secondary thought processes is that each perspective cannot 'know' the other. Primary process by its very existence denies secondary process, and secondary process has no form or experience of primary thinking. Yet, in some way, these two kinds of thought do co-exist in each individual. The notion of incubation might explain one of the ways they co-exist. I would suggest that they have multiple ways of co-existing.

Most of us feel that we 'think' of one thing at a time, in a reasonable way and that if we thought of more things at once we might lose track. I would suggest that while "consciousness is intrinsically single . . . human thinking is a multiple activity" (Wason & Laird, 1968). While an individual may be conscious of only one element of thought, "a number of more or less independent trains of thought usually co-exist." (Wason & Laird, 1968). In this manner primary and secondary processes could co-exist with only a fleeting awareness of the 'difference' arising from these distinct thought processes. It might also be that the secondary thought processes maintain the upper hand in the adult who seeks to establish a logical and orderly impression of his world.

The idea of multiple activity corresponds to an earlier notion of hemispheric functions. The idea presented was that relaxation of one hemisphere would allow for productive use of the other hemisphere. The right and left hemispheres were divided in terms of secondary and primary processes. While I cannot believe that the nature of the human mind can be detailed so simplistically, I do feel that the issue of hemispheric functions points to a fascinating solution, of sorts. If it is true that the human mind works simultaneously on multiple activities could it not be that at certain times, for whatever reason, a synchronicity emerges? By synchronicity, I wish to indicate a state of affairs in which the processes occurring mesh or blend in such a fashion as to alter, in unpredictable ways, the direction of consciousness. Kant implies the effects of such a synchronicity when he suggests that "a representation of the imagination . . . occasions in itself more thought than can ever be comprehended in a definite concept, and which consequently aesthetically enlarges the concept itself in an unbounded fashion" (Rothenberg & Hausman, 1976).

The idea of synchronicity is explanatory rather than descriptive. Terms such as extraconscious or preconscious, incubation or unconscious would obviously play an important part as elements, or functions of that larger process. Synchronicity also implicitly assumes a kind of transformation from various singular modes of thought and of multiple processes, to a momentary larger unity which transcends and enlarges those multiple modes. If it is true that the individual is aware of only one activity of thought at any given moment, he would be incapable of being fully conscious of such a synchronicity. Yet I believe that an individual could sense or feel such a process. Call it insight or call it illumination, call it anything. . . . There must, at that moment emerge within the consciousness of the individual an almost physical sense of unity, of wholeness. Thought, language, mind, and world must at that time blend into a certain indistinguishable knowing. Mystics call it the ineffable. Scientists refer to it as eureka.

Such a synchronicity could not conform to our notions of logic. The process would indicate something larger than our conscious rational understanding, pointing to that which is supra-natural. But "reason does not only consist of its conscious logical tools and manifestations, nor does the will consist only of its deliberate conscious determinations" (Barron, 1969). It is in this sense that the logic of the secondary process will never comprehend the paradox of the primary process. The terms rational and irrational have often been applied, as if that which is not rational must be irrational. Such an either-or category is, when concerned with the issue of mental functions, near sighted and misguided. " . . . The quest of the mind for comprehensiveness . . . is of the essence of the life of reason" (Davis, 1972). The human mind is eminently rational, or a rationality far broader than our conscious comprehension.

The process of that rationality is exemplified by the mind itself. "There can . . . be no reasonable doubt that man's mind, having been developed under the influence of the laws of nature, for that reason, naturally thinks somewhat after nature's pattern" (Fann, 1970). The supra-logic of the preconscious is as much a part of nature's pattern as is the secondary process, if not more so. Hausman in "Creativity and Rationality" insists "that spontaneity as it lies beyond the reach of rational understanding is paradoxical as well as supra-rational." Paradox is a falsehood which is also true, or a true contradiction. Caught in a world that is only reasonable it is possible to see the contradiction and not the truth. It is the creative process which frees us from that reasonable world. It frees us just as the three languages freed the child in the fairy tale.

In attempting to understand how the mind recognizes a plausible combination of ideas when the number of possible ones is unlimited, Charles Sanders Peirce proposes the theory of abduction. "Abduction is a distinct type of reasoning, which is not to be confused with . . . induction and deduction . . . (Fann, 1970). Abduction is the only type of reasoning that can supply new ideas and is, in this sense, synthetic. The theory of abduction proposes that "the mind has a tendency to seek out the unifying features which phenomena exhibit. This apparent thirst of the mind for unity and coherence is most persistent" (Davis, 1972). The theory of abduction states that the mind is a part of nature, and somehow in tune with it. "It is a primary hypothesis underlying all abduction that the human mind is akin to the truth in the sense that in a finite number of guesses it will light upon the correct hypothesis" (Fann, 1970).

The idea of synchronicity and the theory of abduction point to two different aspects of the same process. While the activity of synchronicity would create, or allow for the emergence of knowing, a knowing more complete than any conscious derivative; abduction would then, through a synthetic act, recognize that knowing. These two aspects of the creative process point to the fundamental human features of being and knowing. Synchronicity posits a kind of unity, a blending of multiple activities which alters the direction of consciousness. Such a unity is one of the basic qualities of being, existence, presence. And abduction, in a similar framework, mirrors knowing, through recognition of elements within that unity as relevant, as correct, as truth. These two fundamental elements, being and knowing, echo the two questions asked at the beginning of this writing. First, how does the mind seek out right answers, and second, once found, how does the mind recognize those answers as correct. The creative process reveals, in its essential nature, the duality of being and knowing; integrating that duality, within the mind's form, into a transparent metamorphosis.

References

Arieti, S. *Creativity: the magic synthesis.* NYC: Basic Books, 1976.

Barron, F. *Creative person and creative process.* NYC: Holt, Rinehart & Winston, 1969.

Bettleheim, B. *The uses of enchantment, the meaning and importance of fairy tales* (3rd ed.). NYC: Vintage Books, Random House, 1977.

Burrow, T. *Preconscious foundations of human experience.* Galt, W. E. (ed.). NYC: Basic Books, 1964.

Chomsky, N. *Reflections on language.* NYC: Pantheon Books, 1975.

Davis, W. H. *Peirce's epistemology.* The Hague, Netherlands: Martinus Nijhoff, 1972.

Fann, K. T. *Peirce's theory of abduction.* The Hague, Netherlands: Martinus Nijhoff, 1970.

Gowan, J. C. Production of creativity through right hemisphere imagery. *Journal of Creative Behavior,* 1979, *13(1).*

Henrich, M. Cultural breakthroughs. *American Behavioral Scientist.* 1976, *19*(July-August), 588.

Rothenberg, A. & Hausman, C. R. (eds.). *The creativity question.* Durham, NC: Duke University Press, 1976.

Wason, P. C. & Johnson-Laird, P. N. (eds.). *Thinking and reasoning,* Middlesex, England: Penguin Books, 1968.

C. W. Kaha, 706 West Indiana Street, Urbana, Illinois 61801.

CREATIVITY OR QUALITY: A DECEPTIVE CHOICE

Sharon Bailin

Abstract

The fostering of creativity is currently seen as a primary goal of education, but the view of creativity which underlies this emphasis dictates that creativity must sometimes be purchased at the expense of the quality of the work produced. It is maintained here that this dichotomy between creativity and quality which is assumed in this view is a false one, based on an erroneous theory of creative process. It is argued that the notions of creativity and quality are intimately connected, and thus the question of the choice between the two does not really arise.

In directing the school play, you are forced to make a choice between enhancing the quality of the play or the creativity of the students involved. Which would you choose? This was a question which was actually posed to a prospective dramatic arts teacher in an interview for a teaching position. This was the dilemma: choose between creativity and quality. And the teacher was clearly expected to opt for the former.

I do not think that this question represents an isolated example of pedagogical thinking, but believe that it is, rather, indicative of an entire perspective which pervades theory and practice in arts education and in education in general. Interest in and research on the subject of creativity has been great in recent years,[1] and this trend has been accompanied by the view that the fostering of creativity is a primary educational goal.[2] Contemporary education has come to see as one of its central purposes to make students more creative, and if the quality of work produced must suffer in the process, then this is accepted as an unavoidable consequence. A strict separation is thus established between the creativity of the person and the quality of the product, a dichotomy which, in some circumstances at least, involves a conflict and necessitates a choice.

It will be maintained in this paper, however, that the question posed at the outset is misleading, and that the dichotomy between creativity and quality is a false one. I shall argue that the notions of creativity and quality are intimately and inextricably connected and that, thus, the question of the choice between the two does not arise.

In order to make this case, it is necessary, first, to understand this view of creativity in which the notions of creativity and quality are severed, and to examine its assumptions. It is a view which centers around the idea of process rather than of product. It is assumed that there is a specific process which is characteristic of all instances of creating, regardless of subject matter. Being creative, then, is seen as the ability to engage in this process, and this ability is seen to be associated with certain cognitive and personality traits. Considerations of the nature of the product produced become irrelevant to the assessment of creativity, as personality and process become the focus.

I believe, however, that the very notion of a distinctive creative process can be questioned. There have been numerous attempts to characterize such a putative process, the accounts of Arthur Koestler and of Edward De Bono, for example,[3] and although there are considerable differences in detail amongst the views, nonetheless there emerge certain common assumptions about the nature of the process. It is assumed that most thinking is marked by rigidity and habit and that the creative process involves breaking out of such habitual ways of thinking and disrupting habitual patterns of thought. It is seen, further, to involve making new connections between previously unrelated entities by performing a leap of some sort. It is held that this process is not strictly rational, but involves elements of chance and unconscious processes which loosen the hold of conventional logic. Finally, the process is seen as non-evaluative and involving a suspension of judgment.

Let us begin to examine this basic view by looking at the idea that creativity is characterized by a specific way of thinking which is different from our usual logical way of thinking. I would object that this view draws an artificial distinction between creative and non-creative thinking and that the two are, in fact, not clearly distinct or easily separable. This view distinguishes between two such ways of thinking on the grounds that logical thinking is selective, is confined to established patterns, and involves judgment, whereas creative thinking is purely generative and involves the disruption of established patterns and the suspension of judgment. I would maintain, however, that thinking of all kinds involves a combination of both types of processes, and that, in fact, they are not easily separated.

The 'creative process' model seems to be along the following lines: one is faced with a problem, one suspends judgment and generates new possibilities by the use of disruptive elements (one thinks creatively), and finally, one reinstitutes judgment and evaluates the products thus produced. I would argue, however, that judgment is intimately involved throughout the process of creating. The initial perception of the problem as a problem and the determining of the general direction for solution are very much products of judgment. It is because one has considerable expertise in an area and is immersed in its intricacies that one develops the judgment that enables one to see a certain concatenation of phenomena as in need of exploration, to see it as a problem.

Moreover, the need for a disruption of established patterns is connected with judgment, as well. Theories of creative process base much of their speculation on the single fact that, during the process of creating, we do sometimes suspend one or more of the presuppositions with which we began. Extrapolating from this fact, they emphasize the shaking up of established patterns as the prime characteristic of the creative process, and claim that such a disruption cannot be governed by judgment since its effects would be inhibiting. I would claim, however, that such a departure from established patterns, when it does occur, is not totally free and generated by random external stimuli, but is governed by many parameters. When presuppositions are questioned in real situations, it is not normally as a result of a random shake up of ideas, but is, rather, because one is led to do this as a result of the stage reached in the exploration of a problem. One's thinking to this point indicates the necessity to question a presupposition in order to arrive at a solution.

The idea that judgment must be suspended during the creative process derives support from the view that one cannot be engaged in a process which is creative if one can foresee the outcome of one's activity. According to this view, such foresight would imply a complete plan and would thus rule out the possibility of creativity which is thought to come about spontaneously.[4] This view is characterized by Vernon Howard as the "Unforeseen Theory of Creativity."[5] Since judgment is viewed according to this theory as applicable only within the context of an activity where there is a plan and an end in view, it is concluded that judgment cannot enter into the creative process.

Howard argues, however, that this view is based on a confusion about what it means to foresee an outcome. It is probably true that one does not know exactly what the end product will be like when one begins to create. Nonetheless, it does seem that one can have at least some general or vague idea of the form which this end product will take. According to Howard:

> For even if it be argued that one never *knows* what one will do in advance of doing it, one may yet *intend* in greater or lesser detail to do this or that and know one's intention perfectly well. Only that is required to 'foresee' what one undertakes to create, not a prediction, or clairvoyance, still less full knowledge of results.[6]

One begins with some sort of intention—to solve a problem, to try to execute a work, or simply to experiment in a medium, and one must know when a solution has been achieved or a work completed. Not just any combinations will be generated, but only those which might contribute to the work. Poincare gives a good statement of this point with reference to mathematical invention.

> To create consists precisely in not making useless combinations and in making those which are useful and which are only a small minority. Invention is discernment, choice.[7]

This idea that judgment is suspended during the process of creating seems to be based on a particular view of the role of judgment in thought. The assumption appears to be that judgment can be applied only within a specified framework, but that in creative thought the presuppositions of a framework are abandoned, and so there can no longer be any criteria according to which one can judge. There seem to be problems with this conception however.

Old presuppositions are never all abandoned, nor could they be. It is sometimes the case that one or more assumptions must be rejected in the process of arriving at a creation. Some elements of the previous framework must remain, however, elements in light of which the new structure will make sense and be fruitful. If all presuppositions were abandoned, the result would not be creation but chaos. David Perkins makes this point well.

> . . . the fact remains that no one can depart from much of the preselection at once and expect to make progress. The mathematician cannot discard the familiar axioms *and* conventional notation *and* traditions about which sorts of questions are worthwhile *and* the usual format for proofs. What we perceive as revolutionary innovation in a field always challenges only a little of the preselection. Only because we focus on the contrast rather than the continuity does the innovation seem so much of a departure.[8]

Moreover, the staunch adherence to an idea and the refusal to abandon it may, in some instances, lead to discovery or creation rather than inhibiting them. Einstein's theory of relativity, for example, is frequently cited as a prime instance of the destruction of an existing framework and the overturning of presuppositions. Yet it was Einstein's commitment to the presupposition that the laws of physics are invariant which necessitated his ultimate abandonment of the presupposition of absolute time. Some presuppositions must remain, some elements of the existing structure which give meaning to the enterprise and according to which judgments can be made.

This view also makes certain assumptions about the nature of frameworks and the ways they function in thinking which bear examination. It seems to assume that frameworks are narrow and clearly defined patterns of relationships with rigid boundaries—a kind of closed system—and that we are constrained by force of habit to a specific framework when working out a problem. This highly rigid, habitual way of thinking is considered to be the natural mode, and going beyond the limits of a framework is seen as a leap, as exceptional, as creative. The model of the way we normally think which this view provides seems to be rather inaccurate, however. Instances of going beyond a framework, of breaking away from habitual modes of thinking, are much more common than this view implies. One source of this inaccuracy might be the construal of the notion of framework as clearly defined and rigidly bounded. Certainly some of the enterprises in which we engage do seem to fit this image of a closed system, the game of chess, for example. Here the information relevant to the enterprise is strictly delimited, and any other knowledge or information is outside the framework. Even in this case, however, there is scope for creativity in terms of the specific strategies undertaken. Although, in one sense, the game is totally circumscribed by rules in terms of the specifications for legitimate moves, the possibilities for actual manoeuvres in a dynamic game are wide open.

In most instances of problem-solving and of creation, however, the notion of framework is even less clear-cut. What precisely would be the framework which is involved in the writing of a poem about the poet's experience of war, or in attempts to solve the unemployment problem? There are factors which would be relevant in each case, for example the conventions of poetry in the former case or the prevailing economic models in the latter. But there are many additional sorts of factors which might be relevant, as well. The poet's anger at the belligerence of a colleague might, for example, be relevant to how he frames his poem, or an individual's sense of compassion might be part of the framework determining her approach to an economic problem. In most problem-solving or creative situations, it would be difficult to strictly circumscribe the domain of those factors which are relevant, which constitute the framework. In actual cases, frameworks overlap, shift, and have indefinite boundaries so that the idea of information or ideas being outside a framework is not very helpful.

Tied in with the idea of rigid frameworks is the idea of creative leaps, but this notion is problematic as well. If frameworks were rigid and clearly defined, then some sort of extraordinary leap would be required in order to get beyond a framework. If we construe frameworks in a more fluid manner, however, then the case for leaps is weakened. Creation and discovery can frequently be seen to involve a more gradual process than is often believed. Although it often involves moments of insight and overturning presuppositions to see things differently, these can be understood as features of a reasonable process, rather than as manifestations of an irrational, inexplicable leap.

This phenomenon of seeing things in a broader context, of getting an overall picture, of overcoming blocks to solve a problem, is not a rare occurrence, but is a feature of thinking well in general. As Jerome Bruner suggests, going beyond the information given is an important aspect of how we think, and is not limited to instances of creation.[9] Rather than postulating some extraordinary process to account for creativity, then, it can, perhaps, be seen in terms of the processes which allow us to 'go beyond the information given' in all of our intelligent thought and behavior.[10] Any difference between creativity and everyday thinking is not one of kind but merely of degree. It seems, then, that extraordinary means are not necessary in order to attain extraordinary ends, but rather, it is the skill with which ordinary thinking processes are used and the purposes to which they are put which enable outstanding results to be achieved. This is not to deny that moments of creation are special, but to maintain, rather, that their special nature lies in what is achieved rather than in how it is achieved, that it concerns product more than process. It is when our thinking processes are directed toward exceptionally difficult tasks, when unreasonable demands are placed upon them, that exceptional results occur.

The argument to this point suggests that there is not one unique process which characterizes creating. Rather, we employ a variety of processes, processes which are not specific to creative activity but which are intrinsic to all our thinking. Moreover different types of creative activities may call forth to various extents different processes and so the nature of the individual endeavor is important in determining how creating happens. The specific discipline and the characteristics of the particular work impose constraints and we develop skills and judgment which relate to these constraints. I believe that these findings belie the notion of a creative process which is independent of subject matter.

If instances of creativity do not share a common process, then creativity cannot be seen essentially as the ability to engage in a specific psychological process. The question then arises as to what exactly instances of creativity do have in common. To this I would reply that they involve significant achievement. To be creative is to create—be it a valued work of art, a fruitful scientific theory, an important new economic model, or a viable political system. It is to create a product of quality. This involves satisfying to a high degree the criteria of excellence in the discipline in question and solving its problems in an effective and far-reaching manner.[11]

The idea of originality is one which is frequently connected to the notion of creativity and one may wonder where it fits into this analysis with its emphasis on excellence. I think that our recognition of originality implicitly involves an ascription of value and so is related to the idea of quality. In seeking originality in a product, it is generally not mere novelty which is valued, but rather novelty which is to an end, which meets a need, which solves a problem. A new solution or new sort of solution seems to be considered of particular value, frequently of greater value than a conventional solution, not merely because it is new, but because of the possibility that it will provide a better solution to current problems. It might solve a problem more effectively, solve surrounding problems in the area in addition to the original problem, avoid undesirable consequences of present solutions, or provide a new direction in which the discipline can develop. In the process of accomplishing this, an original production may transcend the limits of the discipline as it exists and contravene some of its rules. This is not, however, a case of arbitrary novelty or random invention, but involves, rather, change which is effective, useful, and significant. This grows out of a profound understanding of the discipline and the problems inherent in it, and is an extension of attempting to solve them in ever better ways.[12]

In questioning the notion of creative process then, I am attempting to break down the distinction between creative thinking and excellent thinking in general. I am arguing that the creative process is just the process of outstanding thinking in a discipline, of achieving extraordinary ends. Creativity and quality are, then, inextricably linked.

Let us now return to the pedagogical dilemma which provided the impetus for this discussion and examine it more closely in the light of the preceding analysis. It must be asked now what precisely is seen to be at issue in the choice between creativity and quality. Why are creativity and quality seen to be conflicting goals in the case of the school play? As we have seen, creativity is equated with engaging in a certain psychological process and this process is thought to involve, among other things, divergent thinking, self-expression, and independence of thought. Fostering these qualities might, however, be totally unconnected with creating a production of high calibre. It might be claimed, for example, that while helping the students to solve acting problems might result in a superior production, nonetheless allowing them to experiment on their own, in many cases unsuccessfully, might involve more creativity.

Now it is doubtless the case that such experimentation education might be valuable in some circumstances, for fostering enthusiasm, independence, or self-concept, for example. This is not, however, necessarily connected with creativity, as has been demonstrated previously. Moreover, this type of experimentation might be a meaningful and effective way to develop skills and thus would contribute to both creativity and quality.

There seems to be a presupposition in the psychological process account that creativity is necessarily free and unconstrained and that, thus, any sort of teaching, coaching, or directing will hamper creativity. Being creative does not, however, involve creation out of nothing, having no antecedents, nor being untaught. Nor is it thrashing about in ineffectual attempts at self-expression. The teacher/director may, through images, cues, and suggestions, help the students to find characters in themselves and their experience.[13] S/he may also help the students to acquire the skills which will allow them to portray and express effectively, and this will give them the freedom to go on.[14]

In connecting creativity with quality, I am taking a stand which runs contrary to the prevalent view of creativity. This latter view has had considerable influence on educational practice, however. An emphasis on process rather than product has resulted in a great deal of educational activity being devoted to the fostering of certain traits of personality, and has transformed arts education into primarily a means to foster psychological well-being. In the process, attempting to foster creativity in terms of encouraging significant achievements has too often been ignored. Now certainly good mental health is a worthwhile goal. The danger, however, is in pursuing this in the name of creativity and thereby neglecting the teaching of the skills of a discipline and the developing and advancing of the traditions in which high levels of achievement are made. It is vital to the continuity of human creating that the idea of quality not be severed from that of creativity.[15]

Notes

[1] The impetus for this proliferation of research was provided by J. P. Guilford in his address to the American Psychological Association in 1950. Guilford, J.P. (1950). Creativity, *American Psychologist 5*, 444–454.

[2] See, for example, Torrance, E. Paul. (1963). *Education and the creative potential.* Minneapolis: The University of Minnesota Press; De Bono, Edward. (1970). *Lateral thinking.* London: Ward Lock Educational.

[3] Koestler, Arthur. (1964). *The act of creation.* New York: Macmillan; De Bono, *Lateral thinking.* Although De Bono himself proposes his theory in the context of creativity in problem-solving and not the arts, it is frequently used as an account of the creative process in the arts as well.

[4] See, for example, Thomas, Vincent. (1964). Creativity in art. In Kennick, W. E. (Ed.) *Art and philosophy.* New York: St. Martin's Press, pp. 283–294.

[5] Howard, Vernon. (1982). *Artistry, the work of artists.* Indianapolis: Hackett Publishing Company, p. 110 ff.

[6] Ibid., p. 120.

[7] Poincare, H. (1970). The foundations of science. In Vernon, P. E. (Ed.). *Creativity.* New York: Penguin Books, p. 80.

[8] Perkins, David. (1981). *The mind's best work.* Cambridge: Harvard University Press, p. 279.

[9] Bruner, Jerome. (1973). *Beyond the information given.* New York: Norton.

[10] This account of creativity is substantiated by the work of David Perkins. Through the use of first person accounts of individuals engaged in creative endeavors, as well as by making use of the psychological literature on the subject, he demonstrates how phenomena such as noticing, recognizing, searching, remembering, and evaluating can, together, contribute to a creative result. Perkins. *Mind's best work.*

[11] For a more complete account of this idea of creativity as creating, see Bailin, S. (1984). Can there be creativity without creation? *Interchange, 15*(2), 13-22. See, also White, J.P. (1968). Creativity and education: A philosophical analysis. *British Journal of Educational Studies, 16,* 123-137; Glickman, J. (1970). On creating. In Kiefer, H.E. & Munitz, M.K. (Eds.). *Perspectives in education, religion, and the arts.* Albany State University of New York Press.

[12] For a further exploration of the notion of originality, see Bailin, S. (1985). On originality, creativity, education, and thought. *Interchange, 16*(1) 6-13.

[13] Cf. Howard's account of the role that such coaching plays in teaching singing. In *Artistry.*

[14] The role of skills in creativity is examined in detail in Bailin, S. (in press). *Creativity and skill.* In Bishop, J., Lochhead, J. & Perkins, D.N. (Eds.). *Thinking: progress in research and teaching.*

[15] I would like to acknowledge the assistance of a fellowship from the Social Sciences and Humanities Research Council of Canada in preparing this paper. A previous version has appeared in *Proceedings of the Philosophy of Education Society. 1984.* Normal, IL: Philosophy of Education Society.

Sharon Bailin, Faculty of Education, University of Manitoba

THE EDUCATION OF THE JAZZ VIRTUOSO

Ralph F. Gleason

I would like to begin with two quotations: A lady once approached the jazz pianist Fats Waller (legend has now made her a Little Old Lady—she was probably a rich matron) and asked, "What is jazz, Mr. Waller?" Waller, a patient man, sighed and said, "Lady, if you don't know, don't mess with it." That is quotation number one.

Here is number two: An alumnus of a conservatory, who later became an outstanding jazz pianist, recalls, "The conservatory not only did not encourage but in every way impeded my interest in jazz and in so doing hampered my musical development. For everything I know today, I am obligated most of all to myself."

The first statement is, as I have said, jazz legend. I have heard it attributed to Louis Armstrong, Lester Young, and Charles Parker and, for all I know, someone may be writing an article at this very moment attributing it to Charlie Mingus or Miles Davis. (I should add parenthetically that if these names are unfamiliar to you, I hope to make them familiar before I conclude. The very fact of their unfamiliarity would support the theme of my general presentation.) The second quotation, which damns the formal educational apparatus, is a statement make by a Leningrad musician who is one of the growing number of young Russians playing jazz music.

The ideas expressed in the two quotations are not unrelated, and these have certainly pervaded the thinking in this country, if not the whole world over. "If you don't know, don't mess with it" is the Zen theme of anti-intellectualism which has haunted jazz since the beginning and made it mysterious (redolent of arcane Negro voodoo practices in old New Orleans on Congo Square). It has been used to reinforce the attitude that jazz is primitive music, possibly not music at all, and certainly not worthy of rank with serious music.

The attitude expressed in the second quotation is the conviction that formal education offers nothing to the jazz musician. Miles Davis, a great, creative jazz improviser and a charismatic figure without peer in the music world, was a student at the Juilliard School of Music in New York for one semester. He spent most of his time downtown on Fifty-second Street in New York's jazz clubs, listening mostly to Charlie Parker, an alto saxophonist, and writing down what he heard on match-box covers. The next day in the rehearsal hall at Juilliard, he would work out the things he had written down the night before. Naturally, with his focus on music outside of Juilliard, he didn't stay long enough to get a degree. Though only time can prove me right, I believe that it is Davis' name that will live as a musical genius and not those of his classmates.

Jazz has been a bastard music, spawned in the brothel, nurtured in the red-light district, and always associated with the sporting life. In the beginning, the entire musical world, with rare exception, screamed out against it. "UNSPEAKABLE JAZZ MUST GO!" was a headline in a music magazine in the Twenties. Public figures raged against it. The word "jazz" itself—which, I might point out, really *does* have four letters—has been traced back by etymologists to sexual connotations.

Today, in a world of shifting values, jazz stands out as a unique American artistic expression, different from that of any other art form. Jazz is now worldwide in its appeal. Jazz musicians like Miles Davis, Sonny Rollins, John Coltrane, Charles Mingus, and Duke Ellington are treated like artists and cultural giants in every country of the world but America. Here, they are really second-class citizens a good deal of the time, and even when they escape this lesser status, at some specific moments, the thought always occurs that the next occasion may bring the trauma and the hurt experienced by all Negro citizens.

In almost every other form of art, certainly in the area of serious music, the American artist is largely indistinguishable from the European. The better he gets, the more he seems to be like another culture's product. The only music which is accepted as art and is indigenously American is jazz. The better a jazz artist is, the more he sounds like a Negro (if he is not already one) and the very best musicians, with but one or two exceptions, are Negroes. Negroes made this music. They created it, developed the basic styles, and are still its leading figures. All whites could be erased from the history of jazz, and the level and quality of jazz would be just where it is today.

The Negro in this country has learned the hard way that no schoolroom really holds much for him. The jazz musician was perhaps one of the first to learn this. He might have gone into other things had he been white, but, being black, he found music and/or entertainment were ways to make money and to grab the "gimmick," of which James Baldwin speaks, and then get out. Sociologists may find in time that the high incidence of superiority in Negro jazz musicians is related in some way to the high proportion forced into a few fields; the talented tenth had fewer alternatives and thus music got more than its share.

Jazz and Education

To consider the topic of formal education and its role in jazz, let's review a list of ten of the greatest-of-all jazz musicians. The qualifications of the persons for such a listing, I submit, would be accepted universally, even though any list of ten is a matter of arbitrary choice. The ten on my suggested list are Louis Armstrong, Duke Ellington, Charles Parker, John Birks "Dizzy" Gillespie, Miles Davis, Thelonious Monk, Charles Mingus, Lester Young, Billie Holiday, and John Coltrane. I, and others, could make up other lists of ten, all Negroes, all similarly qualified, but the general story about their education would be much the same. Here is a very brief account on each of the persons I have named.

Louis Armstrong was a son of the ghetto in New Orleans, a street urchin attracted to music. In his own autobiography he says he was drawn to music because of the whores and the pimps and their glamorous life (seen from the point of view of his own poverty). He learned his music in an orphan's home and then was taught by other musicians with whom he played on jobs. The rest came from himself.

Edward Kennedy "Duke" Ellington has appeared with numerous symphonies and given concerts in the great music halls of the world; his achievements include precipitating a cultural crisis because the Pulitzer Prize Board would *not* honor him. This artist, whose father was a house servant in Washington, D.C., did study music in high school and took private piano lessons, but he has said that he learned, really, from listening to ragtime pianists around Washington. Instead of going to Pratt Institute to study commercial design, he began his phenomenal career as a professional musician in 1918. At sixty-seven he is, I suggest, America's foremost composer.

Charles Parker, who revolutionized the art of jazz as Hemingway revolutionized the art of the novel, studied music in high school like any other kid—he took a couple of semesters of music and played in the school band. At fifteen years of age, he became a high school dropout and launched his professional career in the night clubs of Kansas City.

John Birks "Dizzy" Gillespie, who has been sent by the State Department on long tours of the Middle East and South America as a cultural representative, learned his first music from his father, who died when Dizzy was ten. He then studied in high school and later at a Negro agricultural institute. He doubled between agronomy and music and then left it all to play in Philadelphia night clubs.

Miles Davis, already mentioned, also studied in a Negro high school and then played in bands and went to Juilliard for one semester.

Thelonious Monk, a pianist, who, like Duke Ellington, has achieved the all-American status symbol of a *Time* cover story, studied privately in New York and had no formal education at all.

Charles Mingus, like the others, studied music in high school and then learned from other musicians. Later, long after his reputation was made, he studied the string bass for a while with a classical teacher in New York.

Lester Young, whose style on the tenor saxophone opened the door for much of the vital experimentation of modern jazz, was the son of a professional musician. He studied with his father and played in his band throughout his teens.

Billie Holiday, the only vocalist on my list, is a jazz singer whose style has had the kind of fundamental effect on vocal jazz that the King James Bible has had on English literature. You "hear" her today—even though she's been dead since 1959—in the work of Peggy Lee and almost every other female jazz singer. She was the daughter of a guitar player, became a prostitute at fourteen, and never took a music lesson in her life.

John Coltrane, a tenor saxophonist, is the only one on this list with any sort of real formal training that goes beyond individual lessons. He studied in high school and later at two music schools in Philadelphia, the Granoff Studios and the Ornstein School of Music.

The other examples I could add to this list are overwhelming. Certainly there are some music-school graduates who have reputations as jazz artists, and many of the younger men today have had some sort of formal training. Much of current jazz is highly complex and exacting, and the more complicated it has become, the more sound the musical training that is demanded. For example, John Lewis, pianist with the Modern Jazz Quartet and an internationally known composer, studied at the Manhattan School of Music, and Dave Brubeck studied under Darius Milhaud when he taught at Mills College. But Brubeck, a Caucasian, is a man whose jazz success, curiously enough, has not had any influence upon other jazz musicians. Brubeck, incidentally, is the only jazz musician I know of who ever studied formally with any of the great classicists.

Any close study of serious jazz men—and Duke Ellington has remarked that no musician is more serious about his music than a jazz musician—shows that they were forced to break away from traditional education in order to break through and that they naturally found their own way outside the academics, outside the orthodoxy of musical education. They created their own empirical educational system. Why did Miles Davis, one of the most creative musicians of his generation, spend his time at Juilliard playing what he had heard the night before in jazz clubs if not because the opportunities offered him in the classroom were irrelevant?

The Negro Musician and Jazz Music

When President Johnson assembled his culture session at the White House, critic Dwight McDonald attended and subsequently wrote an account of that event in which he mourned the fact that *no* American composers had been invited. At the end of this long essay, in the usual entertaining Dwight McDonald style, he added that the one bright thing about the White House affair was the delightful playing of Duke Ellington and his orchestra. Obviously, to Dwight McDonald, jazz musician Duke Ellington is not an American composer. In our society, we just do not see these musicians or recognize their accomplishments. We do not know their names.

At the University of California—as in almost all of the leading educational institutions of this country—jazz is regarded with near horror and definite apprehension. Hertz Hall is one of the most benign places I have ever sat in to hear music. I believe I am correct in saying that only one jazz concert has been held in Hertz Hall, and this concert was given last year by several young students. They played the music of Miles Davis, Sonny Rollins, Thelonious Monk, and Charles Parker, but these composers themselves—even though they have played many times in the Bay Area—have never set foot in Hertz Hall or, as far as I know, on the University of California campus. This situation is something like assigning Bach, Mozart, and Stravinsky to play in the Jazz Workshop and Basin Street West (in San Francisco) and then having their music played in Hertz Hall only by undergraduates.

In Berkeley, as in many cities in this country, the nearest major symphony orchestra periodically gives concerts for children in the elementary grades and high school, and the students are excused from their classes to attend the performances. But only when the students themselves have made a deliberate effort to bring jazz musicians to their assemblies—and occasionally to other school affairs—have they been able to hear this form of great music. It is never offered to them as part of their cultural enhancement, nor are courses on the understanding and appreciation of jazz included.

Earlier I mentioned the School of Jazz in Leningrad. There was even a School of Jazz in the United States at one time. Located in Lenox, Massachusetts, it was inspired by the Tanglewood concert series and continued for several summers. The school had the unqualified support of almost all the major jazz musicians, who took time off from concert tours and night-club engagements to work as teachers there for room and board. Applications came from all over the world, the waiting list was enormous, and yet the school died for lack of funds. It simply could not obtain enough money to stay alive. The philanthropic foundations, which reflect the attitude of the academy and the "establishment," did not see fit to provide financial help to underwrite this most interesting and exciting experiment.

In Poland, jazz is taught in the public schools, both at the college and precollege level. Polish jazz musicians alternate between giving concerts and playing in night clubs *and* teaching and performing in the schools on the State payroll. Television programs are produced on American jazz, and jazz per se is in the curriculum.

Yet, only last year in this country, the Monterey Jazz Festival failed in its offer to underwrite, to the total of a $4,000 project, a workshop in jazz education. It was to be under the direction of a music professor from a California state college, with the purpose of providing high school teachers with a three- or four-day indoctrination in ways and means of teaching jazz to their students. Lists of available recordings, recommended books on jazz, and lectures by musicologists and jazz musicians on the history and theory of jazz were to be offered. Demonstrations of teaching techniques were also to be presented by adventuresome teachers who have—on their own—worked out ways to instruct in this area, much like jazz musicians have worked out their own ways to play. The only requirement of the Monterey officials was that the workshop should give the teachers the usual credits for attendance. This instructional project was then presented on the Berkeley campus to the University of California Extension, which did not accept it. It died because no one would fulfill the necessary technical role of sponsorship. A necessary representative of the music department or of the education department could not be found to act as sponsor. Therefore, no credits could have been given.

In answer to the direct question, "Why are there no courses in jazz?", a University of California professor of music last year responded, "We do not offer courses in plumbing either." Yet the University officials are interested in the problems of attrition on campus. How do you keep students who feel little can be gained by remaining in school from dropping out? How often do curricular provisions fail to consider particular students? Sensible answers to these questions might also keep some potentially great music students at the university.

The Changing Picture of Jazz

Some interesting things are being done about the breadth of music programs in some schools and at some levels. There are, for example, thousands of stage bands today in high schools across the country. A stage band is a euphemism for a jazz band. I have been told that they are called stage bands because they appear on a stage and give concerts; but they really go by this title because if they were called jazz bands, the high school music teachers would not be allowed to devote the necessary time and effort to help them. They would be discouraged just as the leaders of the jazz-band workshop at San Francisco State (which produced Paul Desmond of the Dave Brubeck Quartet, Allen Smith, and John Handy) were discouraged a decade ago.

These stage bands are providing a place to go for the young people who want to learn something about jazz. But this approach to jazz in some high schools is only a start—and in a second-class, behind-the-barn kind of way. Still, this development in secondary schools is encouraging. And in time it is going to have a definite effect on American music, if only because of the sheer numbers of students involved.

The jazz musician is somewhat unique as a creative artist. He cannot, unlike the poet, the painter, and the novelist, practice his art in solitary fashion in the proverbial attic. Most of his playing and practicing must be with other musicians, in order to sharpen his own ideas and response. He needs support for his own playing in every possible way. Jazz musicians now rehearse together for their mutual education in a sort of underground. By sitting in on the job in practice sessions, they are defying the union, which demands they be paid for playing. Thus, they do not have the freedom to practice or learn in the only way open to them. They need places where they can gather together and work, experiment, practice, and play without interference and without pressures. But these opportunities are not available to them.

There are jazz courses in a few colleges and universities today, but most of them are not designed for the creative musician but for the interested nonmusician. In contrast, during the short life of the Lenox School of Jazz, students not only studied in classes and in private with the master jazz men but also had the rewarding experience of playing with them. This situation, for example, allowed a young trumpet player to have Dizzy Gillespie, the great jazz improviser and technician, come to him at a rehearsal and say, "Never play a *C* chord here; it sounds wrong and here's why."

But to return to the topic of university music departments. Two years ago, while discussing the possibility of a jazz course, I was asked by the head of a large music department, "Can you *teach* jazz? Can you *teach* art? Can you *teach* a man to be a great composer?" The answer is obvious, and the question would never have been raised if this dean of music understood jazz and this form of spontaneous creativity. He should have realized that it is as much an art as any other music in his department. The rudiments and basic structure of music, as well as fundamental skills, can be taught. But, just this lack of understanding of what jazz is all about prevents essential communication. Jazz is spontaneous, and, like much of American society which it seems to reflect, it is improvisatory. The "art" of jazz and the talent, the creativity of performance, cannot be taught, but colleges could provide the situations where the talent and musicianship might be developed.

Let me pursue this theme a little further. The jazz musician stands up in front of an audience, and he "composes" what he plays as he goes along. He starts with or creates a melodic theme, goes on with a counter melody, and develops a unique composition. It is instant art, a tour-de-force performance. This improvisation is even more impressive when one considers the surroundings in which this art is practiced. The jazz musician works in saloons a good deal of the time, creating his art in front of drunks and many talking, unappreciative customers. He very seldom has even a dressing room to relax in. The backstage conditions of the old Metropolitan Opera House, which Rudolph Bing criticized so severely in an attempt to show the advantages of a new building, would be heaven to musicians working in most jazz clubs.

The jazz musician learns chiefly by doing. He finds out a few fundamentals about the instrument in which he is interested and then he just leaps in and plays. He gets help from those with whom he plays. Other musicians taught Louis Armstrong how to read music. Other trumpet players showed Dizzy Gillespie breathing tricks. John Coltrane says he learned from playing with Thelonious Monk, Dizzy Gillespie, and Miles Davis. The masters of the art pass on their knowledge to the youths coming after them.

Today jazz is a sophisticated music compared with its early folk-music beginnings. Almost all jazz musicians now read music, unlike many of the old Dixieland musicians. Many of the younger ones have had some elementary harmony and even compositional instruction—frequently through the G.I. Bill—in some commercial music studio, which gives them the same kind of education it provides for those who want to play in dance bands.

The jazz musician also learns by listening to others, in person, and on record. This is true in America and in other countries. In Leningrad, where the opportunities to hear American jazz men have been piteously few, jazz records are treasured, and tapes for repeated study are made of the Voice of America broadcasts. In Poland, when jazz was forbidden in the early Fifties, the jazz musicians held secret underground meetings to listen to tapes. This independent and free way of learning—that is, by listening, trying, experimenting, and listening again—has probably made for much more flexibility and innovation than would have been the case in formal educational institutions.

The Creative Jazz Performance

When a jazz musician is finding and developing his own style, he must be ingenious and versatile. He must be able to retain in his memory the chord sequences for hundreds of tunes. He must be able to play changes effortlessly and improvise on them when his turn to solo comes, without the chance to go back and correct his mistakes. In fact, many jazz musicians have made a virtue out of necessity—which is really the story of their music—and have developed a degree of virtuosity so that they can even utilize their mistakes. Dizzy Gillespie, for instance, is known to play a long trumpet phrase, a whirling dervish of notes, and then suddenly to make a mistake. Immediately his "mental computer" shifts, and what he plays after the mistake makes the mistake itself logical in retrospect.

The life of a jazz man is far from easy. Jazz musicians play the job in the honored tradition of show business. The show must go on. A while back at Stanford—which, incidentally, is the only university ever to offer a full year of jazz programs for students—the John Handy Quintet was playing. Suddenly, the bass player became ill, in the middle of the number, before his solo was due. The solo was taken by the alto saxophonist, while the bass player finished the number merely keeping time. An intermission was called and after ten minutes in the open air outside, the musicians returned and completed the program with a performance which brought a standing ovation.

Performing under stress and adverse conditions goes on in night clubs night after night. Jazz musicians play when their bodies have all but collapsed. Errol Garner recorded one of his greatest albums with one finger in a splint, held out above the piano keys like a pencil. Most musicians play through the evening on hot, cramped "stages," with smoke and foul air filling their lungs.

A few anecdotes from the world of jazz will serve most adequately to give a feel for this performing art. At the Monterey Jazz Festival a few years ago, J. J. Johnson, a trombonist, conducted a tremendously inspiring work which he had written for orchestra and trombone and scored himself. Earlier, at rehearsals the musicians who had been added to the orchestra for the occasion from the San Francisco Symphony, had been surprised to discover that Johnson had accomplished the feat of scoring his work without knowing the elementary short cuts which a formal training in composition teaches. Obviously, he had never had the opportunity to learn them, so they had showed him the tricks during the prefestival rehearsals.

Woody Herman, at the end of the Forties, recorded Igor Stravinsky's *Ebony Concerto*. It had been written especially for Herman by the composer, and Stravinsky rehearsed the Herman band for the premiere performance at Carnegie Hall. When the rehearsal was over, Stravinsky, amazed by the virtuosity of the men, said to Herman, "If only I had an orchestra like that!" Numerous jazz artists are without peer on their instruments in the whole world of music.

Some years ago, following a memorable jazz concert at the Hollywood Bowl, Pianist André Previn was approached by Lukas Foss, a composer of modern classical music, who inquired whether the musicians had rehearsed the performance for a long time. When Previn said, "No," Foss asked, "But, surely, you had it all worked out?" He was aghast when Previn said, "No, it wasn't worked out at all. We made the music right up there on the spot during the performance." "But what a chance you are taking," Foss continued. "Sometimes it must be terrible." And Previn agreed. Sometimes a performance is great and sometimes it is terrible. Such alternatives are inherent in the whole concept of spontaneous improvisation, and the product of creativity, as in many another field, may be superb in one case and leave much to be desired in another.

Duke Ellington, whose concert of sacred music at Grace Cathedral in 1965 was one of San Francisco's cultural highlights for the year, has long subsidized his orchestra from his royalties and other earnings. Ellington calls the orchestra his instrument. He uses it and he needs it, he says, to hear the music he writes. And this whole musical "workshop"—this great composer and his orchestra—rattles around the world in airplanes and buses, playing night clubs, dances, concerts, and TV shows, with Ellington working all the while in dressing rooms and hotel rooms, late into the night. The new compositions resulting are then heard soon after as they are tested by the Duke's complex instrument. If we really understood what jazz musicians are doing or "saying" through their music, if we appreciated what they are contributing to the art and culture of the world, if we accepted the contributions of this basic American music, we would subsidize a man like Ellington as a national treasure.

Influences on the Jazz Musician

The jazz musician is an individualist, a highly creative individualist, though he borrows and learns from all sources. For example, the Indian musicians Ali Akbar Kan and Ravi Shankar have had a tremendous influence on jazz in recent years. The works of men like Bach, Bartok, Stravinsky, and some recent European composers have had varying influences on jazz, largely because the great jazz musicians, free of academic restrictions and following their creative instincts, go where their ears lead them and listen to everything. Many jazz musicians are familiar with the broad canvas of the world's music, unlike classical musicians, whose insularity usually excludes a knowledge of jazz. Being less restricted in his whole approach and response to music and having sought a great variety of listening experiences, the jazz musician is freer to experiment and to bring new sounds and forms of expression into his performance. This has been generally true from the beginning of jazz. It is no accident, for example, that the saxophone, a bastard instrument which has not yet been assimilated into so-called serious music, has risen to such heights in jazz. The trumpet in jazz, ever since the rise of Louis Armstrong, has been used to do things that the trumpet is not supposed to be able to do. These "extensions" result in part from the freedom of the musician and his need to explore his musical medium and to follow his ear.

Jazz has operated under a great handicap in America from the time of its beginning in the South. It is Negro music, and the Negro has always been treated as a second-class citizen. In Europe, jazz received a wide reception and was more generally appreciated long before it was recognized here because the European ear was not stopped by color. European composers today are working with advanced jazz sounds and jazz ideas, and some musicians like John Lewis of the Modern Jazz Quartet insist that the only truly imaginative and vital compositional music today is coming from Europe. Lewis also believes that American classical music will die unless it opens its ears and its performance to jazz. This is a radical idea, but some truth may be in it. Jazz musicians can and do play in symphony orchestras, frequently in brass and reed sections and sometimes in other sections. However, very few classically trained musicians are of any use at all in most jazz performances.

Lou Gottlieb, a jazz-oriented graduate of the University of California's music department, once wrote that when the first great American composer came on the scene, he would be a jazz musician or, at least, a musician familiar with jazz. I would go quite a way beyond Gottlieb's conjecture. I think that the great American composers are already with us, that they are on the scene now, and that they are represented in such jazz musicians as Duke Ellington, Miles Davis, Charles Parker, and Charles Mingus. The music these men produce is the music that lives throughout the modern world, and it carries the sense of the American people to the world. I also believe that it is the American music that will last.

The great jazz artists have done what they have done with very little help, if any, from the established educational system. These accomplishments are far superior to the products of the established educational apparatus. Most university music departments are producing performers and teachers whose compositions are written, played, and heard only by other music-department graduates. Jazz has moved the center of gravity in this art outside the academy completely.

It is challenging to contemplate what might be the result of some active, planned effort to encourage, rather than to discourage, the musically creative youth in our society. It is of interest to speculate what might be the result if "jazz education" were brought within the walls of our better high schools and colleges. It may be explosive to reconsider and to design appropriate educational experiences for truly creative youth in any form of art or in any educational discipline.

CREATIVE PROBLEM SOLVING: AN OVERVIEW

Donald J. Treffinger, Scott C. Isaksen, and K. Brian Dorval

Many methods and approaches have been proposed for solving problems creatively; no one has cornered the market on truth. When referring to the efforts any individual or group might make to apply creativity to the task of solving a problem, *creative problem solving* is used. In this chapter, *Creative Problem Solving* (CPS) refers to our specific framework and approach (Isaksen, Dorval, & Treffinger, 1994; Treffinger, Isaksen, & Dorval, 1994). Our approach has emerged from an extensive tradition of theory, research, and practice that spans more than four decades. It has been applied successfully in a variety of settings and by problem solvers of all ages (from early childhood through adult).

This chapter traces briefly the origins of the CPS approach, describes the current CPS framework, and presents a summary of a general model for organizing or guiding systematic instruction or training in CPS. The chapter is intended to provide an introduction to, or overview of, the CPS framework and the Creative Learning model. It is *not* intended as a compendium of research (for which purpose see Isaksen, 1987; Isaksen, Murdock, Firestien, & Treffinger, 1993a, 1993b), nor as a training guide (for which purpose, see Isaksen et al., 1994; Treffinger et al., 1994).

Increasing Access to Creativity: Origins and Development of the CPS Approach

Isaksen (1987) reviewed several myths about the study of creativity, many of which have been quite persistent and difficult to put to rest. From the times of Plato and Socrates, for example, those who sought to create new products or ideas were often regarded as divinely inspired by the Muses or spirits. Others viewed creativity as a mysterious process, breaking away from reality and thus not always easily distinguishable from the bizarre or the insane. Others held that only a very small number of individuals could be gifted with the ability to be creatively productive. Today the mystery and madness myths have been strongly refuted; yet the myths that creativity is a phenomenon that defies scientific examination, and the view that "either you have it or you don't," are still widely held.

Our approach builds on several fundamental principles that we believe are generally supported by theory and research. We hold that:

- Creative potentials exist among all people;
- Creativity can be expressed among all people in an extremely broad array of areas or subjects, perhaps in a nearly infinite number of ways (Torrance, & Safter, 1990);
- Creativity is usually approached or manifested according to the interests, preferences, or styles of individuals (Dunn, Dunn, & Treffinger, 1992; Kirton, 1976);

- People can function creatively, while being productive to different levels or degrees of accomplishment or significance;
- Through personal assessment and deliberate intervention, in the form of training or instruction, individuals can make better use of their creative styles, enhance their level of creative accomplishment, and thus realize more fully their creative potentials.

This does not mean that we believe *everyone will* become a person who attains creative breakthroughs of major human significance; not everyone will be a Rembrandt, a Mozart, or an Edison. It does suggest, however, that *anyone might* become creatively productive in meaningful ways. It also means that we can help people to learn more about their own creative abilities and styles, to learn to apply useful strategies in appropriate ways, and to attain greater success and satisfaction (for themselves and others) through creative efforts.

The roots of our approach are found in Osborn's (1953) novel way of looking at the creative imagination of individuals. He was enthusiastically concerned with promoting creativity for finding new and useful solutions and for developing opportunities for enhancing any situation, whether business or personal. He believed strongly in the potential of every person for creative behavior. Imagination and judgment, as Osborn wisely advocated, are both essential contributors to creative productivity. Because we all need to use both of these processes, might not we be able to use them better?

As Osborn believed strongly in human creative potential and the power of learning, so our approach today maintains a clear focus on nurturing creative skills. One of Osborn's contributions—*brainstorming* (to encourage a free-flowing stream of ideas, while temporarily withholding or deferring judgment)—has become so widely known that it is a part of everyday conversation throughout the world. Alas, in the early years of the development of CPS, and even more unfortunately, still among some people today, brainstorming began to be equated with CPS. This is a serious misunderstanding, because first it overemphasizes the role of divergence in creativity and problem solving, distorting or ignoring the importance of balance between divergence and convergence. Second, it can lead some to view CPS as mere frivolity or undisciplined rambling. Several years ago, a critic was reputed to have dismissed CPS, for example, as "nothing more than cerebral popcorn popping."

In the mid-1950s, Osborn was joined by Sidney Parnes, and the basic ideas of CPS were expanded and organized into a five-step process model (Parnes, 1967). Parnes, with Ruth Noller, Angelo Biondi, and others, devoted great energy and effort to developing the CPS approach from the mid-1950's into the late-1970's (e.g., Noller, Parnes, & Biondi, 1976; Parnes, Noller, & Biondi, 1977) and to making its methods and techniques widely available for application by all people. Parnes and Noller were instrumental, for example, in establishing an academic program to provide instructional opportunities for CPS at both the undergraduate and graduate levels. This program has continued to expand and flourish at the Center for Studies in Creativity at Buffalo State College. Nearly 100 professionals have completed graduate degrees in this program, and undergraduate courses are taken by students from programs throughout the college. The academic programs and their impact or effectiveness have been examined in numerous quantitative and qualitative studies (e.g., Keller-Mathers, 1990; Noller & Parnes, 1972; Parnes & Noller, 1972a, 1972b, 1973; Parnes, 1987; Reese, Parnes, Treffinger, & Kaltsounis, 1976). At a practical level, the impact of CPS has also been extended through the ongoing efforts of many other organizations, including the Creative Education Foundation, the Creative Problem Solving Group—Buffalo, and the Center for Creative Learning. Research and networking among creativity scholars has expanded internationally through a number of conferences and publications (see Isaksen et al., 1993a, 1993b) and through the *International Creativity Network*.

The CPS approach continued to be refined and developed in the 1970s and 1980s, building on the pioneering contributions of Osborn and the "first generation" of CPS developers and researchers. Noller and several colleagues described applications of CPS for a general audience (Noller, 1977), for mathematics (Noller, Heintz, & Blaeuer, 1978), and for gifted education (Noller, Treffinger, & Houseman, 1979). The original formulations for using and enhancing creative imagination, organized into a structured problem solving process model, served as building blocks for several decades of research and development, and thus for many revisions, refinements, and expanding directions. Examples of these continuing developments include resources by Firestien (1989), Isaksen and Treffinger (1985, 1991), Parnes (1981, 1988, 1992), Treffinger and Isaksen (1992), and Treffinger, Isaksen, and Firestien (1982).

Isaksen and Treffinger (1985) expanded the CPS model by describing six stages, rather than five (adding a Mess-Finding stage). In addition, they introduced other modifications: broadening the scope of the early Fact-Finding stage (and renaming it Data-Finding), highlighting the need for both divergence (generating ideas) and convergence (analyzing, refining, and selecting ideas), and expanding the scope and methods for solution development and implementation planning (modifying and expanding the Solution-Finding and Acceptance-Finding stages). The six stages of CPS were refined further by clustering them into three general components, described as Understanding the Problem, Generating Ideas, and Planning for Action (Isaksen & Treffinger, 1991; Treffinger & Isaksen, 1992).

Isaksen and Treffinger (1985) also clarified the definition of the word *problem* as it is used in CPS. A problem for CPS is not merely a puzzle, for which there already exists a novel (or clever, interesting, or even obvious) solution and which only might be termed a problem if, and only if, the person does not already know that solution. In addition, Isaksen and Treffinger contended that a problem should not only be viewed negatively, as an obstacle, with something lacking or deficient, or as something wrong that must be corrected. Problems for CPS were described as opportunities and challenges for successful change and constructive action. The challenges people face each day represent many opportunities for personal and professional growth. Thus, a problem might be any important, open-ended, and ambiguous situation for which one wants and needs new options and a plan for carrying a solution successfully.

CPS Today: A Descriptive Framework

Work on the CPS framework continued to be very dynamic from the 1980s until the present time, and, as a result, the framework has continued to expand and evolve. As we look back at earlier process descriptions, one analogy that presents itself clearly is that their use today would be similar in many respects to solving complex mathematical problems using a slide rule. It *could* be done, and it might even produce acceptable results for some contemporary purposes. But it is much more likely that today's mathematicians or engineers would use an electronic calculator or a computer. Today's technologies help one to work faster, more efficiently, often with a much greater degree of precision, and even to enable the user to undertake much more complex and sophisticated challenges or problems. An alternate analogy (Isaksen, 1994) involves applying the notation system used by software developers and publishers to the CPS framework. In this notation, the first release of a completed program is known as Version 1.0. If there are minor updates and modifications, the number to the right of the decimal point increases (e.g., Version 1.1 or 1.2). When a major revision of the program is released, the number to the left of the decimal point changes (e.g., Version 2.0 or 3.0). Applying this scheme, Isaksen's tabulation sets the current CPS framework as Version 5.2.

Regardless of the informal analogy one might prefer to use to describe it or compare it with its predecessors, today's view of CPS is unique in a number of very important ways. In several respects, contemporary CPS has changed in important and very substantive ways; these include:

- Representing process dimensions in a natural, rather than a contrived way;

- Undergoing a transformation from a prescriptive to a descriptive approach;

- Becoming more flexible and responsive to task, contextual, personal, methodological, and metacognitive considerations.

These developments have been discussed in detail elsewhere (Isaksen & Dorval, 1993; Isaksen et al., 1994; Treffinger et al., 1994).

We have worked toward an increased awareness of, and responsiveness to, the natural methods and approaches individuals and groups use to deal with important, complex, and ambiguous opportunities and challenges. Accordingly, we have moved toward a flexible view of process, in which many tools are available, when and as needed, for an individual or group working on a problem or open-ended task. This has led us away from a process view that prescribes a fixed number or kind of particular "steps" or strategies that must be applied in a fixed, predetermined sequence. We emphasize the need for deliberate assessment of the intended outcomes, the people and situation, and the methods available (which, taken together, we describe as Task Appraisal; Isaksen et al., 1994). The contemporary view of CPS also involves deliberate efforts by problem solvers to make, monitor, and manage specific decisions regarding the stages, methods, and techniques to be used and the order or sequence in which they will be used. The CPS framework is not a simple, step-by-step model in which every group can deal with any problem by "running through" a prearranged set of steps. Today's CPS calls on individuals and groups to invest a substantial degree of thought or reflection, imagination, judgment, and energy in their creative problem solving efforts. At the same time, the framework provides a structured set of operations or tools as resources upon which to draw as needed. Our current graphic representation of the CPS approach is presented in Figure 11.1.

Figure 11.1 depicts three major CPS components (Understanding the Problem, Generating Ideas, and Planning for Action) and six specific CPS stages (Mess-Finding, Data-Finding, Problem-Finding, Idea-Finding, Solution-Finding, and Acceptance-Finding) that comprise our current process framework. We next describe these components and stages briefly.

Understanding the Problem

Although many researchers have focused on problem- finding as a process separate from problem-solving, we consider such a distinction arbitrary and, in the context of a flexible, independent components approach, largely unnecessary and in some important ways inappropriate. A systematic effort to define, construct, or formulate a problem constitutes one of the three major components that should be available to problem solvers. It is not necessarily the "first" step in problem-solving, nor is it necessarily undertaken by all people in every problem-solving session. Rather than prescribing an essential, initial problem-finding process or step, we prefer a construction in which the individual or group analyzes the task at hand (including outcomes, people, context, and methodological options) to determine whether and when deliberate problem-structuring efforts are needed. Typically, then, the CPS component called *Understanding the Problem* will be needed when the individual or group confronts a situation that is (or has become) ambiguous and needs clarity of focus or direction. The problem solver may recognize this initially and so might begin with one or more of the three stages in this component; it is also possible, however, that this component might be undertaken after early efforts to generate options or to implement possible solutions has led to recognition that the problem needs greater clarity, definition, or redefinition. This component includes three specific stages: Mess-Finding, Data-Finding, and Problem-Finding.

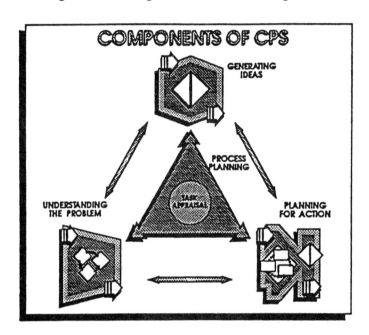

Figure 11.1 *CPS Components*

(From *Creative Approaches Problem Solving*, by S. G. Isaksen, K. B. Dorval, and D. J. Treffinger, 1994, Dubuque, IA: Kendall-Hunt. Copyright ©: 1994 by Creative Problem Solving Group—Buffalo. Reproduced by permission.)

Mess-Finding. Ambiguous challenges and concerns often begin as a *mess*. A *mess* is a broad statement of a goal or a direction for problem solving. Usually, a mess has three general characteristics: It is broad, brief, and beneficial. As an example, a business owner might say, "We would like to reach new customers or include a new target group in our marketing." The mess generally describes the basic area of need or challenge on which the problem solver's efforts will be focused, remaining broad enough to allow many perspectives to emerge as one (or a group) looks more closely at the situation.

Data-Finding. For any opportunity or challenge, many important facts, opinions, impressions, concerns, paradoxes, and circumstances must be considered. In Data-Finding it is important to bring out this information by posing such questions as "Who? What? Where? When? Why? and How?" These questions bring out key data and help the problem solver(s) focus more clearly on the most challenging aspects and concerns of the situation. Converging in Data-Finding involves identifying or constructing one or more clusters of significant data, which will point to the direction that subsequent problem development or solution efforts might take most fruitfully.

Problem-Finding. In Problem-Finding the person or group working on the task will seek a specific or targeted question on which to focus their subsequent efforts. Diverging in this stage involves generating many possible problem statements, phrased in a positive way, by using an *invitational stem* such as "In What Ways Might . . . " or "How Might. . . . ." Effectively worded problem statements invite an open or wide-ranging search for many, varied, and novel options. They should be concise and free from limiting criteria.

Generating Ideas

When an open-ended, invitational statement of a problem has been formulated, or already exists, the problem solver's efforts may be focused on the need to generate options. This component involves one specific CPS stage: Idea-Finding.

Idea-Finding. The diverging phase of this stage involves the person or group in producing many options (fluent thinking), a variety of possible options (flexible thinking), novel or unusual options (original thinking), or a number of detailed or refined options (elaborative thinking). The converging phase of Idea-Finding provides an opportunity for examining, reviewing, clustering, and selecting promising options.

Planning for Action

When a person or group recognizes a number of interesting or promising options, they may need assistance in strengthening those options, refining or developing them, making effective choices, and preparing for successful implementation. Novel or intriguing options are not necessarily useful or workable without extended effort and productive thinking. Thus, the focus of the Planning for Action component is on preparing and developing options for successful implementation. Two specific stages are involved: Solution-Finding and Acceptance-Finding.

Solution-Finding. This stage involves examining promising options closely to determine what steps will need to be taken. If there are a few promising options, all of which might be implemented, the principal focus will be on refining or developing options, making them as strong as possible. If there are several promising options, not all of which can (or may need to) be implemented, the task may focus more on ranking options or setting effective priorities. When many new and promising options exist, the task may be to condense or compress the choices to make them more manageable or to evaluate a number of options very systematically using explicit criteria. For example, to strengthen or refine an option or a cluster of ideas with a common novel theme, it might be appropriate to apply strategies to assess the advantages, limitations, and unique potentials of the options. To set priorities might involve rating each of several options against all the others, one pair at a time. To screen and evaluate a number of specific ideas on many criteria, an evaluation grid or matrix might be employed.

Acceptance-Finding. This CPS stage involves searching for several potential sources of assistance and resistance for possible solutions. Assisters represent people, places, materials, and times that will support the plan and contribute to its successful implementation. Resisters represent potential obstacles—people, places, materials, and things that might resist, go wrong, or be missing at a critical time. Acceptance-Finding helps the problem solver identify ways to make the best possible use of assisters and avoid or overcome possible sources of resistance. Acceptance-Finding also involves formulating an Action Plan that describes the specific steps that will be taken in order to implement a proposed solution.

Learning CPS: A Model for Instruction or Training

We have also worked on the challenge of describing a systematic approach to training and instruction in the use of CPS. A model for learning CPS should take into account the skills involved in learning, practicing, and applying a variety of CPS methods and techniques for all three components and six stages, as well as those involved in Task Appraisal and process planning (Isaksen et al., 1994).

Our approach to instruction and training emphasizes the importance of understanding the characteristics of people and their influence on creative behavior. Thus, we use cognitive and personality measures, along with style indicators, to help individuals and groups identify their own strengths and preferences. We also examine several important context dimensions to model the development of an environment conducive to creativity. These pre-CPS experiences set the stage for effective problem-solving. In addition, they help to create for the learner a usable and effective storehouse of strategies to apply later. Although, of course, there may be many successful strategies for training individuals or groups to understand and use CPS, we believe that the Creative Learning Model (Figure 11.2) provides a systematic, well-structured approach through which we can enhance creative productivity and stimulate authentic learning and meaningful application of CPS.

The Creative Learning Model was first described and illustrated in a journal article (Treffinger, 1979). In 1980, a more extensive description of the model for educational applications, with examples of practical activities or experiences that represented each of the three levels, was provided in book form (Treffinger, 1980). The model was subsequently updated (Treffinger, 1988; Treffinger, Isaksen, & Firestien, 1982, 1983). Feedback from many colleagues and associates has indicated that the Creative Learning Model has been a useful and valuable resource, helping educators, trainers, and group leaders in many different settings to better understand creative learning and to better organize or structure their deliberate efforts to promote creative learning. It has also been a dynamic model that has been modified and expanded as new insights have become available through research, development, and practical work in the field, while retaining much of its original emphasis on balance between theory and practice through nearly a decade of study and application.

Three Levels of Creative Learning

The Creative Learning Model is presented in Figure 11.2. Three levels of creative learning are proposed in the model. These are described (in terms that are functional, even if they are not very imaginative) as Levels One, Two, and Three. The three levels are considered sequential, although the proposed sequence is based on logical analysis and not on direct empirical investigation of a hierarchical structure.

Level One. Level One involves learning to use creative and critical thinking techniques as *tools* for generating and analyzing ideas. Creative thinking tools are those methods, strategies, or techniques that enhance the person's ability to generate deliberately many, varied, or unusual ideas or to extend or elaborate on ideas by adding details or making them more complete. Critical thinking tools are those that enhance the person's ability to analyze, compare, refine, or improve ideas or to make choices and decisions.

The metaphor of the tool was chosen deliberately. Tools extend our own personal capabilities, enabling us to complete a job or task more easily, effectively, or efficiently. One learns how to use tools skillfully, how to identify the tasks for which certain tools are useful and necessary,

120

and how to identify and select tools for various task requirements. Through instruction and practice, one's proficiency and confidence in using tools increases, and more complex tasks can be undertaken. As part of learning how to use tools, a person usually also learns their names and other vocabulary related to their use. There are many different tools, and one ordinarily begins by learning how to use some of the most basic ones, which can be applied in a wide range of tasks. With increasing involvement and experience, however, one's collection of tools, the ease and confidence with which they are used, and the scope of the tasks on which the person works are also likely to increase.

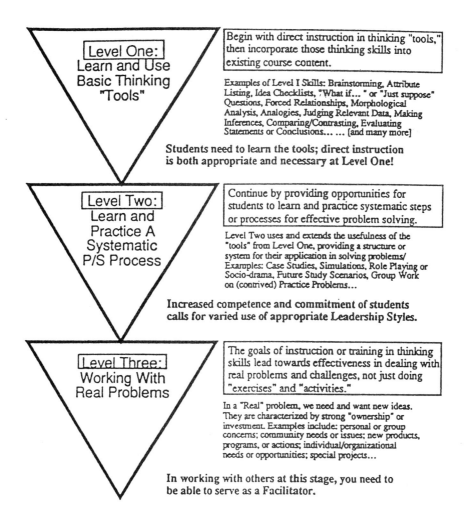

Figure 11.2 *Creative Learning Model*

(From "A Model for Creative Learning: 1988 Update," *Creative Learning Today*, 2 (3). Copyright 1988 by Center for Creative Learning. Reprinted by permission.)

Level One thinking tools include: brainstorming, attribute listing, forced relationships, idea checklists, and morphological methods (for creative thinking or deliberate idea generation); as well as making inferences and applying deductive reasoning, selecting relevant data, sequencing, rank ordering or setting priorities, and making choices or decisions using ALU

(Advantages, Limitations, and Uniqueness) or an evaluation matrix (for critical thinking or deliberate idea analysis or selection). Level One tools can be taught and learned through direct instruction.

Level One skills are not sufficient to insure that a person is an effective or productive thinker. Instructional or training programs that rely entirely on Level One tools are likely to become little more than a collection of relatively meaningless tricks, games, or gadgets unless the learners have structured opportunities to progress beyond exercises and activities by applying the Level One tools in more complex or higher level intellectual opportunities and challenges or task-relevant contexts.

Level Two. Level Two involves learning and practicing a structured process or system for solving problems in which Level One skills can be applied, organized, and extended. CPS, for example, is one approach to defining the process of problem solving that is useful for children, adolescents, and adults, and in which both the creative and critical thinking tools from Level One can be extended and applied in meaningful ways. It is also sufficiently flexible that new tools can readily be incorporated into the problem-solving efforts of an individual or group as they may be learned or designed. Although we represent Levels Two (and Three) of the Creative Learning Model by referring to CPS, other process models might be used as alternatives within the same approach to instruction or training.

In Level Two, the major goals are for students (in any setting and at any age level) to learn a structured approach for using their creative and critical thinking tools to solve problems and to have sufficient experience and practice in using that structured method so they are both confident and proficient. The problems that are presented may thus be preselected, contrived practice problems, intended to be interesting to the students but concerned more with practicing applications of problem-solving strategies than with the actual solutions or their implementation. The problems must be sufficiently realistic so there will be adequate motivation and willingness to work on them; they should also be sufficiently removed from the group's concerns, however, so that the participants will be able to "keep an eye on" the process strategies while they are working on the problem. Effective leadership behavior, taking into account the important aspects of the situation (the task, the relationships among group members, and the developmental level or readiness of the participants), is important for success at Level Two (cf. Blanchard, 1985).

Level Three. Level Three represents the most important desired outcome for any systematic instructional or training program on problem solving: to enable the participants or students to deal effectively with real problems and challenges.

In Level Three, the major goal can be stated very simply: "Solve the problem." Level Three involves problems that really matter and solutions that will really be carried out. There is investment or ownership among the group members, a sense of commitment or concern, and clear recognition that the task is not merely an academic exercise or a group dynamics activity. The problem is real when the challenge is felt personally by the group and the consequences of their efforts matter to them. The role of the teacher or trainer is no longer one of instruction in tools or skills, nor even one of leading the group through a process that is important for them to master; instead, the leadership challenge is now one of effective facilitation.

The Creative Learning Model can be useful in several ways, including: defining the structure or scope of instructional programs for developing thinking skills, planning a systematic approach to working with process outcomes at several levels of complexity, defining the appropriate roles for teachers and students in process instruction, and as a starting point for establishing criteria and procedures for evaluating the outcomes of instructional programs on thinking skills.

References

Blanchard, K. H. (1985). *SL II: A situational approach to managing people.* San Diego, CA: Blanchard Training and Development.

Dunn, R., Dunn, K., & Treffinger, D. J. (1992). *Bringing out the giftedness in your child.* New York: John Wiley.

Firestien, R. L. (1989). *From basics to breakthroughs.* Buffalo, NY: DOK.

Isaksen, S. G. (Ed.). (1987). *Frontiers of creativity research: Beyond the basics.* Buffalo, NY: Bearly Limited.

Isaksen, S. G. (1994). *Versions of CPS.* Buffalo, NY: Center for Studies in Creativity, Buffalo State College.

Isaksen S. G. & Dorval, K. B. (1993). Changing views of creative problem solving: Over 40 years of continuous improvement. *International Creativity Network Newsletter, 3*(1), 1, 4-5.

Isaksen, S. G., Dorval, K. B., & Treffinger, D. J. (1994). *Creative approaches to problem solving.* Dubuque, IA: Kendall-Hunt.

Isaksen, S. G., Murdock, M. C., Feinstein, R. L., Treffinger, D. J. (Eds.). (1993a). *Understanding and recognizing creativity: The emergence of a discipline.* Norwood, NJ: Ablex.

Isaksen, S. G., Murdock, M. C., Firestien, R. L., & Treffinger, D. J. (Eds.). (1993b). *Nurturing and developing creativity: The emergence of a discipline.* Norwood, NJ: Ablex.

Isaksen, S. G., & Treffinger, D. J. (1985). *Creative problem solving: The basic course.* Buffalo, NY: Bearly Limited.

Isaksen, S. G., & Treffinger, D. J. (1991). Creative learning and problem solving. In A. I. Costa (Ed.), *Developing minds: Programs for teaching thinking.* (revised ed., Vol. 2, pp. 89-93). Alexandria, VA: Association for Supervision and Curriculum Development.

Keller-Mathers, S. (1990). *Impact of creative problem solving training on participants' personal and professional lives: A replication and extension.* Unpublished Master's project, Buffalo State College, Buffalo, NY.

Kirton, M. J. (1976). Adaptors and innovators: A description and measure. *Journal of Applied Psychology, 61,* 622-629.

Noller, R. B. (1977). *Scratching the surface of creative problem solving.* Buffalo, NY: DOK.

Noller, R. B., Heintz, R. E., & Blaeuer, D. A. (1978). *Creative problem solving in mathematics.* Buffalo, NY: DOK.

Noller, R. B., & Parnes, S. J. (1972). Applied creativity: The creative studies project. Part III The curriculum. *Journal of Creative Behavior, 6,* 275-294.

Noller, R. B., Parnes, S. J., & Biondi, A. M. (1976). *Creative actionbook.* New York: Scribners.

Noller, R. B., Treffinger, D. J., & Houseman, E. (1979). *It's a gas to be gifted: CPS for the gifted and talented.* Buffalo, NY: DOK.

Osborn, A. F. (1953). *Applied imagination*. New York: Scribners.

Parnes, S. J. (1967). *Creative behavior guidebook*. New York: Scribners.

Parnes, S. J. (1981). *The magic of your mind*. Buffalo, NY: Bearly Limited.

Parnes, S. J. (1987). The creative studies project. In S. G. Isaksen (Ed.), *Frontiers of creativity research: Beyond the basics* (pp. 165-188). Buffalo, NY: Bearly Limited.

Parnes, S. J. (1988). *Visionizing*. Buffalo, NY: DOK.

Parnes, S. J. (Ed.). (1992). *A source book for creative problem-solving*. Buffalo, NY: Creative Education Foundation Press.

Parnes, S. J., & Noller, R. B. (1972a). Applied creativity: The creative studies project. Part I: The development. *Journal of Creative Behavior, 6*, 11-22.

Parnes, S. J., & Noller, R. B. (1972b). Applied creativity: The creative studies project. Part II: Results of the two year program. *Journal of Creative Behavior, 6*, 164- 186.

Parnes, S. J., & Noller, R. B. (1973). Applied creativity: The creative studies project. Part IV: Personality findings and conclusions. *Journal of Creative Behavior, 7*, 15-36.

Parnes, S. J., Noller, R. B., & Biondi, A. M. (1977). *Guide to creative action*. New York: Scribners.

Reese, H. W., Parnes, S. J., Treffinger, D. J., & Kaltsounis, G. (1976). Effects of a creative studies program on Structure-of-Intellect factors. *Journal of Educational Psychology, 68*, 401- 410.

Torrance, E. P., & Safter, T. H. (1990). *The incubation model of teaching*. Buffalo, NY: Bearly Limited.

Treffinger, D. J. (1979). Fostering independence and creativity. *Journal for the Education of the Gifted, 3*, 214-224.

Treffinger, D. J. (1980). *Encouraging creative learning for the gifted and talented*. Ventura, CA: Ventura County Schools/LTI Publications.

Treffinger, D. J. (1988). A model for creative learning: 1988 update. *Creative Learning Today, 2*(3), 4-6.

Treffinger, D. J., & Isaksen, S. G. (1992). *Creative problem solving: An introduction*. Sarasota, FL: Center for Creative Learning.

Treffinger, D. J., Isaksen, S. G., & Dorval, K. B. (1994). *Creative problem solving: An introduction (Rev. ed.)*. Sarasota, FL: Center for Creative Learning.

Treffinger, D. J., Isaksen, S. G., & Firestien, R. L. (1982). *Handbook of creative learning*. Williamsville, NY: Center for Creative Learning.

Treffinger, D. J., Isaksen S. G., & Firestien, R. L. (1983). Theoretical perspectives on creative learning. *Journal of Creative Behavior, 17*, 9-17.

ADVERTISING CREATIVES
LOOK AT CREATIVITY

Sandra E. Moriarty and Bruce G. VandenBergh

Advertising is one of the few fields where professionals carry the title of "creative." The "creative side" of advertising includes copywriters, art directors, "creative directors" and broadcast producers. Their colleagues in the agencies refer to them as "the creatives." One of the interesting things about this side of the advertising profession is that many of the "creatives" are unaware of the literature relating to creative theory and research and few of them know the field is established enough to be served by its own journal, *The Journal of Creative Behavior.*

Creative literature, research and theory is rarely discussed in advertising courses, but most "creatives" don't have degrees in advertising anyway. They come from such diverse backgrounds as English, journalism, graphic design, philosophy, education, sociology and psychology (this last group is more likely to be aware of theories of creativity). Creatives are thought by management to operate with a special "gift," and creatives have been known to encourage this "black magic" view of ideation since that absolves them of having to justify and explain their concepts. ("Trust me . . . I know it will work.")

Some are tremendously well read and devour everything they can find relating to their craft. But still, the overall knowledge of creative theory is often unexpectedly low. At best they may be aware of Alex Osborn's *Applied Imagination* (1963) and James Webb Young's book, *A Technique for Producing Ideas* (1975). Both of the authors, of course, were advertising executives. While some may know of Osborn's book, typically few know that he was involved in founding the Creative Education Foundation in Buffalo, nor have they heard of such programs as CPSI (Creative Problem-Solving Institute) or Synectics.

Given the generally low level of knowledge about creative theory, this study was undertaken to see how professional "creatives" in advertising view their particular type of creative problem solving. Specifically the study investigated their working styles and their descriptions of the creative process.

An Exploratory Study

The question of how creatives in advertising get their ideas is not easily approached through conventional survey research methods. Large sample surveys and structured questionnaires do not allow for the in-depth questioning needed to probe this issue. Personal interviews were preferred, but were prohibitive in terms of generating enough responses for the results to have practical if not statistical meaning.

The option selected was a mail survey to a list of people that could be reasonably identified as representing "creatives" in advertising. They were sent an open-ended questionnaire with certain key questions guiding their exploration of how they get ideas, their working style, brainstorming techniques and methods of getting started and working through mental blocks. While this approach reduced the response rate, it did provide the longer and more thoughtful comments we were seeking.

Method

The exploratory survey was conducted during the fall and winter of 1982-1983. A mailed survey was sent to the most current list of national Addy winners. This list was obtained from the American Advertising Federation (AAF) which sponsors the nation-wide Addy award competition. Addy winners were chosen as a respondent group because the awards represent grassroots advertising in the United States. The competition evolves through a series of local and district award contests. This eliminates the bias of some other award programs focusing almost exclusively on the work from a few large urban advertising centers.

Of the 251 open-ended surveys mailed, 52 or 21 percent were completed and returned. The respondents represent the following job categories: owners of small agencies and creative people now in management positions, creative directors, art directors, copywriters and producers.

Findings

Working Style

"Creatives" in advertising generally know of the concept of brainstorming, but they use a slightly different definition from most creative theorists. Osborn (1963) defines brainstorming as a group ideation process using a conference technique. Most respondents to the survey use the word brainstorming to mean "kicking ideas around." This activity can be done alone, in a team, or in a group. In their lexicon it seems the brainstorming activity has been separated from the group situation. The following comments illustrate this pattern of usage:

- I prefer individual brainstorming followed by group reviews.
- I prefer group meetings for basic input, then I like to go away and brainstorm ideas alone.

For those who use brainstorming in its original form, meaning in a group conference situation, there is a universal attitude of dislike. The following comments are typical:

- Generally I try to avoid "group creativity." But it depends on the group. Each has its own corporate spirit.
- Great creativity doesn't happen in committees.
- I don't like group brainstorming. I only participate as a last resort.
- I don't like brainstorming and feel the best ideas come out of a single mind.
- I feel that a group of more than two or three usually becomes too cumbersome.
- Brainstorming has rarely proved beneficial in groups larger than two.
- A roomful of people can be unfocused and unfruitful.
- I personally have never been a strong believer in brainstorming. Too many egos, too many asides, too many dead ends.
- I don't believe in group creative sessions because I think you lose intensity. I think it gets to be an ego contest.
- I don't like to work in groups although I've had some luck that way. More often so-called "ideation" sessions are too time consuming and often boring.

- I don't think brainstorming is very helpful in a group because the ideas tend to get off track.

Some make a distinction in terms of type of problem solving. For example, many of the creatives note that brainstorming is good for developing strategy and bits and pieces of concepts, the "germ" of an idea. It's also seen as useful for testing concepts once they've been developed and presented. The following comments illustrate these distinctions:

- Group processes are necessary at a certain point. It's a good way to get feedback prior to submitting an idea for final approval.

- Generally I do not see any value to brainstorming. It's good sometimes for ideas; strategies, of course, but not for the development of creative work.

- Brainstorming is only good for getting idea "germs," only one mind working alone can make it "grow."

- I prefer a group discussion of the *problem*. A collective effort usually results in a more accurate, defined creative problem and possible concepts for the solution. But I prefer to develop concepts, scripts, visuals, etc. by working alone. Then after I have arrived at what I feel is the best creative product, I use the objectivity of a group of creative people to test, modify, improve or reject my own solution.

There are a few, however, who are more in tune with the spirit of Alex Osborn and find something positive to say about group brainstorming.

- I prefer to work with an art director but larger groups are effective, too, as well as just plain fun.

- My best idea came as a group project in a meeting where the account team locked themselves up in a brainstorming session away from the office.

Group Size

Osborn recommended a group size of six to eight people. More recent research has found positive results from even larger groups up to 12 or 13 (Osborn 1963; Taylor, Berry & Block 1958; Fox, Lorgi, Weltz & Herrold 1953; Thomas & Fink 1963; Renzulli, Owen & Callahan 1974). None of the advertising creatives, however, favor groups larger than two or three. The universally-approved group size is a team, usually two people made up of a writer and an art director. Sometimes the team may be three and will include an account person who is on the same "wave length" as the creatives or a producer. The following comments are typical:

- I prefer working alone but my secondary preference is for two to three people in a small brainstorming session. That is used when I need other opinions, have to focus on what the client wants (rather than needs), or work out blocks.

- I like to have my art director partner work with me. We complement each other very well.

- I work best with one other brain. Two heads are better than one but three or more aren't. Group brainstorming for me is less efficient that two good people working together.

- I work better as a member of a team: writer, art director and creative director.

- The best thing about working with one or two other people is that we all act as springboards.

- I prefer working with one other person. I find it more stimulating—but not with a committee.

- I believe in brainstorming as much as possible. Two heads are better than one.

- Although I come up with good ideas alone, I prefer sitting down with an art director and "cooking" together.

Occasionally a true loner surfaced in the questionnaires. Even Osborn recognized that individual work is an important aspect of ideation. Some people, however, would rather work alone all the time and find they have difficulty being productive in group situations.

- I prefer working alone, particularly when I'm really interested in the topic.

- My own style is solitary and meditative.

- I enjoy shutting myself off from the world and following my own thought chain.

One respondent admitted working in a variety of different situations and gave an estimate: "30 percent of the time I work with alone, 40 percent I work with a great art director and 30 percent of the time I work with a 'creative' account person."

Osborn (1963) also recommended that in team situations, group work should alternate with individual work. Several respondents described a similar working style. The comment that follows explains how that happens in advertising:

- I prefer sitting down with one other person, a writer, and tossing ideas around. Sometimes I'll come up with the words; sometimes the writer comes up with the visuals. It doesn't matter. After developing concepts we think are right, then the writer writes—alone; and I design—alone. But we constantly check back with one another. If the writer doesn't like the way it looks or the art director doesn't like the way it reads, they talk it out. Because the ad belongs to both of them.

Creative Process

The process of getting ideas was analyzed and described as early as 1926 by Graham Wallas who developed an outline of the ideation process that identified these four steps: preparation, incubation, illumination and verification (Moriarty & Reid, 1983). Taylor identified the steps as a series of mental functions: exposure phase, the predivergent phase where a problem is recognized and an answer sought, the conversion phase where insight is achieved, a postdivergent phase where the insight is revised and redeveloped, and an expression phase where something new is stated and presented (Taylor, Austin, Sutton, 1974). In advertising James Webb Young (1975) described the process for advertising creativity: gather raw materials, organize them, drop the entire subject, wait for the idea to appear and adapt the idea to practical use.

It is obvious that the respondents are intuitively operating with essentially the same processes and key steps. A few of them described the "magic light bulb" or "lightning bolt" phenomenon:

- It rarely takes me more than an hour or two to get five or six ad concepts.

- The most creative ideas usually come suddenly; stunningly . . . First just the beginning but then the whole thing will rush madly into my mind.

- My ideas always come very quickly (If you labor for three weeks on a project, usually the creative idea is less than earth-shaking.)

- They usually come fairly quickly, without a whole lot of screaming and suffering.

128

Most respondents, however, identified a process that demanded lots of hard work and often frustration and tension. The following descriptions are by people who tried to reconstruct the lengthy process they went through when they "got an idea."

- I believe in the "Percolator Process."

  1. Get all the background possible.
  2. Dump it in the brain.
  3. Sleep on it.
  4. Talk it through with other knowledgeable persons.
  5. Keep at it—turning up the pressure as high as possible until the entire mess explodes.
  6. The best idea will usually stick to the ceiling.

- Usually the creative director and I will sit down together, often with the account person and go over the tangibles. Then the CD and I will begin just talking, often laughing, about whatever the problem puts us in mind of. From the hall, it sounds like a lot of hilarity. But from the inside, it's pretty intense. It means listening to every word the other person is saying and keeping your internal monitor turned up full blast . . . so you're sure to detect the wonderful beginning of an idea in a throwaway phrase . . . that half-joke. You have to keep your monitor trained on yourself too. Often . . . something comes out of nowhere. Or, out of something highly personal. Here, we're fortunate enough to be able to speak fearlessly, bravely, about personal reactions and experiences. Often that leads to a great idea. At the very least the process illuminates the creative problem. So, armed with either a great premise . . . or a well-stated problem, I leave to go write the copy. I tend to reappear at the CD's door intermittently . . . with a line, a sketched out ad idea . . . or an incredibly long series of heads or themes. During these early days, many yellow sheets, written over and hardly legible, are studied. Together, we winnow the choices, refine what survives, and occasionally reverse directions. It's pretty exciting.

- My first step is to eliminate all of the obvious "camp" ideas that spring to mind when given the basic information. This process I call "Trash Mind." I let my mind go and get it all out of my system . . . write each headline down . . . or a brief synopsis of the idea . . . and then go on to other things. Sometimes a ridiculous idea has merit . . . but I have to be able to compare it with others arrived at through a logical process.

  Next, research. Get the facts. Write down, in simple sentences, the very basics that need to be conveyed. Set goals.

  Next, meet with my creative team assigned to that account. We all toss out our crazies first and that helps us destroy any ideas that someone else is always perfect and super-creative. Then we settle down gradually to discussions of the fine points from each idea. Meeting ends.

  Individually we work on what we were able to draw from the meeting . . . expanding someone else's idea . . . pursuing our own . . . whatever. Next meeting, the ideas are presented in a more finished form. At that time, a decision is reached as to which concept we will pursue . . . or which ideas. Often we will work on several different concepts for the same job. The decision is never definite but is usually determined by the person with the most enthusiasm for a particular idea. (I have found that the more someone is willing to fight for their idea, the better they will work at perfecting it.)

Next stage is extrapolating the idea into the other areas of the concept—such as possible tie-in materials.

Next stage is a critical review as to whether the concept accomplishes the goals laid down during the research stage—also whether the goals are still valid ones. Then presenting the idea to other creatives and finally to the account executive accompanied by reams of paper stating the creative rationales, projected expenses, proposed production techniques, hints on how to sell the idea to the client, etc.

Critical Steps

Most respondents concentrated on describing certain steps in the process that they found to be particularly critical. These steps mirror the ones identified in the review of creative theories. For example many noted the necessity to do background research at the beginning to gather facts. This is often called immersion:

- We always spend a lot of time up front getting as much information about the product or service as we can before we start concepting. Part of this up front time is spent writing up a creative work plan.

One respondent gave a very graphic description of physically "getting into" the problem. This is how the creator of the famous ad for Vicks described getting the idea for the killer karate chop cough:

- I had been working fruitlessly for several weeks to come up with a good idea. So I decided to start from scratch. While pacing my office I asked myself, "What is it like to have a cough?" I coughed hard and found that I was karate chopping the air with my arms. Voilà, the script practically wrote itself.

Wrestling with the idea is the second step that can be seen in the descriptions of the process. It's trying to tame the beast—a confrontation between the artist and the problem that frequently ends with the artist losing temporarily. This would be similar to Taylor's "predivergent phase." Here's how one writer described this struggle with an idea:

- Once I reach a point where something gels, I'll write the head on a large pad with a magic marker. I like seeing the words big, roughly the same size they'll be set to. I'll stare at them, crossouts leave clues where I've been. Only when the head works, will I go to the typewriter and work out the copy.

One of the most interesting elements of creative thinking is the concept of incubation, getting away from the problem by turning your attention elsewhere while the subconscious continues to wrestle with it. A number of respondents referred to this phenomenon with comments like this:

- I take one or two days to think about the problem. I usually just tuck it away during the period, not spending a great deal of time working on it. The back-of-the-mind mode. Once I meet with the team, the ideas flow pretty easily.

- I let creative ideas simmer in the unconscious until they're ready to come.

- I deposit everything into the conscious, let it filter into the subconscious. Ideas pop out at the oddest times (usually during periods of relaxation).

Illumination, the moment of insight, seems to come in two different situations. On one hand the respondents reported insight while they were wrestling with the problem. Others reported illumination experiences during incubation, when they had put the problem aside.

- Ideas don't always come at the office. They come on the freeway, in dreams, while watching TV, playing tennis.

- Good ideas come when a certain "critical mass" of thought is reached.

- There is no other emotion (other than that which cannot be mentioned in a family research project) like the one that occurs when two people are building on each other's ideas and the solution suddenly presents itself with such force that they stare at each other and wonder where it came from. I think Burroughs called it the "third force in the room." It can be an absolutely hair raising experience and it's very addictive.

The last critical step identified by the respondents is evaluation. Advertising is a very practical business and all creative ideas have to meet the test of the "morning after" with review board presentations, client presentations and copy-testing. This evaluation phase was noted in comments like this:

- The biggest problem is trying not to fall in love with an idea that's only so-so. In other words, when you write it you say, "This is a killer ad" and then two days later you look at it and say, "Did I write something as mediocre as this?"

Mental Set

Some respondents attempted to describe the affective side of the creative process. Their feelings ranged from impatience and frustration to joy and exhilaration. What that suggests is that the creative process with its different steps, engenders various kinds of emotional responses. One respondent noted the necessity to be responsive:

- Being open and perceptive is the most crucial aspect. You never know when a good solution will present itself.

Some noted the positive side of creativity:

- I try to maintain a sense of positive regard and deliberateness.

- Perhaps the most important ingredients surrounding the creative process are joy and pure love.

But more often the comments centered on the effects of impatience and the negative pressures surrounding the creative activity:

- There is frustration and tension at times, usually because of impatience or doubt on my part.

- I sometimes try to dominate my inspiration and force it into my schedule and it doesn't work. I am the servant of *it*.

Deadline Pressure

Without any doubt the negative effects follow from the constant pressure of deadlines. Some respondents noted that this pressure varies with the job. Another said it varied with the stage in the process:

- My routine starts out leisurely, picks up tempo as deadlines approach. When it's all done, nothing is as good as it could be given a little more time. But that's advertising.

131

Surprisingly, most of the respondents recognized a need for pressure:

- I like to put it off as long as possible. I need the pressure and that lets it build up.

- I believe that pressure and the tension it creates helps. It makes me concentrate more and focus my efforts.

- The tensions inherent in a deadline business help make the problem solving more rewarding. Mainly because it's a do or die situation in which the good solution relieves a great deal of pressure.

- There are two important ingredients: one is freedom and the other is pressure. Pressure, frustration and tension can and often do lead to good solutions. It's hard work. It forces you to perform in ways even you didn't think possible.

All good creatives need pressure. Otherwise we would be writing fiction.

Blocks

Another aspect of the mental set, and one directly related to the effect of pressure, is the mental block and these blocks happen to almost everyone in the business—not just writers. There are a few, however, who denied blocks:

- I never had a mental block on anything.

- Mental blocks don't exist. If you can't think of anything, it's an indication of poor input, unclear objectives or some other damn preparation thing.

- In all honesty I've never encountered a mental block that couldn't be overcome by simply refusing to believe it existed.

Several of those who wrote about mental blocks described situations where they are most likely to occur:

- Blocks come when I have more than ample time to produce.

- They usually accompany the dull jobs. I have to try to redefine the problem to make it more interesting to me.

- Mental blocks seem to come when not enough information has been provided.

Several of these respondents, in describing the situation, are also giving their techniques for working out of a block. A number of unblocking techniques were listed, such as going back and getting more information:

- We go back and dig out the research to help coax some ideas out.

- I cure mental blocks by starting over again from scratch, and then exploring new ground.

- I put a piece of paper in the typewriter and start anything: a kid's story, a poem, a grocery list. Just looking at a piece of paper that has something—anything—on it sometimes helps.

Some people cure blocks by reading:

- I rely heavily on my Thesaurus. I compile lists of superlatives.

- I use creative pilfering. I flip through annuals and award books for a spark of inspiration.

- I pore over old creative annuals and my personal morgue (files) of good ideas. Sometimes another person's good idea will help you come up with one yourself. It's like playing golf with someone who is great, you'll play better yourself.

Others just get away from the problem:

- Blocks are best handled by walking away—but not usually for long. I may find it necessary to get into another project. But then my subconscious is working on it and before long I will be back to the "blocked" project.

- I go do something else.

- When we are stumped, we break and regroup. After a break there is always a different avenue that leads to different ideas.

Some use other minds as springboards:

- I get our concept team back together. One person's mental block can usually be broken with the help of ideas flowing from other team members.

- I take the problem to another person who doesn't work on the account. As I explain the thought process, that usually gets me back on the track.

Some find exercise helps—pacing, walking, etc.—or finding a new place to work:

- I take long walks, which almost always clears the mental debris away.

- I work through them by changing the scene.

Others use fantasy and humor:

- I imagine how I would approach the problem if I were a 1,200 lb. gorilla.

- I try to look at it from some crazy perspective. It helps loosen me up.

- I attack with humor. I write the ad I'd really like to see the chicken-hearted client run.

Others try limbering up exercises:

- First I start writing. Anything. Other materials. Press releases. If necessary, depressing letters to friends (or even answers to questionnaires). Usually, an idea will pop into the middle of whatever I've picked up and force me back onto the real project.

Summary

Generally, the respondents differ in a few areas in their creative problem-solving activities from traditional theory. For example, brainstorming is important as an activity used to generate many raw ideas. However, the word is not used to mean a conference activity. Brainstorming is something many of them do alone or in teams. Some creatives like to work with teams but few have any interest in what the larger brainstorming literature recommends.

An identifiable creative process involving such steps as immersion, wrestling with a problem, incubation, illumination and evaluation seems to structure most of their problem solving approaches. Insight, however, may occur at any number of points in the process including at the beginning in research, in the stage when they are actively wrestling with the idea or in the incubation stage when attention has been redirected.

People who work on the creative side of advertising seem to thrive on the pressure, tension and frustration of deadlines. They use pressure as a catalyst. Mental blocks are common and most creatives have a repertoire of techniques for getting back on track.

References

Fox, D., Lorgi, I., Weltz. P., & Herrold, K. Comparison of decisions written by large and small groups. *American Psychologist*, 1953, *8, 351.*

Moriarty, S. E., & Reid, L. N. Ideation: A review of the research. In Leigh, J. H. & Martin, C. R., Jr. (eds.), *Current issues and research in advertising*. Ann Arbor, MI: University of Michigan Graduate School of Business Administration, 1983.

Osborn, A. F. *Applied Imagination* (3rd ed.), NYC: Scribners, 1963.

Renzulli, J. S., Owen, S. V., & Callahan, C. M. Fluency, flexibility and originality as a function of group size. *Journal of Creative Behavior.* 1974, *8 (2)*, 107-113.

Taylor, I. A. The nature of the creative process. In *Creativity: An examination of the creative process*. NYC: Hastings House, 1959.

Taylor, I. A., Austin, G. A., & Sutton, D. F. A note on 'instant creativity' at CPSI. *Journal of Creative Behavior*, 1974, *8 (3)*, 208-210.

Taylor, C. W., Berry, P. C., & Block, C. H. Does group participation when using brainstorming facilitate or inhibit creative thinking? *Administrative Science Quarterly*, 1958, *3*, 23-47.

Thomas, E. J., & Fink, C. F. Effects of group size. *Psychological Bulletin*, 1963, *60*, 371-384.

Wallas, G. *The art of thought*. NYC: Harcourt, 1926.

Young, J. W. *A technique for producing ideas* (3rd ed.), Chicago: Crain Books, 1975.

Sandra E. Moriarty, Director, Jayne Media Center, University of Wyoming, Laramie, Wyoming 82071.

Bruce G. VandenBergh, Associate Professor, Michigan State University, Department of Advertising, East Lansing, Michigan 48824.

SECTION FOUR
THE CREATIVE PRODUCT

Creativity manifests as some sort of "product." A painting, poem, or symphony are obvious creative outputs, as are scientific breakthroughs and engineering innovations. Every product, however, does not necessarily qualify as "creative." In fact, if we want to study "creativity" effectively, we must first agree upon what is a creative product. In our first article MacKinnon identifies three absolute criteria of a creative product:

(1) Novelty: the product must be original.

(2) Adaptive to reality: It must serve to solve a problem, fit the needs of a given situation, or accomplish some recognizable goal.

(3) The product must be produced: from MacKinnon's perspective the idea must be transformed into a tangible product in order to be considered truly "creative."

Susan Besemer asks, "How Do You Know It's Creative?" Based on three dimensions of creativity: novelty, resolution, and elaboration/synthesis, Besemer proposes a point system for evaluating creative products. While the instrument was designed for selecting gifted and talented students for special activities, it could be applied to individual and/or comparative assessment of creative products. Three examples of grade school student work and evaluation are included.

One emerging arena for creativity within the world of business is among professional managers. Barbara Block, a San Francisco-based management consultant reviews the emergence of "intuition" as a trainable management skill. In her article from *Management Review,* "Intuition Creeps Out of the Closet and Into the Boardroom," she reports on several experiments and studies relating to the use and place of intuition in creative management decisions. She concludes by speculating on the future of both intuition and intuition training in management. In "Strategic Planning and Intuition in Unilever," the chairman of this multinational company discusses the important role that experience and intuition can play in assessing the uncertainties in the environment when formulating an organizational strategy. "For a business to remain competitive, the use of intuition (creative problem solving) is inevitable, even where strategic decisions are carefully analyzed." Examples of actual creative problem solving at the organizational level are described.

In our concluding article, "Exploring the Inventiveness in Everyone," Donald Treffinger suggests a shift in the paradigm for assessing creativity from "How creative are you?" to "How are you creative?" He then proposes a four-part model describing the components of creativity as Characteristics, Operations, Context and Outcomes.

Finally, he identifies five indicators of the nature and direction of an individual's creative and inventive potentials. (FD)

135

Of Additional Interest

Besemer, S., & Treffinger D. J. (1981). Analysis of creative products: Review and synthesis. *Journal of Creative Behavior 15* (3).

Brishman, L. (1980). Creative product and creative process in science and art. *Inquiry 23*, 83–106.

Dumaine, B. (1991). Closing the innovation gap. *Fortune,* December 2.

Farnham, A. (1994). How to nurture creative sparks. *Fortune,* January 10.

Fordon, J., & Zemke, R. (1986). Making them more creative. *Training,* May.

McCormak, A. J. (1984). Teaching inventiveness. *Childhood Education,* March/April.

Nelton, S. (1985). How to spark new ideas. *Nation's Business.*

Pearlman, C. (1983). A theoretical model for creativity. *Education 103*(3).

Raudsepp, E. (1985). 101 ways to spark your employees' creative potential. *Office Administration and Automation,* September.

Shlesinger, Jr., E. (1987). Teaching problem-solving through invention. *Vocational Educational Journal,* August.

Shapero, A. (1985). Managing creative professionals. *Research Management,* March/April.

Udwadia, F. (1990). Creativity and innovation in organizations: Two models and managerial implications. *Technological Forecasting and Social Change 38,* 65–80.

Voss, B. (1991). What's the big idea? *Training,* July.

HOW DO YOU KNOW IT'S CREATIVE?

Susan P. Besemer

Teachers involved in the administrative process for selecting gifted, talented, and creative students to receive school enrichment experiences are often advised to use multiple criteria in identifying the students. Intelligence tests, creativity tests, peer nominations and those of parents and teachers are often suggested as possible sources for data relating to identifying the gifted and talented youngsters. Another idea sometimes suggested is the evaluation of a product typical of each student nominee (Renzulli, Reis & Smith, 1981; Treffinger, 1981). These products may include stories, poems, sculptures, paintings, science experiments or any other of the tangible artifacts which demonstrate the ability of each of the students.

Evaluating so many different types of products may seem difficult, if not impossible. But eliminating a nominee because his or her product is unusual or out of the ordinary defeats the purpose of the evaluation, since we are looking for the student who is capable of innovative ideas. What is needed is an evaluation which is general enough to give a fair analysis to all types of products. If teachers had a general checklist of criteria on which to judge we'd probably feel much more confident in making evaluations. This article suggests just such a list. It is a discussion and application of general, all-purpose evaluation criteria for rating quality. These criteria, by the way, are not limited in their usefulness to a juvenile population. They could be used to find the best production of an advertising agency, the most creative art work in a college art show, or the most brilliant editorial in the Sunday morning newspaper. Since many of us like to play the role of the armchair critic, the list could also be used, just for fun, to evaluate TV offerings in the home. Read on if you ever have to pick "the best from the rest."

If we think back on the various products that we have encountered in the last few weeks we are likely to remember one or more that were really outstanding. A trip to a department store or hardware store will sometimes stimulate a laudatory judgment about something on display. We'll think or say "Wow, isn't that creative!" Think hard about a moment like that in your recent past and you will be able to notice some of the characteristics in the product which caused you to smile, to catch your breath, or simply to "ooh and ahh." But first, let's be clear that while all manufactured items may properly be termed "products," the use of the term is not limited to things which are mass-produced. Poems, pictures, sculptures, and even soups are creative products. Abraham Maslow, the noted psychologist, once stated that a first-rate soup is actually more creative than a second-rate painting (1959). Anything, in fact, made by someone is a creative product, although we all know that some products are more creative than others.

Most people state, after thinking about it, that the first characteristic that struck them about the nifty product that they remember was the product's novelty. They'll say that they thought, "This is a really unusual widget." It may be made of a different material, constructed through a different process, or be surprisingly smaller or larger than any of the other widgets that they've seen. Interestingly enough, the research scientists who have written on the evaluation of creative products seem to agree on this criterion. *Novelty* was cited as the prime criterion of creativity in the research studies reviewed in the development of this article.

Novelty

Under the heading of *novelty,* three adjectives are frequently used to describe novel products. The first of these is *original.* While it is ultimately impossible for any person to claim complete originality (since no idea is ever conceived without the benefit of some earlier ideas of others), it is clear that some products are much more original than others. At the very least, there is a new twist to the product; at the other end of the scale, the product is so revolutionary that it bears little resemblance to its predecessors.

Such a product, often shockingly or surprisingly new is sometimes termed *transformational* because it actually transforms the world in the scope of its ramifications. An example of this type of product is the pocket calculator. These are now so widely used that one can hardly remember what it was like to have to balance one's checkbook with no buttons to push.

A third criterion of novelty is described by the adjective *germinal.* This term indicates that the product generates other related new ideas. The idea or product which is the first of a series of similar products is more creative than the subsequent ones. A classroom teacher can quickly spot the trendsetters in the room. The products copied by other children are, therefore, aptly termed *germinal.*

Resolution

Thinking again about that fantastic widget that they recently saw, most people are quick to say that while they were first attracted to it because of its uniqueness, it has to be workable in order for them to think, "Wow, what a fantastic widget." If it doesn't work, function, or do what it is supposed to do, it is not valued. Sometimes items in direct mail catalogs fit into this category. They look great, but they just don't do the trick. This characteristic of "filling the bill" includes many adjectives sought in creative products. The new idea, whatever it is, must be relevant to the problem at hand. A hammer, for example, could be used as a bottle opener, but we don't usually use one for that purpose because it is inappropriate. Most people feel that using a bottle opened with a hammer would be unpleasant, messy, and even dangerous. A solution to a problematic situation must also be adequate. That is, the product must solve the problem well enough to seem like an answer. If it does not take enough aspects of the problem into consideration, then we tend to dismiss it, even if it is a partial solution. One recycled jelly jar filled with water may be an adequate solution to a problem faced by a thirsty person, but it would be clearly inadequate for the stemware needs of a dinner party hostess.

A creative product should be logical in some sense. Some people may question the logic of various works of art, but at a certain level even the most abstract work of art is adhering to a few rules of order. Art or science which is at the forefront of its genre is often shocking in the extent to which it bends or exceeds the established rules of logic for the discipline. The fact that there *are* rules allows for the commonly heard comment, "It's interesting, but is it art?"

In a school setting, teachers are quick to observe which students seem unaware of the rules of composition, balance, and design. Other students recognize and follow the rules dogmatically. The most creative few follow the rules pretty well, but occasionally violate one of the rules. Surprisingly, then, the product still looks fine. It may even seem to be improved by the different twist.

Creative products may also be useful. Of what use, some may ask, is a child's picture of a tree? Just ask the child and you'll be presented with lots of uses. The concept of art for art's sake in the late nineteenth and the twentieth century has nearly obscured the historical fact that until very recently art always has had a clear functional purpose. Whether to celebrate a victory or to pay reverence to a saint, the work of art was not merely an expression of the artist's emotions. With contemporary artists, the art's usefulness is shown as a vehicle for self-expression and self-assertion. In either case, therefore, the work of art is in fact useful—either to the artist himself or to the culture as a whole.

A child's invention or drawing may be less useful to the world than that of an adult, but its usefulness can be more adequately judged by comparing it to the products of other children. The idea of making comparisons only within a delimited set of subjects is clearly important here. Comparing the creative embroidery projects of a group of college home economics majors, for instance, with the embroidery produced by industrial chemists would be as unfair as comparing the chemists' new product formulas with those of the home ec. students. If there is no group standard for comparison, the judge must hypothesize what he or she might expect as the norm for the field. School personnel can usually tell pretty quickly if what they are looking at is below, at, or above grade level.

The criterion of value is one of the very most subjective judgments in the typically subjective area of evaluation. Something which somebody makes can have commercial value, psychological, or even sentimental value. The reason which something is valued is because it fills some need, making this criterion related to usefulness. By asking yourself if you would want to have this or that creative product, you have one sure way of noticing if it is valuable to you. Even if *you* do not value the item, if other people do it is valuable. This value contributes to the level of creativity evidenced. Whether value is the "chicken" or the "egg" in the equation is still a legitimate question, but nonetheless the two are closely allied in many instances.

Elaboration and Synthesis

Let's return for a moment to the hardware store in the widget department. We've noticed a nifty new widget that looks as if it would really do the job. What characteristics can you identify which are "the frosting on the cake?" These are the qualities which make the difference between whether or not you just notice the widget or whether you remember this widget and say to yourself, "The next time I need a widget, this is the one I'm buying." Most people list among these qualities, elements of style or taste. This category of criteria may be termed *elaboration and synthesis*. These characteristics indicate the amount of energy invested in the product. The idea for the product is sharpened, refined, and developed. The criteria sought are concerned with *how* the object is completed—a matter of style. Such words as attractive, and well-crafted come to mind. The word "attractive" does not necessarily mean "pretty" or "beautiful." In the context of this article, the word is intended to denote the quality that *attracts* viewers, listeners, or users to notice the product. Some works of modern art or architecture, for example, are not "pretty," but they do attract our attention.

Another criterion of style is the expressive quality of the product. This factor deals with the success with which the creator communicates with his or her audience. This may be seen as a measure of how clear or how obscure is the meaning or message of the product. Can we easily tell what the creator was "getting at," or is the message so personalized that the creator seems to be speaking only to himself? A product which speaks clearly to more people rates better on this criterion than one, the message of which is obscure.

Let's get back again to discussing the products of children. The objects which have some shock value or which seem out of the ordinary in some way are of a higher level than those which look like all of the others in the "pack." Seemingly on the other side of the coin are those products which are outstanding because of the neatness, care and refinement with which the product was completed. If other virtues are present as well (timeliness and logic, for example) the carefully finished product is superior to that which appears to be "thrown together." The well-crafted product frequently has a sense of completeness about it. That is, there is an organic quality which shows its wholeness and gives a sense of rest or tonality.

Two other characteristics in the category of *elaboration and synthesis* which seem to be at opposite poles from each other are *complex* and *elegant*. *Complex* products contain a number of different aspects expressed simultaneously. This characteristic can also be expressed by the word *interesting*. The mind or the eye has lots to keep it busy when a work is complex, but if this aspect is overdone, the product takes on a frantic look and the eye is distressed. On the other side of this coin is the criterion of *elegance*. Here, this word is intended to denote the refined, pared-down elegance of, for example, Japanese flower arrangements. Contrary to its use in common parlance, the word is not intended to mean, in this context, the opulence of velvets and pearls. A product may have been more complicated in an earlier stage, but if it is an *elegant* product, it has been polished and refined until only the most important essences remain. Charlie Mingus, the famous jazz musician, has said that making a simple idea complicated is commonplace. Mingus stated, "Making the complicated simple, awesomely simple, that's creativity" (Creativity, 1977).

Applying the Criteria

All of the theory outlined above is useful only if it can help us actually evaluate products. Let's look at some of the varied products of a ten-year-old child and see how these criteria may be used as a framework for evaluating different types of products. Using the following three examples, the fourteen criteria are listed with the judgments "low," "medium," or "high" for each category. Final evaluative comments are offered regarding each work.

Interpretation

It is possible, by using the fourteen criteria, to carefully direct the focus of the evaluation to one criterion at a time. This is of great value in the process of evaluation, because a negative or positive judgment on one criterion can often produce a "halo" effect, actually changing the total evaluation if great care is not exercised to isolate the criteria one from another. This focusing of the evaluation can greatly facilitate the comparison of different types of products. In the case of analyzing the work of the child in the examples above, one is struck by the development of factors of *elaboration* and *synthesis* when the child is motivated to focus well on the task. Her visual skills seem well-developed, and on the "expressive" dimension her abilities seem outstanding. One might encourage even more "far out" ideas in her case, and suggest additional development, refinement and attention to completeness. The criteria clearly help in judging among the varied products for this child because they allow for a fairly complete "prescription" for the overall improvement of the quality of creative work done by this youngster. When judging the varied products of a group of children, the criteria can assist in locating the more creative products in the group.

The ratings described above use the very general values of "low," "medium," and "high" to rate the product being judged. It is clear that this system does produce a useful beginning evaluation. Additional details regarding the model and the specific criteria have been provided by Besemer & Treffinger (1981). Presently, a more refined evaluation instrument is being developed and prepared for final testing. On this instrument a numerical score is derived for each evaluation category and for the product's total score. This scale may take a step in quantifying and objectifying the presently subjective business of evaluating creative products. School districts or individual teachers interested in formal validation studies may contact the author for more information.

The Konradgell

There was once a Konradgell named Fibiantricut. Fibiantricut was a very intelligent Konradgell and liked to do homework for school children. He went around knocking on doors and asking if there was any homework to be done for the kids. If so, he would invite himself in the house and usually get soup and crackers all over the new living room rug.

The people in the town that Fibiantricut always visited were against this, because of the fact that in two weeks the new rug would be so dirty that it had to be replaced.

However, there was a boy named Jonathan Jickson who liked Fibiantricut because he always did his homework for him. Jonathan was particularly fond of what Fibiantricut had nicknamed him: Jonjick. So Jonathan nicknamed Fibiantricut "Fibiat." So it happened that Jonathan and Fibiantricut became the best of friends.

One day, as Fibiantricut was approaching Jonathan's house, he heard Jonathan yelling something that sounded like,

"He *can't* stop giving homework to me, even though I know Fibiat. What does he want me to do, bury myself in a 3 million mile hole with 90 thousand tons of homework to do *Alone?*"

Fibiantricut was very hurt by hearing his name mentioned in a negative way, but when he heard his name yelled in a negative way, it *really* hurt him.

Fibiantricut knocked on the door to Jonathan's house immediately. When Jonathan answered, he told Fibiantricut that he couldn't talk to him any more.

That did it! Fibiantricut yanked Jonathan out of his house and started yelling at him. "How can you say what you said in there?! You have no idea how that hurt me!?

"Fibiat, I . . ."

"Be quiet! Do you know how this has made me feel? You will never find out!

Fibiantricut stormed off.

The End of First Volume

The Konradgell #2

Jonathan stood, puzzled, on his doorstep for a moment, then went inside.

But what about Fibiantricut?

He was on his way to the country, looking for more homework to do for kids.

He was also thinking about Jonathan.

Suddenly, he dashed back to Jonathan's house, apologized, and then they both went outside.

The End

Evaluative Comments

Novelty		Elaboration & Synthesis		Comments
Original	high	*Attractive*	medium	This product seems fairly average in most respects, but the basic concept of the story is novel. The problem situation in the story is resolved, but only adequately. While the style is expressive, a certain completeness is wanting.
Transformational	low	*Well-crafted*	medium	
Germinal	low-medium	*Complex*	medium	
Resolution		*Elegant*	low	
Appropriate	high	*Espressive*	high	
Adequate	medium	*Organic*	medium	
Logical	medium			
Useful	medium			
Valuable	low			

Evaluative Comments

Novelty

Original	high
Transformational	low
Germinal	medium

Resolution

Appropriate	high
Adequate	medium
Logical	medium
Useful	medium
Valuable	medium

Elaboration & Synthesis

Attractive	high
Well-crafted	high
Complex	medium
Elegant	high
Espressive	high
Organic	high

Comments

While there are dimensions on which this product may be improved, its stylistic qualities mark it at a high level. Certain refinements of the line in the face of the male mice show an elegance which is unexpected in the work of a ten-year-old.

Drawing, Untitled

Evaluative Comments

Novelty

Original	low
Transformational	low
Germinal	low

Resolution

Appropriate	medium
Adequate	medium
Logical	medium
Useful	medium
Valuable	low

Elaboration & Synthesis

Attractive	medium
Well-crafted	low
Complex	medium
Elegant	low
Espressive	medium
Organic	low

Comments

This product seems to be an "off-hand" artifact. Rather than showing care and restraint, the drawing seems to be merely filling space. Some humor and balance are shown, but overall, this product would not rank well.

144

References

Besemer, S. P., & Treffinger, D. J. Analysis of creative products: Review and synthesis. *Journal of Creative Behavior 1981*. **15** 158-178.

Creativity. *Mainliner,* July, 1977, 25-31.

Maslow, A. H. Creativity in self-actualizing people. In Anderson, H. H. (ed.), *Creativity and its cultivation.* NYC: Harper, 1959.

Renzulli, J. S., Reis, S., & Smith, L. *The revolving door identification model.* Mansfield Center, CT: Creative Learning Press, 1981.

Treffinger, D. J. *Blending gifted education with the total school program.* Williamsville, NY: Center for Creative Learning, 1981.

THE CREATIVE PRODUCT

D. W. MacKinnon

I would argue that the starting point, indeed the bedrock of all studies of creativity, is an analysis of creative products, a determination of what it is that makes them different from more mundane products. This is the problem of the criterion, and only after we have come to some agreement about the criterion, which I shall argue is the creative product, are we in a position to study the other facets of creativity: the creative process, the creative person, and the creative situation. Each of these must be defined with reference to the creative product:

- The creative process or processes are those that result in creative products.

- A creative person is one who brings into existence creative products.

- The creative situation is that complex of circumstances which permits, and fosters, and makes possible creative productions.

In a very real sense, then, the study of creative products is the basis upon which all research on creativity rests and, until this foundation is more solidly built than it is at present, all creativity research will leave something to be desired (MacKinnon, 1975).

To speak of the creative product as though there were only one kind of product is a gross over-simplification. Creative products range from such concrete and tangible objects as a piece of sculpture or a physical invention to such intangibles as leadership or educational and business climates which permit those in them to express to the full their creative potential. Some have even spoken of the person as a product; for example, the individual who makes his own being and life a work of art. It seems likely that agreement among the experts concerning the creativeness of a product will be greater for those products that are public and relatively permanent.

Considerations such as these led us in IPAR's study to draw our subjects from fields of creative endeavor in which the worker creates a public and relatively enduring product. The fields included writing, architecture, mathematics, and physical science and engineering research in industry.

The decision to choose as our criterion objects public and relatively enduring products had been, in part, influenced by our disappointing assessment study of Air Force officers (MacKinnon et al., 1958). Using many of the same tests and procedures which proved so effective in predicting the creativity of architects, mathematicians, and others, we had had little success earlier in predicting the leadership of Air Force officers. In retrospect it is clear that in the study of Air Force officers it was not the predictors that were at fault but rather the several criterion-measures of leadership.

A critical issue for future research in creativity is to find ways and means of studying creativity that eventuates not in objective, palpable, enduring objects but in subjective, intangible, and sometimes fleeting interpersonal relations, educational, social, business, and political climates which permit and encourage those in them to develop and to express to the full their

146

creative potentials. In such a context the problem of studying the creative person is to identify and come to understand those who exert creative leadership. The study of interpersonal and social creativity is a far more difficult and demanding task than the study of personal creativity which so far has been the main focus of our researches. It is, of course, well to start with the investigation of the simpler problem before undertaking the more complex ones, but the time to begin is now.

What does it mean to speak of a leader, a business manager, a teacher, a governor, a general, a college president who is creative? The creativeness of such persons centers more in the realm of interpersonal and social relations than in the realm of ideas and theoretical problems while obviously not ignoring the latter.

At IPAR we have focused on the creativity of persons too much like ourselves, people whose creative products are somewhat like our own. If one thinks of these in terms of the values described by Spranger (1928), all of the creative groups we have studied have had as their highest values the theoretical and aesthetic—and these are the highest values of academicians too. In order to round out our picture of creativity and of creative persons, we need to study fields of endeavor where the highest values of the practitioners are economic, social, political, or religious, or some combination of these. Or, in fields of economic, social, political, and religious endeavor, will it turn out that the most creative workers also will have as their highest values, the theoretical and aesthetic?

What I am suggesting is that in our studies of creativity we, at least at IPAR, have been rather ethnocentric or at least inclined to draw our subjects from our own subculture. There have been some exceptions, of course; for example, the study of Irish business managers conducted in collaboration with the Irish Management Institute in 1965 (Barron & Egan, 1968). This study provided us an opportunity to assess a most fascinating group of men in Dublin. But the criterion was far from adequate, and I am afraid less light than we would have wished was shed on the creativity of Irish managers to say nothing of managers in general.

Anything that is experienced or made by man—an idea, a work of art, a scientific theory, the design of a building—may be a creative product; but if they are to qualify as true creations they must first meet certain criteria.

The first requirement of a creative product is novelty; it must be original. But novelty and originality need further specification. Within what frame of reference or range of experiences is the product original—that of an individual, or of a group, or of mankind? Much that a young child experiences—and many of his ideas will be new to him and in that sense creative for him, but, if these experiences and ideas are had by practically all children, they are not creative products for the society in which the child lives. Similarly, a man may think a thought new to him, yet it may be one of the most common thoughts in the whole world. Thus, the creativeness of a product when judged in terms of novelty, originality, or statistical infrequence is always relative to a given population of products. Those that are most creative are the ones that are novel or original in the experience of an entire civilization or of all mankind.

Mere novelty of a product does not, however, justify its being called creative. There is a second requirement, namely, that the product be adaptive to reality. In other words, it must serve to solve a problem, fit the needs of a given situation, or accomplish some recognizable goal. And this is as true for the expressive arts as for scientific and technological enterprises: in painting, the artist's problem is to find a more appropriate expression of his own experience; in dancing, to convey more adequately a particular mood or theme.

A third requirement that a fully creative product must meet is that the insightful reorganization which underlies it be sustained, evaluated, elaborated, developed, and communicated to others—in other words, the creative product must be produced.

These, as I see it, are the three absolute criteria of a creative product. There are additional and, if you will, optional criteria. The more of them that are met, the more creative the product, for, though there may be many correct solutions to a problem, not all solutions are equally good. Some are more elegant than others. Thus, there is a fourth criterion met by a truly creative product, which demands that the answer which the product yields be an aesthetically pleasing one. The solution must be both true and beautiful.

The fifth and highest criterion for a creative product is seldom met since it requires that the product create new conditions of human existence, transcending and transforming the generally accepted experience of man by introducing new principles that defy tradition and change radically man's view of the world. Products of this level of creativeness would include the heliocentric theory of Copernicus, Darwin's theory of evolution, and Freud's psychoanalysis.

A distinction is frequently made between two kinds of creativity and creative products—artistic and scientific. Artistic creativity, it is said, results in products that are clearly expressions of the creator's inner states, his needs, perceptions, emotions, motivations, and the like. In creating them he has a deeply moving emotional experience or encounter. In scientific creativity, it is argued, the product is unrelated to the creator as a person, who in his creative work acts mainly as a mediator between externally defined needs and goals. He operates on some aspect of his environment so as to produce a novel and appropriate product, but he adds little of himself or of his style as a person to the resultant. Such a description of scientific creativity is, however, more appropriate to technological and inventive activity in which the affective life of the worker plays relatively little role. In the highest reaches of science, as well as of art, it seems clear that there is a connection, albeit a mysterious one, between affectivity and the creative process. In the arts, the great productions appear to be exquisite attempts to resolve an internal turbulence. In the sciences, the important theoretical efforts seem to be personal cosmologies as much as anything else (witness Einstein, the prime example; Sherrington, Cannon, Born, Schrödinger, and others). The validity of the creative product thus is almost (but not quite) incidental to the forces driving its expression. And the forces are largely affective.

There is another sense in which the distinction between artistic and scientific and technological is often obliterated, for surely there are domains of creative striving in which the practitioner must be both artist and scientist-technologist; architecture would be a good example. Great architectural designs are surely expressions of the architect which are very personal products at the same time that they impersonally meet the demands of external problems. Surely, however, creative products are not limited to the realms of art and science and technological invention, but include such intangibles as those educational, social, business, and political climates which permit and encourage those who are in them to develop and to express to the full, their creative potentials. In some cases, even a person may be thought of as a creative product. These are the persons who have been variously called, by both Goldstein and Maslow, the self-actualizing person; by Jung, the individuated person; by Rogers, the fully functioning individual; by Fromm, the productive character; and by Rank, the artist, the man of will and deed who makes a work of art out of his own life.

INTUITION CREEPS OUT OF THE CLOSET AND INTO THE BOARDROOM

Barbara Block

It has been called a gut feeling, a sixth sense. But only recently has the word *intuition* crept out of the closet and into corporate America. Organizations around the country are discovering the benefits that come when they teach their employees to become more intuitive.

"A lot of companies consider intuition a skill and technique they can use to competitive advantage," says Lonnie Helgeson, director of the Hubert H. Humphrey Institute of Public Affairs' Intuitive Leadership Project in Minneapolis, Minn. Companies may be finding intuition useful and teaching the skills needed to use it, but the subject remains a touchy one. The controversy centers around how intuition fits in with more down-to-earth scientific models.

"The message of science is that there is only one way to knowledge—the rational mind," points out Bill Kautz, a trained scientist and the director of the Center for Applied Intuition, in San Francisco.

But 15 years ago, Kautz became curious about how scientists make breakthrough discoveries. As a researcher at the Stanford Research Institute (SRI) in Palo Alto, Calif., he began reading scientists' own accounts of their discoveries. In almost every case, "scientists acknowledged that discovery was not a rational process but an intuitive flash, a blast of knowledge that transcended anything they ever did before," Kautz found. Indeed, Albert Einstein is reported to have said: "I did not arrive at my understanding of the fundamental laws of the universe through my rational mind."

Spreading the Word

To continue his research and "spread the word," Kautz left SRI in 1978 to found the Center for Applied Intuition, a nonprofit organization devoted to the education, research and training of intuition. But spreading the word, Kautz is quick to admit, is not always easy—especially in the business world.

"You won't find someone talking about intuition here," one pharmaceutical executive says. "It is not something that can be demonstrated with paper and pencil, in test tubes or trials," he says. "How do you explain a gut feeling when you are held accountable in terms of dollars?"

Outside consultants are equally nervous about discussing their work. For example, when a story about a Texas-based expert who teaches intuition to employees of major companies appeared in the press, one of her clients, a *Fortune* 30 company, immediately canceled its contract with her.

Despite these problems, the corporate community is beginning to take a new look at intuition because it is discovering that intuition—which the Random House dictionary defines as "direct perception of truth or fact, independent of any reasoning process; quick and keen insight"—does in fact make business sense.

Landmark studies have found a correlation between business success and intuition. At the New Jersey Institute of Technology in Newark, N.J., parapsychologist E. Douglas Dean and engineer John Milhalasky spent a decade studying the relationship between executive intuition and profitability. They asked CEOs to guess a 100-digit number randomly generated by computer. Indeed, 80 percent of the executives who scored above average in intuition had also doubled company profits in the last five years.

Similarly, Weston Agor, at the University of Texas in El Paso, found that of 2,000 managers studied, top-level leaders scored higher on intuition than those ranking lower in the organization. In a follow-up study of 70 executives, all but one acknowledged using intuition—but were reluctant to admit the fact to colleagues.

As one executive of a *Fortune* 100 company confided, "If I told you everything we were doing in this area, you could ruin my career."

"What breakthrough product ever came out of market research?" asks James Milojkovic, organizational consultant with San Francisco-based Human Factors. "Market research defends the status quo" but does not result in innovative thinking, he believes.

Milojkovic spent a year as a visiting scholar at Stanford University studying the role of intuition in strategic decision-making processes by CEOs of Silicon Valley companies. "I would debrief them, at the end of the day, about how they made their decisions," he says. "Over 60 percent were willing to say explicitly they used intuition." The rest, Milojkovik observed, were uncomfortable admitting that intuition played a major role or would have difficulty verbalizing it. "But by and large," he concludes, "most successful people frequently call upon their intuition. Then they justify [their decision] with charts, graphs and spreadsheets [and other objective data]."

A Rose by Any Other Name

Today, intuition training often takes place under the guise of creativity or leadership skills.

Innovation Associates, of Framingham, Mass., has had over 5,000 executives from large corporations, including Digital Equipment Corp., General Foodsand Clorox Co., go through a three-day leadership training program that spends a considerable amount of time honing intuitive skills. "All through the course, when we talk about dealing with complexity, developing a vision, taking effective action in a complex environment, we talk about how intuition relates to that," says Joel Yanowitz, director of consulting services at Innovation Associates. "We believe intuition is an important skill component for successful leaders."

And in the MBA program at Stanford University, there is a long waiting list to enroll in the Creativity in Business course, which focuses on intuition training. "Our approach is very different and very experiential," says Michael Ray, who created the course in the early '80s and who authored *Creativity in Business* (Doubleday).

When Dupont Industry manager Herman Maynard first looked for a course on intuition with Minneapolis-based consultant Lonnie Helgeson in 1987, he ran up against the negative stereotypes associating intuition with the mystical, irrational and subjective—all business taboos. "At the time," he recalls, "we couldn't even use the word 'intuition' in the title of the program. It wasn't considered acceptable in business."

Budget Crisis Resolved

Still, in June of 1988, Maynard took 15 professionals through a pilot program to learn about intuition. A few months after the course, his department was facing a "severe budget issue" for which no obvious solution could be found. Using nontraditional, visualization techniques learned in consultation with another Minneapolis-based consultant, Magaly Mossman, he came up with a way to approach senior management.

The results: "We got nearly full funding and we were one of the few businesses [units] that did," Maynard says. Furthermore, "we are getting breakthrough inventions every two or three months. And it is not just affecting the chemists. People all through the organization, including the secretaries, are being more creative."

At Griffin Health Services, a healthcare holding company in Derby, Conn., more than 40 of the senior staff have taken courses designed to help them become more intuitive. "The key to accessing intuition is to be relaxed and turn off the voices of [objective] judgment," says Executive Vice President Jerold Sinnamon.

Procter & Gamble's director of communications, Bill Lambert, a 17-year veteran with the company, at first viewed intuition training with skepticism. But after taking Innovation Associates' three-day leadership course, he has a new respect for his intuition.

"I am much more aware of it and quick to say, 'hey, don't put down the gut side,'" Lambert says. "Previously, I would only go with the facts. Now I pick things up with no rational explanation of how I did it and with amazing accuracy."

"It is sometimes unsettling for people to get useful insights without knowing how they got them," observes Yanowitz. "But we encourage people to be experimental, to keep an open mind, to see if they get helpful insights."

Yanowitz and other experts are emphatic about using intuition in conjunction with rational, logical analysis. "You don't blindly follow hunches; you test them out, ask yourself 'Does it make sense?'" Yanowitz cautions. "You wouldn't want the corporate treasurer balancing the company checkbook with intuition, would you?"

"Intuition can be a wild card unless you learn specific ways to make it consistent, pragmatic and reliable," says Karen Wilhelm Buckley, a Redwood City, Calif., management consultant. "The primary thing is to work in an environment where you can get immediate feedback. It's just like learning to play golf; you have got to swing and hit, swing and hit."

Economic Realities

Despite the possibilities, tough economic decisions may keep intuition training from becoming a sweeping trend, says Charles Hess, president of Inferential Focus, a New York- based consulting firm that specializes in forecasting change. "Today, companies are under a lot of pressure with competition, acquisitions, cutbacks, and they go back to what they are comfortable with—logic, sequential and bottom line thinking."

And Charles Clark, training director of Dow Chemical's Agricultural Products Department, hasn't the least bit of interest. "I have never heard the two words— intuition and training—used together," he chuckles. "We have 10 topics we have to cover. Intuition is not on the list. It sounds like a very elegant frill."

Or is it? A report for the year 2000 issued by the International Management Institute in Geneva, Switzerland, in 1986 specifically called for increased training in intuition.

In response, executives from all over the world convened in Geneva in 1987 to discuss the implications and applications of intuition in business. Representatives from Digital Equipment, Phillips Petroleum, Shell Oil, SAS Airlines, among others, were present. The group initiated a research project on the role of intuition in business vision and decision making. A follow-up questionnaire has been sent to 250,000 managers in four continents, and more roundtables have been scheduled.

Where will intuition go in the '90s? Kautz predicts intuition training will continue to show up in increasing numbers of employee development programs. This will happen, he believes, as executives increasingly recognize that intuition has been significant in their own business experiences.

"Executives are making good decisions, [backing the decisions up with data] and then asking themselves where the decision came from," Kautz says. And the answer frequently falls beyond the rational ways they were taught.

Barbara Block, based in San Francisco, consults on employment issues and emerging business trends.

STRATEGIC PLANNING
AND INTUITION IN UNILEVER

F. A. Maljers

The Chairman of a multinational company discusses the formulation of management strategy in general, and then in particular strategy formulation at Unilever—the organization structures and implementation and communication. He emphasizes the important role that experience and intuition can play in analysing the complexities facing businesses in an uncertain environment.

Managers have to operate in a world that is always changing. Nothing is constant for long, whether in technology, politics or society. The change that surrounds us presents new strategic challenges, but also alters the environment in which these must be resolved. While business strategy is as important as ever, it is getting even more difficult to implement.

Strategic management is not easy for any company. For a global business the size of a company like Unilever it can be daunting. In 1988 Unilever had sales of over $30bn, with businesses ranging from household name consumer products to industrial operations in specialty chemicals and agribusiness. In all there are production facilities in at least 75 countries (and exports to most of the rest). All this is run by 17,000 managers with 277,000 other employees.

The largest companies in the world all have to take strategic management seriously. However, management methods and styles vary enormously between companies. Each is run in their own characteristic way. A view of how any one company operates may offer a useful lesson, but is only a single example. It would be an illusion to think that there is only a single correct model of strategic management of a global business.

The Process of Strategic Management

There are two distinct stages to the process of strategically managing any business. Firstly there is the formulation of the strategy. This includes analysis of the environment, identification of possible options, and choice of which alternative is preferable. Secondly, but equally important, is the implementation of that strategy. The two aspects are clearly interdependent. However, this is worth stressing; the literature on strategic management has often overlooked the importance of implementation of the formulated strategy.

The two steps of formulation and implementation are faced wherever strategic decisions are made. All companies must go through the same process. However, in large companies this may need to take place at several different levels. In Unilever, for example, three main groups are involved in strategic management; operating companies need a strategy, but so do the management groups that oversee them, as well as the corporation as a whole.

If a global company is to function successfully strategies at different levels of the business need to inter-relate. The strategy at corporate level must build upon the strategies at lower levels in the hierarchy (the bottom-up element of strategy). However, at the same time all parts of the business have to work to accommodate the over-riding corporate goals (the top-down approach).

Because, these two forces work in opposite directions they can present a dilemma to the person who has to oversee strategy formulation. The requirement is to find the right equilibrium for the particular circumstances. Excessive instruction from the top stifles management creativity. Yet, at the same time there must be sufficient direction to allow for the interests of all the corporation's stakeholders.

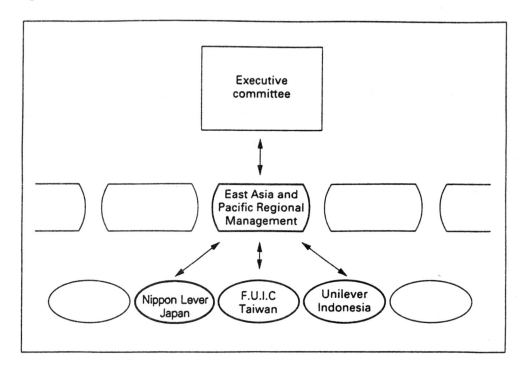

Figure 1 *Unilever's Organization*

In searching for the desired equilibrium it should be remembered that compromise may not lead to the best solution, particularly if it requires combining the worst aspects of different approaches.

The balance between 'top-down' and 'bottom-up' is often determined by the culture and philosophy of the company involved. Unilever's basic approach to organization is decentralization. Unilever consists of hundreds of individual operating companies—each with their own identity. Yet some coherence is necessary and is provided by a common corporate culture and some common services such as research, finance and management development. Such linkages are vital, they ensure that the total is worth more than the sum of the parts.

Formulation of Strategy

Academic literature has often described strategy as if it were the end product of a long development process. Firms are supposed to make strategic decisions only after exhaustive analysis of both their competitive advantage and the industrial environment. However, examination of actual company behaviour suggests that many firms operate in a very different way.

Decisions are made quickly, based on *experience* and *intuition* as well as thorough analysis.

The real, dynamic and highly competitive world of business places great demands on all scarce resources, especially time. Increasingly business decisions having to be made at great speed. In such an environment it would be impossible to expect firms to use complete analysis as the only tool in strategic decision making. Careful analysis is vital, but it is necessary to avoid spending excessive time analysing at the expense of action.

The Time Dimension of Strategy Formulation

Complete analysis of a business problem is further constrained by the complexity of the problem faced. Businessmen, like chess players, sometimes find that a problem can have many solutions in theory. The time dimension, however, imposes a limit and intuition is necessary to select the practical option. The identification of the realistic planning horizon then becomes the fundamental first stage in the formulation of a business strategy.

Planning with a very long horizon obviously has its dangers. Long-run changes are not well understood and are poorly forecasted. Those 20 or 30 years in the future are of little relevance to many companies.

Unilever, as a consumer goods company, has generally stuck to a time horizon of about 3-5 years. However, other businesses who work in very different situations do need to take a longer view. Shell have to consider the long term impact of their investment in the North Sea, while the Anglo-French Channel Tunnel would not be built if investors only looked a few years ahead.

In business there is no single strategy horizon that is always right. The need is to be both realistic and pragmatic, the difficulty is in getting the right balance.

The Role of Intuition

The combination of uncertain time horizons and unavoidable pressures lead to an important role for intuition within the formulation of business strategy. Intuition is a vital and integral part of thinking. It gives the benefit of a holistic approach to problem solving, and reflects the value of cumulative experience. This is especially important when choices are based on expectations of an uncertain future and unpredictable competitive behaviour.

There is no reason to expect intuition to get any less important. Information technology means that companies are faced with growing quantities of information, but often its quality is not much improved. This technology also increases the pace at which decisions need to be made. For a business to remain competitive, the use of intuition is inevitable, even where strategic decisions are carefully analysed.

The benefits of intuitive thinking can be seen within Unilever. As part of the Agribusiness operations, research had been done into certain animal vaccines. During the early 1980s it was suggested that the expertise that had developed in monoclonal antibodies might also be applicable to humans. There was great uncertainty about the commercial and technical problems that the application of research in a new environment would bring. However, the consensus within Unilever was that the idea felt right. Resources were invested, commitments made. As a result a revolutionary home pregnancy test was launched in Britain that brought the test time down from 2 hr to 30 min; at the same time the technology made the product available in a form that was much more convenient for the user.

As a result of an intuitive decision, Unilever has established itself as a world leader in this area. The technology has been further improved, so that the company is now leader of a growing market in Europe, with a substantial business being built in the United States and elsewhere.

The experience within Unilever is that the benefits of research activities are as much in the success of spin-off effects as in the well briefed programmes. Sometimes such successes are called coincidence, in practice they are the result of the skills and intuition of the company's employees.

Strategic Fashions

A further illustration of the limits of complete logical analysis can be seen in the changing fashions of strategic management.

The 1970s were typified by the popularity of conglomeration and diversification led by companies such as ITT and Litton Industries. Courtaulds diversified into battery farming. Greyhound greatly expanded the scope of their operations. Unilever, although generally not a dedicated follower of fashion, moved into transport and packaging, and even considered moves into construction and car hire.

More recently there has been a concerted move back towards an emphasis on core businesses. Gulf and Weston needed a major restructuring programme with a big one-time loss and divestments of well over $1bn. Another example is Dart and Kraft, who merged before being split back into Kraft and Premark. Kraft also sold Duracell batteries, which was a highly successful business but inappropriate to their business mix. They ended up as a major food company dominating the U.S. cheese market. For Kraft this proved not to be enough, for they have subsequently been acquired by Philip Morris. The resulting integration with General Foods has further strengthened their position in the U.S. food industry.

However, even while companies continue to divest operations that are inappropriate to their business mix there are signs that the pendulum is swinging back again. Mercedes and General Electric have both moved towards diversification.

These fashions in corporate strategy should not be undervalued. They are partially a reflection of rapid changes in the environment in which firms operate, they are also influenced by the codification of new business principles. Books such as *In Search of Excellence*[1] express in simple ways strategies that were previously not identified as such. Yet the same book also illustrates the impermanence of any advice on what is optimal, for many of the firms that Peters and Waterman identified as most successful have subsequently encountered severe problems. Such impermanence is not surprising, for success in business means doing things better than the competition, not matching them. A firm's strategy is successful only as long as it is not being copied by the competition.

Strategy Formulation in Unilever

Unilever were one of the pioneers of the back-to-core strategy. At first this was not the result of a conscious decision. The move started when a large capital investment was proposed in an area in which the executive committee realized that management had little experience or expertise. This realization led to a re-assessment of Unilever's capabilities and skills in all areas of the business. This process led to the divestment of a whole range of peripheral activities including transport, oil milling, wallpaper, floor-covering and even turkey breeding.

With hindsight it appears that Unilever required a catalyst before the strategy became fully apparent. The realization of what was wrong with a single proposal led to the crystallization of a very important element in the corporate strategy.

In developing the strategy Unilever's executive committee tried to keep an open mind in dividing between core and non-core. The past performance of the relevant businesses played a role, particularly in areas where it was perceived that Unilever had both technological capability and management expertise. These areas included, for example, most of the food businesses as well as the specialty chemical operations. In addition some room was also left for both compromise and intuition. The profitable U.K. animal feeds business was retained while the Continental European business was divested. The long-established British packaging business was sold while a similar operation in West Germany was retained.

Throughout the criterion for retaining a business was the company's ability, as perceived by the Board, to add value to an activity. This could come from expertise in the product, the region or both. These operations were retained and supported, but activities where value could not be added were targeted for divestment.

Organizational Structures

At the time that Unilever were refocusing on the core, there was some concern that the strategic direction had developed informally through a process dependent on coincidence. As a result a thorough review of the strategy formulation process was initiated.

There are a number of organizational structures that could be adopted to encourage strategic management. The possibilities could include:

- a Corporate Strategy department staffed by professional strategists,
- a single senior executive with a think-tank of company managers or specialist outsiders,
- a combination of strategy management with line responsibilities.

Each option presents a different balance of dangers and advantages. Some encourage the splendid isolation of an ivory tower; others do not allow sufficient independence from operational loyalties. Furthermore, the success or failure of any one format is frequently as dependent on the characters of the individuals concerned as on the structure itself.

Over a period of time Unilever experimented with a number of structures with varying success. The company has now settled for a full time Corporate Development board member free from major line responsibilities. However, within Unilever the most important realization was that Corporate Development is a staff function, with an advisory role, regardless of the organizational structure. Strategic decision making cannot be delegated. In Unilever the ultimate strategic responsibility remains in the hands of the three-men Chief Executive.

Implementation of Strategy

The formulation of strategy within whatever structure, and be it the result of fashion, intuition or careful systematic analysis, is only the first stage of strategic management. Any strategy can only be counted as successful once it has been satisfactorily implemented.

The process of strategy implementation can be more difficult than the initial strategy formulation. Recent work at the London Business School seems to support this[2]—the firms studied undertook projects that failed to match their clearly stated company strategies. Deviation from the agreed strategy can be presented with various explanations. Probably the most respectable is the need for flexibility, adapting to the needs of rapidly changing circumstances. However, even this may be used as an excuse for behaviour that is nothing more than unplanned and opportunistic.

Managerial Resistance

When implementing strategy there is a danger that managers may resist the new strategy. Occasionally this is seen in explicit action. More often it is reflected in subconscious behaviour that can frustrate the corporate aims. This can be seen in the inclination of managers to postpone the moment when the success of a proposed project or strategy has to be demonstrated. In some cases there can even be a danger that the strategic processes can become counter-productive and hinder a company's development.

Unilever discovered that when faced with creating a 5-year plan, managers liked to propose significant capital expenditure in the early years (see Figure 2a). This was justified by planning ambitious results for the last couple of years of the period. The combination of certain early investment and uncertain late return could have dire consequences on the corporate cash-flow (Figure 2b).

Within the company this phenomenon was popularly known as the 'hockey-stick' effect. Although it was actively discouraged it took a long time to disappear. To avoid its recurrence Unilever now emphasize the importance of the third year in all discussions for company 5-year plans.

Communication of the Strategy

In order to maintain managerial support an important stage in the implementation of a new strategy is the communication of the strategy to senior executives. Their cooperation is vital, failure is likely if they are not convinced that the new direction was right.

There can be no single prescribed way of presenting a strategy to a company's managers and work force. Corporate cultures differ between countries, between industries and between individual companies. The immediacy of the problems that companies face are different, some require instant action, others allow time to fully enlist management cooperation. Furthermore, with a company as disparate as Unilever the strategy has to provide coherence, a goal towards which all can work. All companies need to present their strategy in the way that is most appropriate for them.

For Unilever, with a move back to core businesses it was particularly important to communicate the strategy effectively. Although the new strategy was coherent and credible, this was not sufficient. It had to be presented in such a way that made management feel that it was acceptable and worth working for. Many new skills had to be developed to make the new strategy a success. This involved facing difficult decisions. The company had to learn how to deal with restructuring, including disposals and job-losses. Organic growth had to be stimulated, and supplemented where possible with selected acquisitions. At the same time fundamental decisions had to be taken on how to reallocate R & D and marketing expenditure in support of the new strategy.

Unilever was fortunate in that the problems called for a strategy implementation that fitted well with the underlying corporate culture. Unilever emphasizes the relative independence of operating companies. Sharp changes of direction are only imposed from the centre in cases where there are very clear advantages. Unilever was in a position where the senior managers could proceed comparatively gradually. The problems did not require an immediate strong reaction, which fitted the culture demanding a gradual dosage rather than a sudden shock.

In practice Unilever attempted to give as many executives as possible the opportunity to feel a part of the strategy process. The company was as open as possible. A major conference was held of senior managers to discuss and refine the strategy, which also gave people a feeling of greater commitment to the concern's strategy.

The Next Challenge: 1992

Business is continually facing new challenges. One that is currently raising significant strategic issues for Unilever is the prospect of Europe 1992. It will bring lower transport costs, greater harmonization of standards and a further impetus towards the Europeanization of tastes and fashions. 1992 will offer many companies opportunities, most notably in a new found ability to exploit economies of scale.

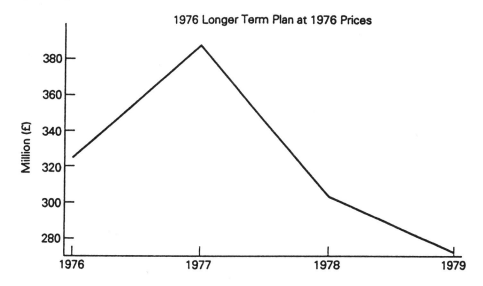

Figure 2(a) *Unilever Capital Investment 1976-1979*

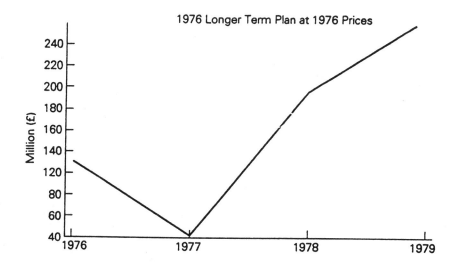

Figure 2(b) *Unilever Operational Cash-Flow 1976-1979*

159

Unilever is looking forward to 1992. For the company it means the acceleration of a process that was started in the 1960s. At that stage the management structure was altered in anticipation of change. Subsequent investment decisions have been based on the assumption that European borders would eventually disappear. Unlike many Japanese or American companies Unilever has the advantage of having many operations throughout Europe, giving a deep understanding of the area and its consumers.

However, to fully benefit from the new developments it will be necessary to adapt the current strategies even further. Most fundamental will be a change in mentality. 1992 will force a change from and emphasis on national organizations and markets to a greater perception of a more united Europe. This will take time, human habits are slow to change, but ultimately organizations and attitudes must alter.

Unilever has tried to apply the lessons from the past. A conference has been held of senior executives to improve understanding, encourage cooperation and develop new ideas. Careful analysis has been combined with concerted actions to implement decisions once made. An attempt has been made to manage the strategic balance: actions that come too late will leave missed opportunities and eroded competitive advantage, while moving too fast runs the danger of leaving the consumer behind. The regional differences in the U.S.A. illustrate just how slowly consumption habits may change.

Unilever like all companies must also react to the dichotomy of Europe 1992. For while there will be great opportunities for economies of scale trends in tastes will require greater diversity in some respects, but may converge in others. This will require both more concentration and flexibility from manufacturers. Thus the process of developing a strategy for 1992 is, like that for any business strategy, the challenge of finding the right equilibrium.

Conclusion

Strategic management of a global business is not a simple task. There is no single approach or solution that will always provide the right answers. Every company is different, and each will need to tailor their approach to their own requirements.

Thorough logical analysis can never be the only tool of strategic management. The complexity of the problems faced ensure that both experience and intuition play important roles, even though these are often less well defined.

The experience of many companies shows that strategic management plays a vital role if a company is to survive and thrive in today's world. It is not easy to develop or implement successful business strategies. However, by taking a balanced view of the surrounding world and integrating business experience and intuition with rigorous analysis, executives can successfully build coherent and value-adding business strategies.

References

T. Peters and R. Waterman, *In Search of Excellence,* Harper and Row, New York (1982).

P. Marsh, P. Barwise, K. Thomas and R. Wensley, *Managing Strategic Investment Decisions in Large Diversified Companies.* Centre for Business Strategy. London Business School (1988).

Mr. Maljers is Chairman of Unilever.

Exploring the Inventiveness in Everyone

Donald J. Treffinger

The terms creative and creativity seem to mean something different to almost everyone who uses them. They are used and misused so much, and so often, that they have become for many people mere "buzz words" of very little importance—and often, words that suggest foolishness or chicanery. There are many myths and misunderstandings about creativity, in any of its manifestations. Many of those myths carry over to inventing, which might be described as a *process* that takes place when creativity is brought to bear on a need or opportunity to do something new, better, or differently in any applied field. Let us look briefly at three of these common myths.

1. Creativity or inventiveness are mysterious experiences that just "appear out of the blue sky."

2. Inventors, like most other kinds of creative people, are a rare group—a few special geniuses specially endowed with a gift that was not given to most mere mortals. Like other highly creative types, inventors are eccentric, odd, socially inept, "flaky" or maybe even bizarre, and right out there near the edge. Inventors are odd, and they are born, not made.

3. The process of inventing is necessarily mystical, defying rational description, predictability, or nurture. You can't really say how to do it, and in fact, if you try too hard to study or control or manage it, it might vanish entirely.

If these were truths, rather than myths, we might hold some very specific expectations about how researchers and practitioners should approach or deal with the topic of creativity. In some ways, in fact, looking to the literature of the field reveals that theory and research has often appeared to treat these myths as if they were credible.

If these myths were truths, for example, it would seem to be reasonable to attempt to distinguish the characteristics or traits of a few rare geniuses who are successful, creative inventors from other more ordinary people. In fact, many studies of the creative personality approached the issue in exactly that way, from the 1950's well into the 1970's and 80's. Many researchers went on a search for the characteristics of definable groups or categories of interesting and presumably unusual people: inventors, creative artists, scientists, or managers; gifted people. They wanted to find out the difference between those who were "really" or highly creative, and those who were not.

It has been a merry, if frustrating chase. It is not that the research did not reveal some interesting characteristics—which were subsequently formulated into many impressive check lists and rating scales—but rather that researchers and practitioners have nearly drowned in all the characteristics that have been described. In an informal, unpublished search several years ago, we combed the literature in search of as many "creative characteristics" as we could possibly find. The list numbered more than 300, and we stopped there more because we ran out of the will to keep listing than because we were certain we had exhausted the possibilities. (And, no, the list is not available for anyone to use in making up the biggest, grandest identification check list yet. We fear the consequences: "Whoa! You only have 235 of these characteristics—sorry Mr. Edison, you'll never be a creative inventor.")

Even more interesting than the sheer quantity of characteristics, however, was their nature and variety. It would be simply impossible for any human to possess all of the traits or qualities that turned up on our list. With apologies to Clark Kent, just about the only items we did not find were, "Walks on water" or "Leaps tall buildings with a single bound." Many of the items were contradictory—so inherently opposite that one could not possibly be both. Some researchers were quite clever in resolving that concern; they included, "deals effectively with tensions, disharmony, and paradoxes."

With the increase in attention to learning styles in education in the mid- to late- 70s (e.g., Dunn & Dunn, 1972, 1978), some creativity researchers were intrigued. Perhaps these newly-emerging tools would help us better to understand the differences between more and less creative people. Alas, more frustration: no single learning style pattern seemed to characterize adequately all creatively productive people.

Since then, there has been considerable new progress in research, which has been facilitated greatly by a new way of thinking about the challenge. The turning point has really been the conclusion that we had not been asking the right question; this has opened the door for a number of very new and different research pathways. Most simply put, we learned that instead of asking, "How creative are you?" it would be much more productive for us to ask, "How are you creative?" Although this seems very simple, and looks on the surface only to be a little semantic sleight of hand, its consequences and benefits have been substantial. It may yet, in the long term, prove to be the most significant new finding about creativity of our generation of scholarship in the field, and it might not be too bold to suggest that, in fact, it can be the cornerstone of a very substantial paradigm shift. The basic form of that paradigm shift holds up quite well across almost any talent or ability domains with which we have tested it. That is, it seems just as plausible in relation to giftedness (from "how gifted are you" to "how are you gifted"), any talent area, or a specific domain of applied creativity (from "how inventive are you" to "how are you inventive").

Creative productivity, such as inventiveness, is best viewed, not merely as a set of "hard-wired" traits within the mind or personality of the individual, but as a composite of many factors that are in constant, dynamic interaction. This challenge has been discussed in the literature in relation to proposals for an "ecological" view of creativity (e.g., Harrington, 1990; Isaksen, Puccio, & Treffinger, 1993). Consider, for example, the interaction among four constellations, keeping in mind the brief acronym, COCO; these are portrayed in Figure One (from Treffinger, 1994).

Each of the four components of the COCO model can help us to discover ways to set aside one or more of the myths, and to explore the potentials for inventiveness and creativity in everyone.

• **Characteristics.** Rather than viewing characteristics as limiting traits or qualifications, we might instead view them as ways to understand and manage diagnostics: gaining better knowledge of one's strengths, interests, styles, and personality to enable someone (teacher, mentor, supervisor, person for oneself) to focus, guide, and direct inventive efforts and energies productively. That is, we should look at characteristics as one source of information to help us understand people and to guide us in helping them learn and grow, not just as a means of sorting them into groups or categories. Viewed in this way, the potential for meaningful creative productivity and inventing is not just the province of a few isolated geniuses. It is within everyone. This does not mean everyone is (or even will necessarily become) creatively productive, or a successful inventor. It does mean, however, that *anyone might!* In addition, not everyone will be creative or inventive in the same way or in the same domain. Knowledge of individuality and learning styles suggests that creativity and inventiveness can be expressed in a variety of ways and applied in a very extensive array of talent domains (Dunn, Dunn & Treffinger, 1992; Feldhusen, 1992; Gardner, 1983; Kirton, 1976).

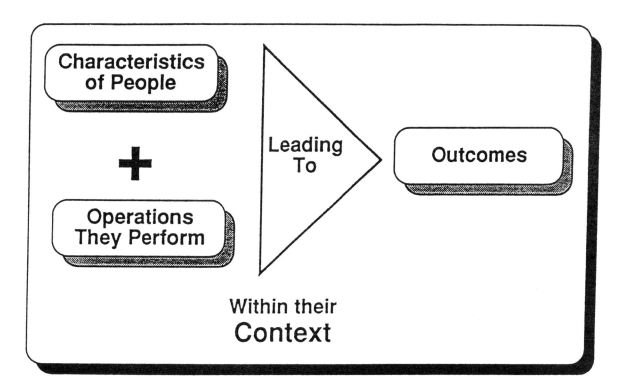

Figure 1 *COCO: Components of Creative Productivity*
Source: Treffinger (1994); reprinted by permission.

•   **Operations.** For years, there has been heated debate about the question, "Can we teach creativity?" In the old paradigm, this was an elusive and challenging question, primarily because it was often addressed at the level of seeking "deep core changes in the inner make-up of the person." If only a few people really had the traits and abilities of creativity, then anyone who purported to be teaching creativity was boldly asserting that they could modify and change the deepest, inner workings of the person... putting something in that was not there before.

In a more contemporary, ecological view, that issue has lost much of its vigor. Today, the question might better be stated as, "Can we help people to increase or enhance their ability to think creatively and critically, to solve problems, and to make decisions?" There is ample research to support the view that deliberate efforts to enhance creative and critical thinking and Creative Problem Solving can be effective and powerful (e.g., Isaksen, 1987; Isaksen, Murdock,

Firestien, & Treffinger, 1993a, 1993b; Torrance, 1972, 1987; Treffinger, Sortore, & Cross, 1993; Van Gundy, 1987).

A person's creative productivity does not depend only on some fixed set of internal personality traits or level of cognitive abilities; it also reflects the extent to which the person knows and uses effective strategies appropriately. To do so, one must be *competent* (knowing the strategies, when and how to use them, and monitoring the results), *confident* (aware of one's ability to use the strategies successfully), and *committed* (willing to engage in using them).

• **Context.** The setting and environment in which one functions, and one's reactions to that context, also work to encourage or inhibit creativity and inventiveness. Creative characteristics and a rich array of strategies can be the foundation for success in one setting, at a certain time, and in relation to a task or goal, or they can be a design for frustration, lack of productivity, and disengagement in unsupportive environments and situations. Effective problem solving and creative productivity are influenced by a number of specific context or climate dimensions, including such factors as freedom, challenge, idea support, dynamism, debate, conflict, and idea time (see: Isaksen, Dorval, & Treffinger, 1994, for example).

• **Outcomes.** Our goals, aspirations, and expectations, and those of others who are involved in any tasks upon which we work, also play a role in influencing inventiveness and creativity. We create and work— upward, downward, or horizontally ("marching in place")— in relation to the goals and visions we establish and accept. We also define and apply, for our work and others', the criteria by which we will assess the merit and impact of our efforts (e.g., Besemer & Treffinger, 1981; Besemer & O'Quin, 1987; Treffinger, 1988).

In sum, then, creativity is not just the result of a rare and esoteric genius, expressed through a mysterious and unpredictable muse, even though in process or in retrospect it may sometimes seem that way. It is just as much the result of deliberate, sustained efforts by individuals or groups to recognize and use their own styles, strengths, and skills to attain a meaningful and important outcome, at a time, in a context, and for a purpose.

Indicators and Implications for Strategies

If we begin to look seriously at the goal of exploring the creativity and inventiveness in everyone, what are some of the characteristics that might be indicators of the nature and direction of one's creative and inventive potentials, and what are some of the implications for teaching, mentoring, or personal learning?

One recent effort to synthesize research on the nature and characteristics associated with creativity, in relation specifically to inventing and inventors, yielded five broad, descriptive sets of characteristics, which were termed "Inventor's Principles" (Treffinger, 1992). The five principles, with brief descriptions of several of the characteristics in each set, are presented below. Each set also includes examples of implications of those characteristics for nurturing or developing creativity and inventiveness.

1. Inventors demonstrate openness and courage.
   • Being aware of, and challenging, assumptions
   • Challenging accepted or "obvious" beliefs
   • Being unafraid to make mistakes and willing to learn from them
   • Willing to take risks

- Making "leaps" in their thinking
- Disbelieving those who say, "It can't be done"
- Turning negatives into positives (setbacks into opportunities, obstacles or problems into challenges)
- Being open-minded to new possibilities
- Skeptical of "pat answers"

From this set of characteristics, the rationale emerges for linking creativity and inventing through activities and experiences such as *breaking limiting mental, perceptual, social, behavioral sets; questioning assumptions; challenging ideas constructively; asking "how might we…" rather than saying "we can't because…;" overcoming habit-bound thinking;* and *recognizing and overcoming internal and external blocks and barriers.*

2. Inventors observe skillfully and deeply.
- Looking beyond the obvious
- Looking at things and experiences in different and varied ways
- Using all the senses available
- Asking, "why," "why not," "why else," "how," and "how else."
- Experimenting
- Finding and making patterns
- Watching for (being alert to) details that others overlook or ignore
- Perceiving gaps, paradoxes, needs, or missing elements
- Noticing where ideas might lead

From this principle, the related activities and tools for creativity and inventing emphasize skills of *sharpening or improving breadth and depth of observation; digging deeper in many ways;* and, *joining opposites (strange and familiar).*

3. Inventors acquire and use much information creatively.
- Going beyond the information given
- Being exposed to (and seeking out) many ideas and experiences
- Seeking breadth and variety of activities and experience
- Experimenting, and testing ideas, hypotheses
- Asking many, varied, and unusual questions
- Taking old answers as starting points for posing new questions
- Gathering knowledge/data from many sources and domains
- Making connections that transcend ordinary "boundaries" of disciplines, fields, or modes of inquiry

From this principle, the related activities and tools for creativity and inventing emphasize *making connections across content domains; learning many ways to gather, organize, analyze, display or present, and interpret data; searching widely for information and ideas,* and *asking probing questions.*

4. Inventors know how to generate and analyze possibilities.

- Asking "what if" or "just suppose"
- Thinking of many, varied, and unusual possibilities
- Turning ideas around playfully
- Predicting, speculating, forecasting
- Combining or changing parts to make new possibilities
- Using metaphors or analogies
- Trying different possibilities to get "unstuck"
- Looking at one thing and seeing something else
- Making inferences and deductions
- Sequencing, categorizing, and judging the relevance of data
- Analyzing possibilities in balanced and constructive ways
- Defining problems and sub-problems constructively
- Deciding, evaluating, choosing promising options
- Translating ideas into actions

From this principle, the related creativity activities and tools for inventing emphasize *learning, practicing, and using (authentically) many idea-generating techniques (divergent/creative thinking) and idea-analyzing (convergent/critical thinking) techniques; learning and using structured approaches for problem-solving and decision-making.*

5. Inventors know and listen to their "inner voice."
- Trusting their own judgment
- Having confidence and persistence in pursuing their own ideas and goals
- Trusting their own hunches or intuitions
- Becoming absorbed in their passions—losing sight of time and place
- Not giving up in the face of disdain, discouragement or ridicule from others
- Refusing to be beaten down by dismay when things aren't working
- Being skeptical of others' ideas—and their own
- Investing great effort, energy, time, and personal resources in their ideas and work
- Holding their commitments strongly
- Seeing their efforts through to conclusions, products, or outcomes

From this principle, the related creativity activities and tools for inventing emphasize awareness of challenges and opportunities; recognizing t*alents, strengths, and sustained interests; providing time, encouragement, resources, and support to pursue talents and interests; perceiving gaps and needs; building self-confidence, trust,* and *perseverance.*

Personal and Educational Implications

Let us consider some of the implications of these principles, and the strategies or methods associated with them, for individuals who wish to discover and develop their own creativity inventiveness, and for teachers or others who seek to develop the skills and talents of inventive thinking among others.

First, think of these principles as *invitations*. Your own personal creativity and inventiveness can be at work when, in your own areas of talent and interest, and through your own preferred style of working, learning, producing, and sharing, you draw upon any of these characteristics and use them in dealing with new tasks, opportunities, or challenges.

At the personal or self-directing level, the most obvious implication (which may nonetheless be worth stating) seems, then, to be: *seek out, and make deliberate or systematic efforts to discover and use the creativity and inventiveness within yourself.*

The investment you make in knowing yourself—your style, your interests, your "driving force"—will help you to be that person as well or as authentically as you are able. Focus your efforts on knowing who you are, and capitalizing on your strengths, talents, sustained interests, and best ways of learning and working. You need have little or no concern about trying to be creative in ways that fit some stereotyped expectations about "the creative person." Find and immerse yourself in what's best and right for you. Dr. E. P. Torrance has spoken for years about finding and focusing on your "passion," and his emphasis is well-founded. What about being "well rounded"? It's fine—if your goal is to grow up to be a golf ball.

For educators or others who seek to nurture creativity and inventiveness among their students or colleagues, there are several important implications. These include:

- Give more time and much more deliberate effort to seeking all students' best strengths and talents, and respond to them in appropriate and varied ways.

- Worry less about trying to get everyone sorted and gathered into the correct "bins." Don't assume that a level playing field means that you have to teach everyone as if there were no differences among people. Respond to who people are, and what they need, not to categories.

- Take time to monitor your instructional efforts and to evaluate their impact and effectiveness; reflect on and debrief your activities and programs, as a foundation for continuous improvement.

The educational or instructional implications of new views of operations or strategies focus on the question, "What works best for whom, and under what circumstances?" This view challenges us to explore such issues as:

- How do we use our knowledge of students' characteristics to design and deliver instruction more effectively?

- What kinds of productive thinking operations or methods are most successfully learned and applied, and in what ways, by different learners, at different times, and for different purposes?

A final recommendation for educators or trainers is to become critical consumers of information and resources on creative and inventive thinking, making deliberate efforts to compare and evaluate various approaches. Treffinger, Feldhusen, Isaksen, Cross, Remle, and Sortore (1993) presented an extensive set of 15 criteria for reviewing and evaluating published materials. These criteria can guide educators in their efforts to make informed decisions. The field includes a diverse array of offerings, from the enthusiastic, engaging, and charismatic entrepreneurial creators of a variety of unresearched, untested packages, to many other approaches that are based on, and supported by, many years of theory development, research, and practice. Many new research efforts are also in process, which will continue to help educators expand

and enhance their efforts. These include, for example, investigations of ways to link process skills more effectively to learner characteristics, specific task or outcome parameters, and varied environments or settings (e.g., Isaksen, Puccio, & Treffinger, 1993). Recent developments have also included searching for ways to help people select and apply various methods and strategies in natural and flexible ways that construct meaning personally rather than presuming it can be imposed externally upon the problem solver (e.g., Isaksen, Dorval, & Treffinger, 1994; Treffinger, Isaksen, & Dorval, 1994). Critical consumers need to be aware of the variety of, and differences among, many models and approaches, and to study the alternatives carefully in order to make effective decisions.

Summary

1. Everyone has the potential or capability for creativity and inventiveness.

2. Know your style and strengths, and commit yourself to them with vigor and singleness of purpose. Discover and pursue your passion, and don't let anyone beat you away.

3. Consider the context in which you will be operating. If it isn't conducive to creative efforts, change it—or change where you are (get away from it).

4. Make a deliberate effort to learn, and to be able to select and choose for yourself, many different strategies or operations for productive thinking.

5. If you're an educator, work always to create and sustain opportunities for all your students to do all these things, too.

References

Besemer, S. P. & O'Quin, K. (1987). Creative product analysis: Testing a model by developing a judging instrument. In: S. G. Isaksen (Ed.). *Frontiers of creativity research: Beyond the basics.* (pp. 341-357). Buffalo, NY: Bearly Limited.

Besemer, S. P. & Treffinger, D. J. (1981). Analysis of creative products: Review and synthesis. *Journal of Creative Behavior, 15* (3), 15–178.

Dunn, R. & Dunn, K. (1972). Practical approaches to individualizing instruction. Nyack, NY: Parker Publishing.

Dunn, R. & Dunn, K. (1978). T*eaching students through their individual learning styles.* Reston, VA: Reston Publishing.

Dunn, R., Dunn, K., & Treffinger, D. J. (1992). B*ringing out the giftedness in your child.* New York: John Wiley.

Feldhusen, J. F. (1992). T*IDE: Talent identification and development in education.* Sarasota, FL: Center for Creative Learning.

Gardner, H.(1983). Frames of *mind.* NY: Basic Books.

Harrington, D. M. (1990). The ecology of human creativity: A psychological perspective. In: M. A. Runco & R. S. Albert (Eds.). Theories of *creativity.* (pp. 143–169). Newbury Park, CA: Sage.

Isaksen, S. G. (Ed.). (1987). Frontiers *of creativity research: Beyond the basics.* Buffalo, NY: Bearly Limited.

Isaksen, S. G. & Dorval, K. B. (1993). Changing views of creative problem solving: Over 40 years of continuous improvement. *International Creativity Network Newsletter, 3* (1), 1+4-5.

Isaksen, S. G., Dorval, K. B. & Treffinger, D. J. (1994). *Creative approaches to problem solving.* Dubuque, IA: Kendall-Hunt.

Isaksen, S. G., Murdock, M. C., Firestien, R. L. & Treffinger, D. J. (Eds.). (1993a). *Understanding and recognizing creativity: Emergence of a discipline.* Norwood, NJ: Ablex.

Isaksen, S. G., Murdock, M. C., Firestien, R. L. & Treffinger, D. J. (Eds.). (1993b). *Nurturing and developing creativity: Emergence of a discipline.* Norwood, NJ: Ablex.

Isaksen, S. G., Puccio, G. J. & Treffinger, D. J. (1993). An ecological approach to creativity research: Profiling for creative problem solving. *Journal of Creative Behavior, 27,* 149-170.

Kirton, M. J. (1976). Adaptors and innovators: A description and measure. *Journal of Applied Psychology, 61,* 622-629.

Torrance, E. P. (1972). Can we teach children to think creatively? *Journal of Creative Behavior, 6,* 114-143.

Torrance, E. P. (1987). Recent trends in teaching children and adults to think creatively. In: S. G. Isaksen (Ed.). *Frontiers of creativity research: Beyond the basics.* (pp. 204–215). Buffalo, NY: Bearly Limited.

Treffinger, D. J. (1988). *Student invention evaluation kit: Research edition.* Honeoye, NY [now Sarasota, FL]: Center for Creative Learning.

Treffinger, D. J. (1992). *Base document on education.: A report based on the national think tank for the advancement of scientific creativity.* Akron, Ohio: Inventure Place.

Treffinger, D. J. (1994). *Professional development module: Creative and critical thinking.* Sarasota, FL: Center for Creative Learning.

Treffinger, D. J., Isaksen, S. G., & Dorval, K. B. (1994). *Creative problem solving: An introduction.* Sarasota, FL: Center for Creative Learning.

Treffinger, D. J., Feldhusen, J. F., Isaksen, S. G., Cross, J. A., Remle, R C., & Sortore, M. R. (1993). *Productive thinking handbook: Rationale, criteria and reviews.* Sarasota, FL: Center for Creative Learning.

Treffinger, D. J., Sortore, M. R. & Cross, J. A., Jr. (1993). Programs and strategies for nurturing creativity. In: K. A. Heller, F. J. Mönks & A. H. Passow (Eds.). International handbook of research and development on giftedness and talent. (pp. 555-567). Oxford: Pergamon Press.

Van Gundy, A. B. (1987). Organizational creativity and innovation. In: S. G. Isaksen, (Ed.). *Frontiers of creativity research: Beyond the basics.* (pp. 358-379). Buffalo, NY: Bearly Limited.

SECTION FIVE
THE CREATIVE PRESS

"An environment can help a person be more creative. It can inspire by being beautiful or unusual. It can foster creativity by allowing freedom." This quote by Hucker from his article on the Hallmark Innovation Center succinctly describes the key elements discussed in this section. If the "place" or environment where creativity and innovating happen is to be successful, certain physical and psychological needs of its inhabitants must be fulfilled. This section provides insight about these factors and advice on how to incorporate them into the design. Authors use such terms as culture, atmosphere, social climate, and emotional climate in referring to the creative environment.

Physical factors range from a simple but safe and comfortable work area with adequate lighting to an architecturally designed space with art work, lush foliage, and classical music. Hallmark finds visual humor an excellent stimulant to creativity as well as adding variety to its work spaces. Thompson (1992) suggests that instead of adorning walls with diplomas and past rewards, individuals might hang pictures that represent personal or organizational vision or place toys on desks as a reminder of the creative self.

Kanter and Ekvall describe the emotional or psychological factors needed to encourage creativity in individuals or organizations. A partial list from Ekvall includes challenge, freedom, idea-support, playfulness, and risk-taking. Amabile and Gryskiewicz (1989) through their Work Environment Inventory also found freedom and challenge to be strong stimulants to creativity. These studies agree with the report from the 1993 *Business Week* President's Forum that successful companies are advocating empowerment and autonomy for employees, openness and flexibility in organizational structure, and the use of cross-functional teams to meet ever-changing market demands. Kanter includes in her "facilitating conditions" a list of power tools: information through open communication patterns, support that connects people across diverse areas, and resources that are easy to acquire.

Resources are mentioned by Amabile, Hucker, and Kanter as essential to eliciting creativity. These include people and skills, materials, facilities, information and funds. Resources can affect both physical and psychological factors. For example, if risk-taking is to be encouraged, failures must be expected and planned for in the budget. Yong tells of three essential steps necessary for managing creative people: (l) understand the creative process, (2) appreciate the creative person, and (3) encourage a creative work climate. Kanter labels a corporate leader as one who makes change happen and improves business, a "change-master." Change masters have many personal skills, such as being able to communicate and sell creative ideas as well as team building and idea realization. Since creativity and non-conformity are inseparable, individuality must be cultivated and encouraged by management. The animal metaphor used by Grossman and Ring provides an example of identifying individual needs in providing appropriate motivation and recognition. These eagles, otters, and unicorns are archetypes of innovators. By understanding their styles and needs, the leader can encourage creativity by providing the appropriate environment. (CC)

Of Additional Interest

Amabile, T. M., & Gryskiewicz, N. D. (1989). The creative environment. *Creativity Research Journal* 2(4), 231–253.

Amabile, T. M., & Gryskiewicz, N. D. (1989). Creative human resources in the R&D laboratory: How environment and personality affect innovation. In Robert Kuhn (Ed.), *Handbook for creative and innovative managers*, 501–523. New York: McGraw-Hill.

Farnham, A. (1994). How to Nurture Creative Sparks. *Fortune 129*, 94–100.

Geis, G. T. (1989). Making companies creative: An organizational psychology of creativity. In Robert Kuhn (Ed.), *Handbook for creative and innovative managers*, 25–33. New York: McGraw-Hill .

Kirton, M. J. (1991). Adaptors and innovators: Why new initiatives get blocked. *Creative Management*, 209–221.

Lehr, L. W. (1989). Encouraging innovation and entrepreneurship in diversified corporations. In Robert Kuhn (Ed.), *Handbook for creative and innovative managers*, 221–220. New York: McGraw-Hill.

Miller, W. (1987). *The creative edge: Fostering innovation where you work*. Reading, MA: Addison-Wesley.

Raudsepp, E. (1989). Creative climate checklist: 101 ideas. In Robert Kuhn (Ed.), *Handbook for creative and innovative managers*, 173–182.

Shapero, A. (1985). Managing creative professionals. *Research Management*. March-April, 23–28.

Thompson, C. (1992). *What a great idea: Key steps creative people take*. New York: Harper-Perrenial.

Van Gundy, A. G. (1984). How to establish a creative climate in the work group. *Management Review*, August, 24–38.

THE ORGANIZATIONAL CULTURE OF
IDEA-MANAGEMENT: A CREATIVE CLIMATE
FOR THE MANAGEMENT OF IDEAS

Göran Ekvall

The appearance of the concept and phenomenon of idea-management or idea-handling is due to several forces of change in industrial developed societies. One is the accelerating rate of development in technological fields, which enforces almost continuous changes in products and processes. Another is fast, world-wide commerce, giving the individual company a more flexible and uncertain market to compete in. A third force is the frequent fluctuation in the life-styles and preferences of customers due to international media, communications and travel, secularization, affluent conditions and so on. A fourth is new values, ambitions and attitudes at work, which result in demands from employees to participate in problem-solving and decision-making. Companies need the ideas and the support of all their employees in the implementation of the new. Idea-management then becomes a necessary activity.

The concept of idea-management is about finding and taking care of ideas for change in the organization's operations, concerning both products and processes. It is a much broader concept than R & D management, as ideas are sought from all quarters. Idea-management has two sides. One concerns general features of the organization which stimulate or hamper innovation, the other includes special formal systems and procedures for idea-finding and use.

I have, for the last ten years, been carrying out a research programme about organizational conditions for creativity and innovation, covering both soft aspects like values, climate and leadership styles as well as harder qualities of the organization like structure, strategies and special systems for innovation. Studies have been done in small and large industrial organizations, banks, airlines, newspaper offices, broadcasting corporations, universities and hospitals.

Among the general features of organizations my research group has especially focused on, one of the more subjective, softer aspects is the emotional climate. Among formal structures and procedures for idea-handling, we have studied suggestion systems extensively, but also touched on several others, such as innovation offices, internal development funds, idea-hunts, idea-promotors, and training programmes in entrepreneurship.

Climate has to do with behaviour, attitudes and feelings which are fairly easily observed. Culture, on the other hand, refers to more deep-rooted assumptions, beliefs and values which are often on a preconscious level, things that are taken for granted. If we include climate in the culture concept, we can look upon climate as a manifestation, on a more superficial level, of the deeper, basic cultural element.

I regard organizational climate as an intervening variable which affects the results of the operations of the organization. The climate has this moderating power because it influences

173

organizational processes such as communications, problem-solving, decision-making and the psychological processes of learning and motivation. The organization has resources of different kinds—people, money, machines, etc.—which are used in its processes and operations. These operations bring out effects of many kinds and on different levels of abstraction: high-quality or low-quality products or services; radically new products or only small improvements in the old ones; high or low job satisfaction among employees; commercial profit or loss. Climate has an important influence on these outcomes. But the effects in turn influence both resources and climate. The causal picture (seen in Figure l) becomes complicated.

We measured creative/innovative climate through a questionnaire, consisting of 50 items forming 10 different scales with 5 items in each. The organizational climate score is an aggregated score based on the scores of the members of the organization. This instrument was thoroughly constructed and standardized by a series of factor analyses.

To give you some insight into the kind of research we have been doing in order to grasp the concept of innovative climate, I will present two sets of data.

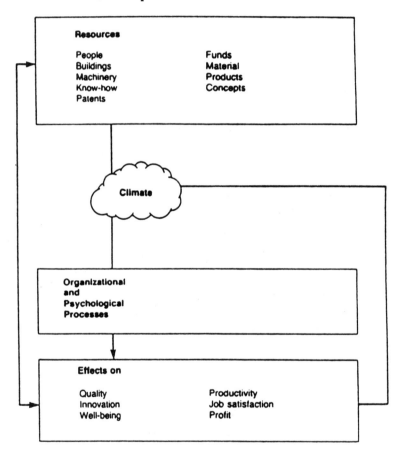

Figure 1 *The Relationship between Climate and the Organization*

Table 1 shows the mean scores for the climate dimensions from 27 different organizations. 'Organization' here stands for a separate small company or a self-governed part of a large company. All employees or a representative sample answered the questionnaire. The figures in the table are thus mean scores of the means for the organizations in the three groups. Very rigorous criteria were applied when putting organizations in the 'innovation' and 'stagnated' groups. The criterion of innovation is based on product innovations. (The classification was of course made independently of the climate scores, by a researcher from a business school who had developed a method to rate the innovativeness of a company's strategies and products.) The reliability of the climate scales permits a mean score difference between any two organizations of 0.25 to be considered significant (provided that the means are based on a substantial sample of individuals).

Table 1 *Mean Climate Scores for 27 Swedish Organizations*

Climate dimension	Organizations Innovative N=8	Stagnated N=4	Average N=15
Challenge	2.35	1.64	1.90
Freedom	2.17	1.52	1.74
Idea-support	2.09	1.31	1.64
Trust	1.82	1.37	1.60
Dynamism	2.31	1.30	1.55
Playfulness	2.16	1.29	1.69
Debates	1.54	0.92	1.28
Conflicts	0.71	0.85	0.88
Risktaking	2.34	0.95	1.12

The tendency in the table is evident. The innovative group has the highest mean scores of all three groups on all dimensions, with the exception of 'conflicts', and the stagnated group has the lowest mean scores, also except for 'conflicts'. But the opposite difference on the 'conflicts' scale is not strong. The 'conflict' climate aspect is a tricky one in relation to creativity and innovation. Personal, emotional conflicts can be seen as blocking creativity whereas ideas-controversies ('debates') are stimulating but in some highly creative organizations both types of tension are markedly present. Those organizations, however, seem to be creative in spite of the personal tensions, not because of them.

Research results of this kind indicate that climates are different in innovative and stagnated organizations.

In Table 2 the results from a study in an American industrial company are presented. A translation of the Swedish version of the creative climate questionnaire was applied in eight independent product departments belonging to the same division. The top management of the division rated one of the departments as creative and innovative and one as very problematic from that aspect. In the table only the results from these two 'extreme groups' are included. The scores are the means of the group members' scores. The results are very much the same as in the Swedish material, with the exception of 'challenge', where no difference was observed. Compared to all the other seven departments the 'stagnated' had the lowest score on all dimensions except 'challenge' (where it was in the middle) and 'conflicts' (where it had the highest score). The 'innovative' department, however, did not show the most supportive climate of all departments.

Table 2 *Mean Climate Scores for the Extremes of a US Industrial Company*

Climate dimension	Innovative dept.	Stagnated dept.
Challenge	2.32	2.25
Freedom	1.92	0.95
Idea-support	1.85	1.00
Trust	1.62	1.25
Dynamism	1.97	1.50
Playfulness	1.62	1.35
Debates	1.52	1.10
Conflicts	1.10	1.40
Risktaking	1.27	0.40
Idea-time	1.50	1.00

On the relation between organizational climate and formal systems for idea-handling (such as suggestion schemes), our results are clear-cut and the conclusions straightforward:

- No idea-handling system can work successfully without a supportive climate in terms of the dimensions I have referred to.
- An idea-handling system can make a good climate even better.
- An idea-handling system which is set up in an organization where the climate is bad tends to make that climate still worse. The system becomes another area of conflict and distrust.

When it comes to the more basic aspects of organizational culture—the beliefs and values concerning leadership and organization—that lay behind the concrete organizational phenomena, a model relating culture to idea-management has evolved in our research efforts.

The three broad value orientations affecting leadership and organization that have appeared in western societies during this century form different patterns which distinguish organizations from each other. These patterns imply very differing conditions for idea-management. Let me label the orientations 'structure', 'people' and 'change'.

'Structure-orientation' was the first on the historical scene of industrial society. It is articulated in Taylor's 'scientific-management' concept, in Weber's bureaucratic principles and in Fayol's classical management teachings. It is also seen in leadership-style concepts such as 'initiating-structure' (the Ohio leadership studies), and production-centeredness' (the Michigan school). In Burns' and Stalker's famous book *The Management of Innovation* (1961), structure-oriented organizations are described by the metaphor 'mechanistic'.

'People-orientation' is based on human relations and has had many variants. McGregor's theory Y is perhaps the strongest. 'Participation' is another but it also has other sources. The leadership style described as 'consideration' (Ohio group) or 'employee-centered' (Michigan) belongs here. Nowadays the concept of 'human resources' seems to be the most vivid representative of this orientation.

'Change-orientation' is the youngest and it is gaining ground. It is prevalent in the 'organismic' organizations described by Burns and Stalker. Leadership terms such as 'entrepreneurial' and 'transformational' leaders mirror this orientation. The modern distinction between leader and manager, between the person who creates meanings and goals for others and the one who administrates information and decisions, is clearly a result of this value-orientation being strong.

In the Swedish industrial culture where I do the main part of my research, four types of profiles on these three orientations are discernible. They are presented in Table 3.

Table 3 *Profiles of Value Orientations*

Value orientation	Culture Patterns			
	A	B	C	D
Structure	++	++	0	0
People	0	+	0	++
Change	0	0	++	+

Type A is a *bureaucratic* culture with an *authoritarian* face. In such an organization in Swedish society it is not possible to run an idea-handling system successfully. The employees keep their ideas to themselves. If they hand in an idea, by mail or in the suggestion box, they do so anonymously and the idea is a joke or an impertinence.

Type B is a *bureaucracy* with a *human* face, a well-ordered culture where people's needs, feelings and relationships are considered, mostly in a formal, administrative way. Our research shows that in such a culture an idea-handling system can work. Many of the large Swedish industrial companies are of this type. Several of them have effective systems of idea-handling. But because of the weak change-orientation in these cultures, the idea-handling remains at a relatively low level of creativity. Improvements and refinements of processes and products turn up but no radically new concepts.

The type C pattern constitutes the classic *entrepreneurial* culture headed by a pushing, idea-rich and dominating person. This situation often characterizes the early phases of an organization's history. In a culture of this kind there is no need for a special procedure to handle ideas. Everything that occurs in the organization is in one way or another idea-handling. The pace of ideation is for the most part so great that a more formal procedure of idea-handling would be obstructive and pointless.

Type D may best be described as a culture of relations and *co-operation*, where opportunities exist for creative thinking. Innovation is seen as vital for the survival of the organization. Expansion through innovation is the main strategy. Renewal is sought in team-work and networks. It is assumed, in this type of organization, that creativity and innovation result when different people and their differing thoughts and experiences meet. Patterns of this kind have been called 'greenhouse cultures'. As long as the organization is small, there is no need for a formal idea-handling procedure. But as it grows and the number of people and ideas becomes large, even in an idea-stimulating culture and climate such as this one, a more formal procedure seems required to take care of the creative potential of the employees. In a type-D culture we have no doubt the best conditions for a successful idea-handling system, one that brings forth both improvements and new concepts.

Idea-management thus has very different prospects according to the cultural pattern of the organization. In some organizations it is futile to try to implement an idea-handling procedure of any kind, because it will be rejected like an unfit transplanted organ, the immune defence being the prevalent values, norms, attitudes and analogous actions. In other organizations formal procedures of idea-handling are possible but not necessary. When the organization is small, the people-orientation strong and the change-orientation marked, then a climate exists which allows all members of the organization to speak and have their ideas considered as a matter of course.

But when organizations grow to a level where it is impossible for all the members to know each other, where the division of work between individuals and groups becomes more strict, where communications are restricted by physical and administrative distances and boundaries—in such a situation the need for an idea-handling system arises even in an organization where the cultural and climate conditions support creativity and innovation.

This is a paradox, that formal procedures are needed to take care of employees' ideas in organizations with creativity-stimulating values and climates. Bureaucracy and formalism are enemies of creativity and innovation, but nevertheless we do need formal procedures and routines to be able to utilize the creative potential existing in the organization. It seems that formalism must be resisted by its own means.

The paradox can be explained in two ways. One explanation is that human beings as well as organizations function far from perfectly. Even in organizations that work well, correctives are needed for inappropriate actions. Formal procedures of idea-handling are, in this perspective, correctives of inadequate behaviour such as idea-suppression, force of habit, status-quo thinking, self-righteousness and territory protection. The formal procedure is seen as a substitute for a more spontaneous flow and nurture of ideas.

Another explanation is that organizations are systems that are structured and composed of separate sub-systems, which are of vital importance for the survival of the total system, the organization. Idea-handling is such a structured sub-system, and it is becoming more and more important.

Reference

Burns, T. and Stalker, G. *The Management of Innovation* (London: Tavistock, 1961).

EAGLES, OTTERS, AND UNICORNS: AN ANATOMY OF INNOVATION

Stephen R. Grossman
Margaret J. King

Introduction

Of all trainable skills in business life, innovation is in the highest demand today. Eagles, otters, and unicorns are the three archetypal "players" who will solve problems as well as develop competitive new product and service concepts. Business can discover and promote these innovators from within by providing the appropriate culture for the recognition, teaching, and regarding of their respective talents and tendencies. Based on extensive consulting in innovation, creativity, and problem-solving, this survey identifies the typology of innovation through basic skills and styles, and describes both motivators and blocks to successful achievement.

With the accelerated rate of technological change, social and economic instabilities in the marketplace, and continued challenges and threats from foreign competition, for the majority of American businesses, simple hard work is no longer equal to the task of competing. Working smarter, by innovating and creating, seems to hold the most promise. What has become clear to many business leaders is that they and their constituents are called upon to innovate merely in order to survive. Human capital must be seen as a resource as never before.

In response to this need, many organizations have set up "innovation programs", which can be found anywhere from suggestion boxes and quality circles for hourly workers to inside ventures and "skunkworks" where small groups are spun off from the mainstream business to operate under a special set of formal and informal cultural norms. With a few exceptions, these efforts have been at best marginally successful and at worst catastrophes that not only have failed but have done much worse in demotivating those involved.

Important reasons for this lackluster performance can be offered: innovation is no single classed entity, as often assumed. There are several different types, and depending upon which type is sought, different players are needed: their cultural needs are unique and have to be accommodated.

This overview will attempt to give decision-makers a clearer understanding of what is needed in any given situation to harness innovative potential.

The Innovation Process

If we accept as a working definition that innovation is a *unique idea implemented profitably,* then that uniqueness is primarily the achievement of the individual contributor, and the implementation process is in large part dependent on the business culture. Operating under these assumptions, we will explore three modes of innovation, the individual needed to best execute each, and the role played by corporate culture for implementation.

Three Modes of Innovation

I. The first mode may be broadly classified as *"innovation by improvements."* These may be process improvements; making things run more efficiently, cost-effectively, or faster; or making product improvements, such as higher overall quality, fewer rejects, or increasing an already existing product benefit. Excellence, quality, and productivity are most often the nomenclature used to characterize innovation by improvements. Innovation by improvements starts with existing methods, products, or services and modifies them to generate more bottom-line effectiveness while maintaining their conventional attributes.

II. The second mode may be termed *"innovation by extensions."* In terms of methods or processes, innovation by extensions may initiate new ways of performing existing manufacturing or service schemes, such as using microwaves to dry materials or reconfiguring product components (as in front-wheel drive in a car) to yield some new benefit. In new product development, the extension may take the form of putting a fairly well developed technology to work in new areas by modifying some base material—for example, making highly absorbent tissues and towels derived from a technology for disposable diapers. Other cases provide a unique customer service by transforming some business strength from one arena to another, as in the development of "phone mail" that combines technologies in communication and computers in some novel way. Hence, innovation by extension may be viewed as the creative manipulation of existing technologies to extend what already exists.

III. The third mode is *"innovation though paradigms."* These are totally new patterns for doing business, or a singular new product line filling a need that not only has never been filled before, but has had life only at a dimly conscious level. These emerging products, processes, and services that follow a paradigm shift might be considered answers to the questions, "I know it's impossible, but I wonder if there is any way to– – –?"

At its core, innovation by paradigm concerns itself with reversing the fundamental unconscious assumptions we all make about our own sector of the business environment. Whether product, process, or service, it is something that has not before been consciously conceived as belonging in the realm of possibility, because of the self-limiting ways in which we ordinarily think. Examples of such innovations are rarer than the first two types, but might be typified by the development of the transistor, or the Manhattan Project, or animation in films, or transplants in medicine, and the like.

Not only did these breakthroughs call for different technologies than were currently available, but perhaps more important, introduced new methods of personal and professional interaction. A totally different pattern of mental, physical, and attitudinal behavior ensued.

In summary, then, innovation manifests itself as three distinctly different expressions. Each makes a different demand of the culture and the individual contributor. Before proceeding to define and describe the prototype and culture needed for each, it is important to emphasize that no value judgments are implied as to the importance or value of one model of innovation over another, either in terms of the quality of products or service, or with regard to the bottom line benefit. It is further important to see innovation as a thinking *process,* one not necessarily represented by the end product. Therefore, improvements may be just as valuable as a total paradigm shift. It is simply pragmatic to regard these styles as distinctive in the executions that make them work.

Player Profiles

Individual contributors may be regarded as the source of illumination. He or she may be anyone from an hourly worker with an idea for inspecting more products per hour to a CEO who develops a new vision for the company. All contributors, however, share some essentials. Everyone, for example, shares both right and left brain processes. Only when the cultural climate is favorable, however, can the whole brain be brought into play to draw effectively on both hemispheres for maximum results.

The Innovators: Eagles, Otters, And Unicorns

In our consulting work, we have discovered three types of innovators: eagles, otters, and unicorns. Each is identified with a different combination of knowledge and manipulative skills, each motivated by different values, and each innovating in a different realm.[1] The characteristics of the eagle are ego strength, power, and tenacity; for otters, cleverness, playfulness, and indulgence; for unicorns, mysticism, brilliance, and individualism. Sometimes what distinguishes eagles, otters, and unicorns is not their intrinsic separateness but simply the duration of time spent in character.

Eagle, otter, and unicorn are styled as prototypes here to profile their key characteristics. They are not intended as orthodox stereotypes without variation or flexibility.

In general, we find that eagles innovate by improvements, otters by extension, and unicorns by paradigm. With training and the right emotional equipment, one can move from one style to another, or unfortunately, under the influence of the prevailing company culture, even become stripped of the motivational aspects, lose intellectual interest, and become "drones".[2]

For all three orders of innovation there are three general characteristics that the individual contributor must exhibit at least to some extent. They are: 1. domain-relevant skills; 2. manipulative thinking skills; and 3. motivation. (Amabile, 1983).

Domain-Relevant Skills

These derive from a depth and breadth of information about situations of interest, along with the ability to do critical thinking about the information. With some notable exceptions, most innovators have a strong historical knowledge base in their fields.[3] They know what works, what doesn't, and have the thinking skills to figure out why. Attempts at "innovation by musical chairs," moving people with long-term knowledge of one area into something new in hopes that the change of venue will make them more creative, rarely work. In this scenario, it is lack of accumulated knowledge that proves fatal.

Manipulative Skills

Manipulation involves being "childlike": looking at a situation that is well known as if for the first time. A point of view change can often solve problems where conventional views have failed. One thinks of Land's five-year-old daughter asking him why he didn't put his darkroom inside the camera—the question that inspired the Polaroid.

Motivation

A complex of needs, values, goals, and objectives drive us to perform the task at hand; innovation requires a high degree of motivation. The right motivation will produce the two traits necessary for innovation: passion and perseverance.

Coming up with new ideas is not enough. True innovators also need other attributes to see the organization and the perseverance not to give up in the face of adversity. These attitudinal "skills" can, in many cases, actually step in to compensate for gaps in domain and manipulative skills.

Motivation operates in two modes: intrinsic and extrinsic. Intrinsic motivation is the problem itself, simply because it is inherently appealing or intriguing. Extrinsic motivators are goals, rewards, and recognition (the carrots) along with the penalties, fears, or obligations (the sticks) that operate, positively or negatively, to resolve the problem—or to keep it from going unsolved. These two modes might be thought of as the difference between playing (volition) versus performing (obligation).

Innovation is highest when domain-relevant skills, manipulative skills, and motivation intersect to act in concert.

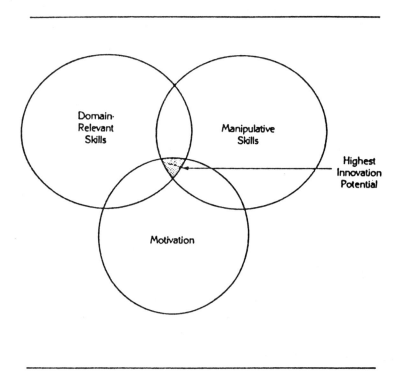

Figure 1 Source: Amabile, T. *The Social Psychology of Creativity*

Note: The original model (1983) created by T. Amabile used the term "Creativity-Relevant Skills" not "Manipulative Skills."

Following are profiles of each corporate character, and finally, what the business culture needs to provide for each to innovate within their optimal modality.

The Eagle: Truth, Justice, and the American Way

Domain-Relevant Skills

Eagles have well developed knowledge of disciplines pertaining to their work. For example, the eagle in marketing knows how well the product has performed and also has a thorough knowledge of the field of marketing itself. As mentioned, they know what works, what doesn't, have the ability to reason about these cause/effect relationships in this area. The additional knowledge and interest for the eagle tends to center on the business as a whole in a bird's-eye view, seeking understanding of the workings of other departments which only indirectly involve them.

For it is their working premise that an overall knowledge of the business strategies and the formal and informal organizational norms will provide them with the added grist for their intellectual mills to make them productive employees. It is not unusual, therefore, to find them changing perches within the business with a view towards getting ahead. One might find an engineer in the research department taking an MBA or marketing degree at night with a view towards moving into finance, operations, or marketing to position themselves closer to the decision-making center of the business. For the agile, domain-relevant skills are paramount. For this category of innovation, information and knowledge about function, department, and overall company, including work in progress in other sectors of the business that may at first seem outside their bailiwick, is the fuel for the fires of creativity.

These employees also tend to concentrate on management skills, reading all the most current intelligence on productivity, quality, excellence, and other management issues. They tend to pursue courses given either in the training department or in some adjacent academic facility dealing with current theories for managing people. In sum, the domain-relevant skills for eagles tend to be 1) knowledge of their area of work; 2) ability to reason, to understand and track cause-effect relations; 3) knowledge of the overall business philosophy and power structure; and 4) management skills.

Manipulative Skills

Every creative act is a manipulative exercise (Pames, Noller. Biondi, 1977). Unlike the God of the Old Testament, we mortals do not create something from nothing. We take what exists, reshaping or reconnecting it in some new way to solve a problem.

There are three basic manipulations possible, some synthesis of which will be found in every creative encounter. These manipulations are *making something larger, smaller, or rearranging its components*. Other terms of manipulation are reversing, adapting, modifying, putting to other uses, transposing, extending, miniaturizing, deleting, substituting, or combining. However, all of these acts fall into three transformations: making larger, smaller, or rearranging. Many products, from instant coffee to microchips, have probably been results of one or more of these mental exercises.

Eagles possess three skills that contribute to their manipulative prowess. They are *fluency* and *flexibility*, together with the eagle's-eye *powers of observation*.

Fluency is the knack of generating large numbers of responses or ideas when a problem or challenge is posed. Flexibility is the ability to generate ideas that span many different categories when faced with obstacles and challenge. For example, when asked to improve a desk calendar, the fluent mentality can with ease generate a high-volume stream of notions about changing the aesthetic qualities: i.e, color, configuration, geometry, and clarity, whereas the flexible mind will take flight not only with aesthetic models but ideas for functionality and cost efficiency as well.

Degrees of fluency and flexibility depend in large part on powers of observation; that is, having the ability to look at a system and describe it in diverse ways. The more ways in which a system can be described, the more potential manipulations can be performed. Description and manipulations travel hand in hand. Of the three characteristics needed for innovation in the improvement mode, these manipulative/descriptive skills are the easiest to teach and to put into practice on the spot once they are grasped.

Motivational Aspects

For all of our characters, intrinsic motivation is significant. However, the importance of intrinsic versus extrinsic depends on the nature of the individual contributor. For eagles, it is extrinsic motivation that is the stronger of the two in releasing passion and perseverance. Money, power, and a sense of security are the leading influences. Eagles are primarily concerned with how a successful resolution of the problem is going to bring them increases in salary and standing in the pecking order of the company. For them, the question is one of how innovation will expand their power and territory.

Eagles tend to think futuristically—a future viewed in terms of personal and corporate rewards for problem solving. Competitors of a high order, eagles need to show that they perform better than their colleagues in a given situation. However, they are also consummate team players, believing that, headed by a strong leader, the whole convocation can perform more effectively than any individual member. Sparked by a need to belong, they feel a high loyalty and bring an esprit de corps to the business, often sacrificing personal time to put in long hours of hard work. Dress may be best categorized as "appropriate," from the workers in uniforms on a production line to middle managers on up who "dress for success."

Eagles enjoy soaring highest, being number one, the leader in whatever market the business has chosen to compete. They tend to get many of their ideas and philosophies either from "father figures " in the organization, outside consultants whose credibility is acknowledged in the power structure, or cultural heroes. The reward system most motivating for them is power, influence, and money (typified by promotions); increased responsibilities (new vistas of influence); perks in the form of invitations to participate in glamour events such as national sales meetings in Hawaii; and sizeable bonuses and profit sharing. The plurality of innovators in large corporations fall under this heading. Their guiding attitude is that problems can be solved by "overwhelming" them with time, money, and additional people marching to the same tune.

The Otter: The Play's the Thing

In contrast to the eagle as an "improver", the otter may be expected to innovate in the area of *extensions*. This is not meant to imply that otters are not innovative in the first mode of *improvements* or the third of *new paradigms*.

Dominant-Relevant Skills

As with the eagle, the otter has a broad-based knowledge of the subject area. Otters have all the historical perspectives on what works and what doesn't, with the logical facility to know why. However, this is where they part company with the creativeness as it operates in the eagle mode. The otter is no longer concerned with information about the power structure of the organization and the general state of the business as a whole. Instead the focus is a knowledge of many subjects that, on the surface, have little or no relevance to the field in which they are actively employed. These are the "deep trivia" buffs who devote their leisure hours to reading and studying such arcane topics as medieval history and armaments, or the Greek philosophers, or the care and feeding of spiders.

You rarely catch them with a copy of the *Wall Street Journal*. Instead, observe them bent over on the lawn outside the corporate center totally absorbed in watching a group of ants building a mound. The otters wide-ranging interests correlate highly with significant degrees of creativeness. The reason for this correlation lies in the basic mechanism of the creative act. The great writer and philosopher Arthur Koestler, author of *The Act of Creation.* has coined the term "bisociation" as the essence of creativity. According to Koestler, bisociation is the ability to find associations and connections between two or more ideas, concepts, or things that were previously unassociated in order to solve a problem; that is, finding common elements in uncommon systems. Therefore, the more diverse the knowledge base, the more bisociations can be found—and the more inventive the individual.

Manipulative Skills

Aside from the attributes of fluency and flexibility that identify the eagle, the wide-ranging otter is also a visual thinker. That is, otters tend to think about ideas and concepts in mental pictures, as metaphors or analogies for their experience of the world. Otters are "imaginative" thinkers, who develop their own images of the world born of highly personal experience, yielding unique representations and insights. The breakthrough idea of velcro came when an otter scientist was looking for new ways of attaching things to each other for the space program. He noticed how tenaciously cockle burrs attached themselves to his sleeves and cuffs. At once he imagined a whole series of cockleburrs lined up along one panel of a garment to allow it to attach to another. Versatile and quick, the otter can also manipulate these images, extending something or reversing something else to develop yet another novel image in the service of solving a problem.

A study of creative people conducted by Gordon & Poze (1981) demonstrated that these thinkers held two features in common. Along with the ability to "fuzz" or purposefully distort those images to create new ones that could solve some long-term problems or lead to a new insight about the way things could work. The otter has both the visual skills to develop images and the fluency and flexibility to turn these images into something never before glimpsed.

Motivational Aspects

The biggest motivational differentiator between eagles and otters is the degree to which intrinsic motivation provides the passion and perseverance otters thrive on. While outside motivators tend to drive eagles much of the time, for the playful and clever otter, the dominant motivation is an intrinsic one. The problem is sufficient unto itself, without the "add-on" incentives of money, power, and prestige.

Otters are inherently very curious and curiosity drives them. They want to find out why things are the way they are and what it might take to change them. A vision of the future is as important as it is to eagles, but otter vision assumes a different focus. This view is more concerned with what things might be like *if some problem were solved* rather than the accrued benefit to them *when the problem is solved.* Theirs is a rich fantasy life, many times preferring their own company over that of others, and finding it easier to work on solutions to problems alone rather than as part of a task force. Given a choice, their working hours tend to be erratic because "the spirit", not the clock, must move them to solve the problem. Demands to produce within set hours is anathema to their free-floating minds. Oftentimes they are night people, not morning types, who resonate to the Oscar Wilde adage, "Only dull people are brilliant before breakfast". However, they do have enough "organizational consciousness" to show up in the office on time most days, but are often found working late—not because the informal norm so dictates, but because they get their best thoughts later in the day when they can be alone at last.

185

For the otter, money and benefits are not motivators; lack of money, however, does act as a demotivator. They regard such considerations as "hygiene factors", much like desk and chair, pen and pencil, that someone else provides for them.

Otters also pride themselves on their problem-solving ability and like to be recognized for it by solicitation of their opinions and ideas about matters that do not necessarily fall within their working bailiwick. They tend to look slightly disorganized, perhaps with the sign on their office wall declaring, "A Clean Desk is the Sign of a Sick Mind".

They can also appear to be unreliable or forgetful, getting so absorbed in a task that they arrive late for meetings and events in a caricature of the absent-minded professor, oblivious to time and place, engrossed in an elaborate interior life all their own.

In sum, they are motivated mainly by the problem itself but also require intellectual excitement on the job. Otters are nourished in environments where they are learning, and tend to leave settings where they feel mentally stagnant. Though a far smaller percentage of the population of business cultures than the eagles, they do make a showing in most large businesses. All that need happen is that the culture remove the coverings, shake off the dust, and let them explore the waters.

The Unicorn: A Children's Story

Unfortunately there are not enough of these around in corporations. It is from the unicorn that the totally new concept, the breakthrough paradigms, will come (see section on third mode of innovation). Although scarce, unicorns are worth cultivation; recognizing who they are and their cultural requirements might lead to a watershed in the form of some new and exciting breakthrough—the kind that can turn a "flat" organization around and throw the competition into a tailspin.

Domain-Relevant Skills

The unicorn, like the eagle, has both breadth and depth of subject-area knowledge, and, like the otter, deep knowledge of many apparently nonrelevant areas. However, the widest divide between these two and the unicorn is the ability to abstract concepts to arrive at newfound generalized principles. This talent resides in the ability to think in terms of integrated systems and global concepts rather than in the narrower formats of deductive logic. This ability to think at high levels of abstraction and in generalized patterns is strongly correlated with what is commonly and erroneously called high IQ. In truth, most intelligence tests tend to measure two components of intellect-linguistic and logical-mathematical intelligence (Gardner, 1983) with the higher value assigned to the ability to abstract. In this evaluation, unicorns do find themselves classified as genius-level.

Manipulative Skills

Along with the fluency and flexibility skills of eagles and the imagery skills of otters, unicorns are able to engage in an activity called "self-watching" (Grossman, Rogers & Moore, 1988). They have the uncommon ability to step outside themselves "in process" to observe what they are doing and how they're thinking, while at the same time bringing to the surface the preconscious assumptions being made about the problem under consideration. Spending a fair chunk of time at the "meta" level, unicorns can make adjustments in their own perceptions that others cannot.

A classic example of someone who used self-watching technique to solve problems was the famous scientist Nicholai Tesla. Tesla designed a new machine, built it, saw what worked well and what failed, made repairs to it, and retested it. He repeated this cycle relentlessly until no flaw remained. What is so astonishing about this feat is that it was done entirely in his own head without touching one piece of equipment!

As with otters, unicorns lead active fantasy lives, but unique to themselves, they are an active part of their own fantasies. Many tend to personalize the analogies and metaphors that they use to view the world or to solve problems. The great physicist Richard Feynman developed some of his ideas by "shrinking" himself to the size of a sub-atomic particle. Einstein came to his theory of relativity by asking himself what the world would look like if he took a ride on a beam of light. In keeping with their mythological image, unicorns seem to inhabit another world.

Motivational Aspects

With money the notable exception, the unicorn is almost exclusively intrinsically motivated. The work itself must drive the engines of productivity. Unicorns need the freedom to pursue even those lines of thought remote from the reaches of the organization's self-image. The ancillary spinoffs of such pursuits may well provide extraordinarily positive, but quite unforeseen, benefits. The unicorn is a fiercely independent creature who often follows a private dream in preference to the more popular benefits of security and job stability that large organizations offer.

Were we to select one word to describe the personality and motivation of unicorns, it would be *paradox*. Because their perceptions are unique and so distinctive, unicorns also tend to be somewhat insecure. They put more emphasis on money than do otters, who regard money as a "hygiene factor" (see motivational aspects of otters). However, although important to both eagles and unicorns, money has quite distinctive meanings for each. For the eagle, money may translate into power. For the unicorn, money is symbolic of acceptance and love, proving their value to the outside world. Most unicorns want the world to love what they create; from this love they derive temporary boosts to their self-esteem. They must then live with the paradox of believing in their own internal vision largely to the exclusion of others, and simultaneously, needing a high degree of affirmation from others, because sometimes deep down they feel that they may be totally wrong.

This paradoxical existence, a precarious balance between belief in self and self-doubt, is what makes them so creative; for every creative act is the resolution to some paradox (Gordon, W. J., 1980). The recognition that mutually exclusive states can functionally coexist has lead to some of the greatest breakthroughs in technology, art, and in new ways of doing business. The unicorn is a constant reminder of this fact.

Creating the Culture for Innovation

It is clear that for innovation of any type to occur, the right people have to be brought together in the appropriate culture. The question is invariably raised, "How do I identify these eagles, otters, and unicorns in my own business so that I can support them in a way that will make my company innovative?"

The question is a good one, but the answer is not easy. Because they are so rare, the unicorn is the easiest to spot; everyone is familiar with the company's resident genius eccentric with the unbelievable mind that never shuts down. Eagles and otters are harder to identify. They are more easily concealed in the bullrushes of daily corporate life, and tend to blend more closely with the cultural norms. The point, though, is that there are plenty of "undiscovered" innovators hidden out there waiting for the call to arms. For that call to sound, the culture needs to change as follows.

Cultural Needs for Innovation: The Eagle

If we could sum up the needs of the eagle in one or two words, they would be "organizational information". Eagles need to know how the power is structured, which way the organization is headed, how they will help the business to get there, and what the personal payoff will be. They need access to information from other departments that they feel might influence their work. The eagle needs to be given a clear vision of where the organization projects itself to be in the future, and what part each employee is expected to play along the flight path. This need can be termed *1. Strong Visionary Leadership.*" This is far and away more important than anything else a culture can provide—for both eagles and otters. Unfortunately, in most large corporations this is what is most lacking. Strong visionary leadership gives company players a window into the future—the ship of state or winning team metaphor—of where the organization wants to go and how both journey and destination will be achieved. Ideally, that image is conceived and developed at the top and carefully communicated to all organizational stakeholders (employees, owners, stockholders, and any client the organization seeks to serve). In reality, it is not that our business leaders are not bright, willing, and strong; in most cases they simply lack the guiding vision to promote innovation in modes 1 and 2. Why is this vision so important?

Vision Provides Alignment

A major block to innovation in any business is the interactions between departments. Each department has its private turf, seeming to operate independently of the others. But it's a costly war for independence.

About six years ago we were contacted by a large insurance company that was having difficulty achieving its main business goal. Two years before that, the key decision-makers had created a definition of the company's future. Their goal was simple: to become the "number one" insurance company in the U.S. When they called us, they were even further from their goal than when they began.

After some analysis, it became clear that divisions and departments were working at cross-purposes. The sales staff's idea of "number one" was different than the marketing group's; the actuaries and accountants had still other definitions. Because the groups didn't share a "visual definition" of the goal, they were finding it difficult to work together to achieve it. A common vision was needed which would yield a single purpose and the inter-departmental alignment necessary to achieve that purpose. Contrast this problem to Walt Disney's incredible success record due in large part to his ability to communicate his vision of the future to the world at large.

Visionary Leadership Aids in Creativeness

Every complex act of innovation involves change. Because the change involves a new departure from standard operating procedures, conceiving it is part of the creative act, one that relies on the ability to reevaluate or "reperceive" current reality. The innovator must ask, "How can I use what I have in some new way to get where I want to be?" However, if the goal is not sufficiently visual or specific, the individual contributor will have trouble shifting perceptions of present conditions to determine whether new ideas are synchronous with the goal. The cloudier the vision of the future, the more firmly rooted in the present is the individual contributor— and the more problematic the whole innovation process.

Vision Provides "Innovation Insurance"

A vision is a metaphor or analogy for some desired state. For a metaphor or analogy to work for a company, it should be an apt symbol of the desired state. One multifunctional group in an ad agency saw themselves as "MASH 4077". A technical/ manufacturing team in a large corporation seized upon the 1980 U.S. Olympic Hockey Team as their metaphor, while in still another corporation, one project team, lacking a designated leader, saw their interaction as a New Orleans Jazz jam session.

These analogies are powerful because they provide a base for problem solving in difficult situations. They become a continuing and fruitful "fountain of solutions" to unforeseen problems, providing a cheap form of "innovation insurance". For these reasons and many more, having a company or group vision and thinking in images about the future, is like reading a treasure map. You are shown the route, the milestones, and the X that marks the spot. What is left for the individual contributor is simply to read carefully, following the dotted lines, and dig.

Decision Makers as "Angels' Advocates"

A group of management people in a small midwestern corporation were having their weekly discussion of production problems and what to do about them. One of the talking points involved production loss due to the apparent lack of motivation or the packers group.

The packers were responsible for wrapping the product in newspaper, then packing it in boxes for shipping. The problem was that these workers spent more time reading the newspaper than packing the product. Needless to say, the packers' efficiency was far below par, regardless of how up to date they were on the news.

After the customary subject of motivational talks had been tossed around and wrestled to the ground, someone suggested using blank paper to wrap the product. The management group was interested at first, but later discarded the notion because of the unacceptable expense. Someone else proposed foreign-language newspapers. Although this was not a bad idea, it failed to pass muster because such papers are difficult to come by anywhere near the plant location. Finally, in final exasperation, one of the team's junior members blurted, "Let's just poke their eyes out! That'll stop them from reading".

No sooner had this "idea" been uttered than the head of the group said in his calm way "Let's hire blind people for the job". Eureka! Management spent the rest of the meeting discussing how to implement the "blind" revelation. Questions such as what do we do about the workers already on the line and how to keep the unions happy called for resolution, but after some modification the idea was implemented as a resounding success. Not only did the packers' efficiency show significant improvement, but the company rose to an important civic responsibility in the bargain.

The critical turning point in that meeting, the innovative idea, was *hiring blind people.* While "poking eyes out" was certainly an imaginative new perception, it took a second thinker

189

to modify and recast that idea into a viable plan of action. This is because the *Angel's Advocate* approach means looking at new ideas in terms of what is useful about them rather than why they won't work. It also involves taking what won't work and modifying it to develop an alternate idea that will. If we look at the mental mechanism that might have gone on for the Angel's Advocate in our management meeting, what's useful about "poking their eyes out" is that they would no longer be able to see. Now it became a relatively short mental jump to move on from "not seeing" to "hiring the blind". In other words, becoming the Angel's Advocate means looking for value in an idea that goes partway toward solving the problem, then fine-tuning it to fix deficiencies.

Contrast this case to what generally happens in business when new ideas are solicited from employees via the conventional suggestion box. The first week there are fifty ideas inside. The second week there are five ideas. The third week there is a wad of used chewing gum wrapped in an employee notice. Why does this happen? The reason is simple; we all have a natural tendency to go the other direction, to be "Devil's Advocates", looking for why ideas won't work instead of why they are useful. Why do we do this, when it does not really serve our best interests? Quite simply, because most of us don't really like to think. (When someone says that they are "lost in thought", it's generally because they're in unfamiliar territory!)

We look for "something wrong" with an idea for the reason that it can then be laid to rest so that we don't have to consider it further. Finding something wrong is an act of closure. On the other hand, when we see value in an idea, we then have to keep thinking about it. Since most bright people have their own thoughts and problems to work on, they have a need to dismiss unusual ideas, throwing the baby out with the bath water. But whenever the business culture (who really are the top decision-makers) can institute a mindset of Angel's Advocacy, it pays enormous dividends for innovation in all three modalities.

There is another angle. If we can discipline ourselves to keep from holding any one person responsible for 100% of any idea, not only will we be significantly more innovative as a company, but we need not ever compromise. In summary, then, the cultural norm needs to take the step from *"We give our entrepreneurs the freedom to fail"*, to *"We refuse to let our entrepreneurs fail"* by taking some of the responsibility for making their ideas work.

Rewards Based on Performance

One of the most important characteristics of creative people is what we might call the "fairness doctrine". The creative mind holds a slightly romanticized view of life, believing that great work should be rewarded and mediocre work should not. These are the types of people who, standing in line at the movie theater, will speak up and get highly agitated if someone tries to sneak into the line ahead of them. There is nothing so disheartening to the creative person (especially eagle and otter) than to see some "fair-haired boy" win a promotion every two to three years, when it is clear to everyone in the business that he has done nothing exemplary.

Creative people take things personally! They are sensitive to all that goes on around them and get depressed and demotivated when someone moves up whose work performance isn't consonant with his newly acquired position. As a result, the individual performers mentally "retire" from the business—either by leaving, or worse, by staying in place and simply failing to notify the personnel department of their attitudinal separation from the company.

Having consulted with close to 50 large corporations and small businesses, the most astounding thing we've discovered is the legions of the wonderfully creative who are actively in residence but whose lights are obscured under many bushel- baskets of organizational arbitrariness—what are perceived as unjust policies.

The way to resurrect them is to have clearly defined performance standards for all employees, and to reward them solely as a function of their adherence to these standards. This apolitical stance promotes the "fairness doctrine". When someone gets promoted, aside from announcing the event on the bulletin board, the addition of a clear rationale giving the reason for promotion goes a long way toward resurrecting many a mental retiree.

Creative Problem Solving in Training

As stated, it is relatively easy to develop the manipulative skills of eagle and otter. A number of companies specialize in doing this. Once people have in hand the domain-relevant skills, together with the cultural requirements necessary to release passion and perseverance, the largest payback from the training investment involved will be the sharpening of manipulative skills. Employees will see the power to create inside themselves that may have been dormant for a long time. The other benefit of this type of training is that employee attitudes about their work will change as they begin to appreciate problems as creative challenges to be overcome rather than as obstacles that shackle and trap them in a state of low-level frustration.

Cultural Requirements: The Otter

Like eagles, otters need visionary leadership and a culture of Angel's Advocacy, but the culture can motivate them best if they themselves are invited to participate in the development of the key vision. Otters pride themselves on their skills for imagining, but more important, there will be the greatest degree of overlap between their intrinsic motivation and the needs of the business, thus increasing the chances of innovation.

The most important thing the culture can do for them is to match their business work with their natural central interests, because otters create from the inside out, not from the outside in. Creativity for otters is a personal expression of solutions to their own discomfort with the way things are, not merely a targeted response to business problems.

Otters also need to be rewarded for performance, but not with the stress on money or power. Recognition is what they are after. Since by definition their perceptions are unique, there is always that insecure part of them that feels alienated from the world. They therefore need to be assured of the importance of their contribution and to feel valued for themselves. Dinners in their honor, or technical awards from peers, go farther to motivate them than raises or promotions.

Because of their need for blocks of time alone, otters require private inviolate spaces within the workplace where they can just put their feet up on the desk and daydream outside the view and hearing of others, tantamount to basking on the riverbank, mudsliding, or swimming to explore underwater. Many large companies provide just the opposite scenario by inserting everyone into modular cubicles on the "open plan" without "closure"—sometimes with a genuine interest in being more democratic. However, priding themselves on being different, otters must be treated with respect for that individuality. They do not flourish in bullpen settings.

Training Needs

The largest block for otters derives from their need to work outside the team structure. Unfortunately for them and for the business, while individuals create, innovation is ultimately a team effort, based not only on ideas but on implementation. Otters need the help of others to bring their ideas into the world as viable constructs and to be willful about implementing them in order to bring unique visions to life as commercial successes.

What is therefore needed above all in the human development sense are courses in "Creative Team Building" where otters can learn how to work productively and effectively with others to implement their ideas without compromise. A course promoting "Angel's Advocacy" will sensitize them to the needs and values of coworkers, whose support is essential to putting their ideas to work.

It might also be valuable for otters to sharpen their management skills, since their value to the company will multiply if they can creatively input on many projects, not just those of which they are the "sole proprietors."

Cultural Needs: The Unicorn

Unlike the other two types, unicorns don't need clear visionary leadership because they march to the beat of a different drummer. What they do need, however, is excitement! Stimulation must be built into the job or they get bored and mentally retire into their own baroque internal existence—where they would much rather play anyway.

How can the business culture optimize the atmosphere of excitement of unicorns? It can insure that they're turned on by what they're doing, as well as surround them with a select coterie of kindred spirits. According to a high-ranking Vice President of Research for a Fortune 500 company, there needs to be a "critical mass" of these people in close proximity. They continually stimulate and support each other, not only in the obvious intellectual ways, but also engender in one another a sense of belonging and trust, necessary preventives to ward off the strains of self-doubt and the onslaught of organizational nay-sayers who are so detrimental to the process of innovation. One other factor the culture needs to provide for these people: a high-ranking organizational sponsor, the modern-day equivalent of "patron," in the mold of the 17th-century European sponsors of artists and composers. This should be someone skilled at manipulating the organizational power structure, with influence over the resources necessary for the minimum of test-market implementation of a new idea. Because unicorns are so often obsessed with the problem and challenge of their work, they don't bother with the streetwise politicking and selling that also needs to be done. They are at times insensitive to the needs of others; thus the patron provides the "lubrication" necessary to clear the implementation pipelines.

Training Needs

The deepest gap for unicorns in leading rewarding and productive business lives is a lack of empathy and sensitivity to others. This occurs because they are such devoted slaves to their own internal visions. Courses in creative team building or high-powered sales training seminars given by dynamic and knowledgeable presenters go a long way towards helping them to engage other "less talented" employees in productive encounters, whether in meetings or one-on-one chance encounters in the halls, where so many important business decisions are in fact made.

Action Steps for Businesses

Businesses will be best served by identifying their in-house blockages to the innovative process, removing them and letting the creators emerge naturally. There are five main aspects influencing blockage:

1. The degree of intrinsic motivation in the work;

2. The type of decision-making system that deals with new ideas;

3. The degree of visionary understanding of organizational goals and how each worker fits into that picture;

4. The type of reward and recognition system that exist within the business;

5. Accessibility of inter-departmental information.

By far the most important of these is number 1. Following is an Innovation Audit that covers these five areas that we have developed and used in companies. Decision makers might consider having all key employees respond to this audit. As a result of that response, appropriate steps can be taken to modify the culture, and finally, reap the rich rewards that change yields.

Innovation Audit

Name (optional) _____

Department _____

Position _____

Please say as much as you want in response to these questions. Your responses will be kept confidential.

1. How excited are you about the work you do?

2. What are the things you value most about work in general and to what extent are they satisfied or missing in your day-to-day activities?

3. a) What are the things you dislike most about what you do? b) How might you change them and still get the work accomplished?

4. What else could be done to make your work more stimulating? (Don't limit yourself only to what seems practical.)

5. a) When and under what conditions do you get your best ideas? b) How may we translate that to the work environment?

6. a) In general, what kind of a hearing do new ideas get in the division? (Both yours and others.) b) What problems exist "selling" new ideas? (Both up the ladder and across departments.)

7. What is your personal view of where the organization is going and how you fit into the picture?

8. a) How available is information to you? a) About the general state of the business; b) From other departments that might impact on your work?

9. a) How consistent is the reward/recognition system in the division? b) Where are the problems and how might things be improved?

10. a) If your division could be compared to an animal, what animal would it be most like? b) What animal would you prefer it to be like.

11. a) What would you say are three important things we might do to increase our creative importance and that of others in your division? b) What might be some important first steps?

Summary

Innovation is not a simple entity. There are three basic types, each different in style and scope. In order to innovate, organizations need to decide a) what type is sought; b) what breed of creator is most likely to provide the breakthrough ideas, and c) how the culture can support the individual contributor. The environment in which productive work occurs varies from company to company, depending mainly on the motivational needs of individual contributors and their innovation profiles.

For each type of contributor the culture must supply three basic elements:

1) *Clear visionary leadership.* The culture must provide each individual with a clear picture of where the organization is going and how each person contributes to implementing that vision.

2) *Angel's Advocacy.* People in the business who evaluate new ideas must be disciplined a) to look for what's useful about the idea, and b) to help the individual modify the idea to fill in what's missing.

3) *Designated rewards for performance.* Rewards and recognition must be based on performance. Clearly articulated criteria for success must be in place so that employees know what is expected of them as well as what to expect from the business.

While the three different types of contributors in this review are sketched as strong and distinct profiles, it is recognized that creative people can be uneven blends of all three aspects (domain, manipulative, and motivational) as they play a role in innovation. However, experience teaches that the most important of these by far is the motivational component. ("It's your attitude, not your aptitude, that determines your altitude",) and also that the easiest to acquire with training is the manipulative component. We were all children once and can reawaken the instinct to play that is so important, as adults, in our work.

Notes

[1] These terms derive from asking business people to use metaphors for self identification during creative sessions.

[2] One or the biggest problems in organizations is that people change and grow, but the organization refuses to recognize the change, forever viewing them with that first impression made early on in their careers.

[3] One exception is the field of higher mathematics, where many key breakthroughs have been made by "newcomer" contributions under the age of 21.

References

Amabile, T. *The social psychology of creativity.* Springer Series in Social Psychology, Saratoga, NY: Springer-Verlag, 1983.

Gardner, H. *The concept of multiple intelligence, in frames of mind.* NY: Basic Books, 1983.

Gordon, W. J. J. *Private communication, lectures on creative performance.* Buffalo, NY: 1980.

Gordon, W. J. J., & Poze. T. *Conscious, unconscious interaction in the creative act, Journal of Creative Behavior,* 1981, *15,* 1–10.

Grossman, S. R., Rodgers, B., & Moore, B. *Innovation, Inc.: Unlocking creativity in the workplace.* Plano, TX: Wordware Publishing, 1988, 133–161.

Parnes, S. J., Noller, R. B., & Biondi, A. *A guide to creative action,* NY: Scribner Sons, 1977.

Stephen R Grossman, Double Dominance, Inc., Maple Shade, NJ (609-779-702)
Margaret J. King, Thomas Jefferson University, Philadelphia, PA.

Managing Creative People

Leonard M. S. Yong

Abstract

This article discusses three essential steps that are necessary for effective managing of creative people. It recommends that attention be paid to understand the nature of the creative process. It also suggests steps that can lead to better appreciation of the creative person. Thirdly, the paper outlines action that can assist to encourage a creative work climate.

In today's fast-moving and competitive business environment, most managers acknowledge the importance of being able to manage creative people in their organizations. Proper management of creativity is crucial for the development of an organization that can rejuvenate itself and implement continuous improvement in its business. It creates a work environment in which creativity is encouraged rather than inhibited.

Since creativity is so important for the organization, one needs to understand the nature of creativity. Just what is creativity? Can creativity be developed in individuals in the organization and how does creativity benefit the organization? These are some of the questions that often arise when this subject is discussed. Creativity entails the act of providing an inventive or original response to a problem that cannot be solved in a simple and straightforward procedure. Most people are not using the latent creativity that they have been endowed with hence resulting in performances much below their potential. And organizations are now learning to tap the creative potential of their employees for the benefit of the organization by managing creative people in a productive manner.

In order to manage creative people and to harness their creative energies for the mutual benefit of the individual as well as the organization, it is important to understand the creative process and appreciate the creative person. This in turn leads to steps that can be taken to encourage a creative work climate and finally to result in innovative breakthroughs for the organization that can give it a cutting edge in business enterprises.

Understand the Creative Process

What causes creativity in the individual? Can the creative process be managed and focused for the organization's benefit? Research in the last four decades suggests that the creative process can be understood. Joseph G. Mason sums up the research to indicate four principal characteristics: problem sensitivity, idea fluency, originality and flexibility. Studies on the creative process indicate that these characteristics can be developed to some degree in any individual.

Problem sensitivity is the ability to organize our perception and identify the real problem that exists. It is important for managers to develop problem sensitivity in themselves and their subordinates. Problem sensitivity can be developed when one appreciates the fact that every man-made situation, business operation or human relationship can be improved and someday would probably be improved. The creative process involves the ability to be sensitive to the existing problem or situation and to seize opportunities to recognize the challenge within an existing problem.

Idea fluency is the ability to generate a large number of ideas from which to choose. Research has indicated that the more ideas one has, the greater the likelihood of finding a usable solution. Delaying evaluation of the ideas during the process of generating ideas can facilitate idea fluency. Some devices can assist in the process of idea fluency. Note-making by writing down ideas that flash across our minds at odd moments or recording our observations of circumstances or opinions of problems can be one such device. Another technique for developing idea fluency is to use special times or locations in which we tend to be more creative.

Originality in the business context is the ability to find new ways to adapt existing ideas to new conditions. The manager can facilitate the development of originality in himself and his subordinates by encouraging an atmosphere of curiosity. The habit of always asking questions about a situation is a healthy one. Creative people are always asking questions such as: "Why do we do this?" "How can we improve this procedure?" "Is this really necessary?" Originality is nurtured when we are willing to challenge the obvious.

The fourth characteristic of the creative process is flexibility. Flexibility is the ability to consider a wide variety of rather dissimilar approaches to a solution. To be flexible, one needs to be aware of mental blocks that can lock a person into a fixed way of doing a particular thing in a specific manner.

Appreciate the Creative Person

After four decades of research, behavioral scientists have concluded that despite their unconventionality and individualism, creative people share a lot of common traits. They tend to be self-confident, independent and are risk-takers. This is not surprising since the creative person must dare to be unconventional in order to break free from the customary ideational constraints that make innovations impossible. In doing so, the creative individual risks putting himself open to criticism, failure and embarrassment.

Research data suggest that creative people can be extremely intense in their endeavors. They are able to be so engrossed and absorbed in their creative activities that they may lose their sense of time, working well into the night on an exciting project. They exhibit a high level of energy. They are also noted to be adventurous, playful and full of curiosity. They have a strong urge to understand the world about them.

Creatives can play a greater role in their work environments when their creative potential is harnessed and directed in the right direction. Then, instead of dissipating their creative energy, the creative executive can then be an asset to the organization as an innovator and idea generator. Furthermore they can then play a vital role in the organization whether they are the subordinate or the leader.

Managers who deal with a creative person should try to be very clear as to what the parameters are that they should work within. This can be done without stifling their creative potential if the existing limits are clarified at the beginning of the project. To enhance teamwork in a work team which comprise creatives, the team-leader may need to earmark special projects which can benefit from the extra efforts that will be put in by a creative person.

Creative leaders should consciously avoid being perceived as terse and abrupt with subordinates and colleagues in their intense desire to bring about improvements and changes to their work environment. They should develop more warmth and tact in their communication with others. Furthermore they need to be more aware of their tendency to sound condescending in their interaction with others.

Encourage a Creative Work Climate

It is important that managers encourage a work climate that can nurture creativity rather than inhibit it. Gary K. Himes (1987) suggests that an organizational climate that encourages creativity is characterized by seven attributes. (i) Good supervisor-subordinate relationships which can nurture an atmosphere of mutual respect for each other's ideas. (ii) Open communication that will enable free flow of information throughout the organization. iii) Active support and cooperation from management. A definite procedure is established for fair and consistent consideration of ideas conceived by subordinates. (iv) Attention to highly creative personnel. The person who has exhibited creative behaviors may be assigned work which enables them to have a respite from daily operating pressures. (v) Time to think. Allow moderate slack time which can provide opportunities for staff to think and engage in creative work. (vi) Avoidance of premature criticism. A manager should attempt to avoid premature criticism of creative ideas from subordinates. (vii) "Loose-Rein" management style in which management tolerates and expects a certain degree of reasonable risk-taking.

Perhaps the most significant element for encouraging a creative climate is the environment of trust that is developed by good supervisor-subordinate relationship. Michael Badawy, professor of technical management and applied behavioral sciences, gives some guidelines for managing a good supervisor-subordinate relationship. (i) Continuous feedback is essential for encouraging creative subordinates to persevere in their attempts for continuous improvements. Lack of feedback may cause frustration and indicate lack of interest on the part of the supervisor. (ii) Provide appropriate direction. The supervisor should be tolerant but not pamper. He must be able to distinguish between a creative person's legitimate impatience with unrealized possibilities and his petulance over failure. (iii) Know how to handle failures. The supervisor must know how to give his subordinates a wide margin for error in order for them to experiment, create and innovate. Without this, their fear of failure will destroy true initiative and stifle creativity. The fear of failure is more intense in larger bureaucratic organizations than smaller entrepreneurial settings. (iv) Maintain an intrapreneurial climate. Large companies are encouraged to nurture in-house entrepreneur development among their employees. Intrapreneurship has been adopted or tried by companies such as IBM, Hewlett-Packard, Texas Instrument and AT & T. (v) Balance the need for freedom and the necessity of structure. A combination of freedom and structure is necessary for the proper cultivation of creativity in the workplace. While freedom is important for innovation, structure is crucial for productive business.

Conclusion

In the decades ahead the business environment will have a greater need for creative and innovative management more than ever. It is clear that creative activity is imperative in the present competitive business environment. Organizations that neglect to nurture and cultivate creativity in their work place do so to their detriment. Those organizations which have already implemented some form of program to encourage creativity and to manage creative people within the organization have begun to reap benefits.

One of the immediate advantages for an organization that practices encouraging creative people in their midst is to harvest a greater commitment of the creative employee to the organization. This commitment serves as an invaluable resource that in the long run can yield unmeasurable benefits to the organization.

References

Badawy, M. K. (1987). How to Prevent Creativity Mismanagement. In A. Dale Timpe (Ed.) *Creativity.* New York: Kend Publishing.

Himes, G. K. (1987). Stimulating Creativity: Encouraging Creative Ideas. In A. Dale Timpe (Ed.) *Creativity.* New York: Kend Publishing.

Kuhn, R. L. (Ed.) (1988). *Handbook for Creative and Innovative Managers.* New York: McGraw Hill.

Mason, J. G. (1987). How to Develop Ideas. In A. Dale Timpe (Ed.) *Creativity.* New York: Kend Publishing.

Yong, L. (1989). *Creativity: A Study of Malaysian Students.* Petaling Jaya, Malaysia: Cordia Publications.

Yong, L. (1990). Creativity for Productivity in the Malaysian Context. *Jurnal Productiviti,* Malaysian National Productivity Centre. December 1990, n7, p. 37-43.

Yong, L. (1992). Characteristics of Malaysian Business Executives with the Creative Classical Profile Pattern. *Learning 2001,* Minneapolis, Spring 1993, v4, n1, 20-21.

Leonard M. S. Yong, Ph.D., Associate Professor, Faculty of Education, University of Malaya, 5910 Kuala Lumpur, Malaysia.

Leonard M. S. Yong, Ph.D., Associate Professor, Faculty of Education, University of Malaya, 5910 Kuala Lumpur, Malaysia.

CHANGE-MASTER COMPANIES: ENVIRONMENTS IN WHICH INNOVATIONS FLOURISH

Rosabeth Moss Kanter

Innovation and new venture development have no special origin. They may begin as a deliberate and official decision of senior executives, or they may be the more or less "spontaneous" creation of mid-level managers who take the initiative to solve a problem in new ways or to develop a proposal for change. Of course, highly successful companies allow both, and even official top-management decisions to undertake a development effort benefit from the spontaneous creativity of those below. But regardless of origin, for an idea to be turned into living reality capable of generating financial returns, certain organizational characteristics must generally be present. Those companies with high levels of enterprise tend to reflect these "facilitating conditions" for change more widely in their ongoing practices, as I show in *The Change Masters*.

Broadly Defined Jobs

Innovation is aided when jobs are defined broadly rather than narrowly, when people's ranges of skills to use and tasks to perform give them a "feel" for the organization, and when assignments focus on results or goals to be achieved rather than rules or procedures to be followed. This, in turn, gives people the mandate to solve problems, to respond creatively to new conditions, to note changed requirements around them, to improve practices—rather than mindlessly following "book" routine derived from the past. Furthermore, when less constricted definitions of jobs permit task domains to overlap rather than diverge, people are encouraged to gain the perspective of others with whom they must now interact. Such communication leads to employees taking more responsibility for the total task rather than simply their own small piece of it. This in turn generates the broader perspectives that help stimulate innovation. In areas that benefit from more enterprise and problem solving, bigger jobs work better. This is the principle behind work systems that give employees responsibility for a major piece of a production process and allow them to make decisions about how and when to divide up the tasks. Pay-for-skill systems similarly encourage broader perspectives by rewarding people for learning more jobs.

A proliferation of job classifications and fine distinctions between steps in what are really connected processes (e.g., the differentiation among many types of engineers specializing in only one step in a conceive-to-design-to-build process) has inhibited innovation in many large, segmented American companies. Individual jobholders need take no responsibility for ultimate outcomes as long as they perform their own narrow task adequately. When jobs are narrowly and rigidly defined, people have little incentive to engage in either "spontaneous" innovation (self-generated, collective problem solving with those in neighboring tasks) or to join together across job categories for larger, top-directed innovation efforts—especially if differences in job classification also confer differential status or privilege. Companies even lose basic efficiency as some tasks remain undone while waiting for the person with the "right" job classification to become available—even though others in another classification may have both skills and time. And people tend to actively avoid doing any more work than the minimum, falling back on the familiar excuse, "That's not *my* job"—a refrain whose frequent repetition is a good sign of a troubled company.

Examples of high-level entrepreneurial effort make clear this link between job definitions and the enterprise necessary for innovation. In some high-tech computer companies, people in professional and managerial jobs are regularly exhorted to "invent" their own jobs or are given broad troubleshooting assignments to "fix it" by "doing the right thing." Organization charts can be produced on demand, but by the time people add all the exceptions, the dotted lines reflecting multiple responsibilities, and the circles around special teams or task forces, the whole thing resembles a "plate of spaghetti," as one observer put it, more than a chain of command. While this situation can also appear chaotic and undisciplined, it does result in more people assuming responsibility to solve problems and make improvements, generating high levels of innovation in every function.

A major manufacturer of household products can cite numerous instances of spontaneous problem-solving effort by employees who are part of self-managed "business teams" responsible for producing their product in their part of the factory without supervision. Over the last 10 years, work teams have gradually taken responsibility for every function in the factory, and they conceive of themselves as "owning" and managing their own small business. To capture such benefits, New United Motor Manufacturing, the GM-Toyota joint venture in Fremont, California, has enlarged production jobs. Teams of five to twelve workers, guided by a team leader, get broad responsibility and divide up the specific tasks themselves; each worker is theoretically able to do any job. In contrast to the dozens of job classifications that existed when the plant was run by GM, there is just one classification for production workers and three for skilled trades.

Small but Complete Structures

When it comes to innovation, "small is beautiful," and flexible is more beautiful. Or at least small is beautiful as long as the small unit includes a connection with every function or discipline necessary to create the final product, as well as the resources and the autonomy to go ahead and do it. In order to get the kind of interfunctional or interdisciplinary integration that innovation requires, close relationships are required among those dedicated to a common business goal—working teams or venture teams that are functionally complete, on which every necessary function is represented.

This is why the idea of dividing into smaller but complete business units is so appealing to organizations seeking continual innovation. All the players are right there, linked closely in the innovation process. (And for all their cumbersomeness in practice, "matrix" reporting relationships acknowledging multiple responsibilities nurture interfunctional links.) In smaller business units it is possible to maintain much closer working relationships across functions than in larger ones—this is one of the reasons for Hewlett-Packard's classic growth strategy of dividing divisions into two when they reached more than 2000 people or $100,000,000 in sales. Even when economies of scale push for such larger units, the cross-functional project or product team within a single facility (captured in such ideas as the factory-within-a-factory) helps keep communications alive and connections strong. Similarly, the skunk works of creative innovators given their own charter and territory speed the development process.

Finally, it is important that those with local knowledge have the ability to experiment based on it—within whatever guidelines or limits are set at higher levels. Innovation is discouraged when those with the responsibility lack the authority to make those changes they feel will benefit their business.

Culture of People Pride

High-innovation organizations have in common the high value they place on people and their potential—what I have come to call a "culture of pride" that expects and rewards high levels of achievement and assumes that investments in people pay off. A mutual adjustment system of management, in contrast to a command system, requires a high degree of respect for people—not only on the part of the company but also on the part of all the players who must back and support one another's ideas.

The investment in people that characterizes high-innovation settings is slightly different from the more paternalistic principle of lifetime employment. While many high-innovation companies try to maintain lifetime employment policies that certainly offer security in exchange for loyalty, this by itself is not responsible for the level of enterprise found in them. Instead, it is the expectation of continuing growth of contribution over time that fosters more entrepreneurial stances. This is reflected in large dollar amounts spent on training and development—and in the emphasis on having the best human resource system possible.

Operationally, a "culture of pride" is fostered through abundant praise and recognition—a proliferation of awards and recognition mechanisms that continuously hold up the standards for display and publicly acknowledge the people who meet and exceed them. High-innovation settings are marked by celebrations and award ceremonies and trophies and wall plaques and merit badges and awards (e.g., "local hero" awards, "extra mile" awards, "atta-boys") that visibly communicate respect for people and their abilities to contribute.

Merit reward systems (as opposed to automatic cost-of-living adjustments with little or no merit component) also convey the company's recognition of performance. And so does rewarding people by giving them new challenges. Data General engineers say the rewards are like pinball—you win a free game, a chance to do something on your own.

Low-innovation settings, by contrast, seem begrudging about praise; they operate in ways that signal that all important knowledge comes from outside the company, and they expect people's recognition for achievement to be the fact that they have kept their job. I have even found a company that gives significant monetary awards for above-and-beyond contributions—but keeps these all secret.

Power Tools

The entrepreneurial process requires three kinds of "power tools" to move ideas into action—information, support (backing or legitimacy, appropriate sponsorship or championing), and resources. Of course, when large projects are initiated at the top of the organization and handed a staff and checkbook, there is little issue about acquiring the tools to accomplish innovation—although even in this case, managers can run across problems of access to things they need, whether people or facilities. But for instances of spontaneous entrepreneurship, generated within the organization and still lacking the status of a major and official project, access to power tools can determine whether bold new initiatives are ever seeded. Access to

202

power tools is easier in high-innovation settings because of organizational structure and practice.

Information

Information is more readily available in high-innovation settings because of open communication patterns that make data accessible throughout the organization. For example, operating data may be shared down to the shop floor or face-to-face communication may be emphasized or norms may bar "closed meetings"—all common practices in some high-technology companies. Both GE Medical Systems and Wang Labs have declared all meetings open to anyone. And Hewlett-Packard emphasizes on-line "real time" face-to-face communication through meetings instead of writing.

Support

Support or collaboration is encouraged in high-innovation settings by the dense networks of ties that connect people across diverse areas of the company—such as cross-discipline career paths, membership on task forces and cross-area teams, frequent conferences or meetings across departments, or even whole-unit parties like Silicon Valley's Friday beer busts that bring everyone together to rub elbows as equals. Easy access to potential sponsors or champions is also more likely when title-consciousness is minimal and the chain of command is not a pecking order. Tektronix, for example, has everyone on a first-name basis. Digital Equipment has its own helicopter service to allow everyone easy travel across seventeen New England facilities.

Resources

Resources are easier to get in high-innovation settings because they are decentralized and loosely controlled. More people have budgetary authority and can make commitments for "seed capital" for new activities. Or there are more sources of slack—uncommitted funds—that can be allocated to innovation. There are discretionary time and discretionary resources that can be managed flexibly, used for experimentation, or reinvested in new approaches. 3M is most noted for its internal seed capital banks and its 15 percent rule for technical people—up to 15 percent of their time can be spent on projects of their own choosing.

Overall, high-innovation companies are what I call "integrative"—pulling people together rather than apart. The jobs, structure, and culture all promote a wider feeling of responsibility and team consciousness that not only encourages the development of new ideas but also gives people the tools and the confidence to act on them.

Rosabeth Moss Kanter, Class of 1960 Professor of Business Administration, Harvard University

Change-Master Skills: What It Takes to Be Creative

Rosabeth Moss Kanter

Corporate entrepreneurs are people who envision something new and make it work. They don't start businesses; they improve them. Being a corporate entrepreneur, what I call a "change master," is much more challenging and fun than being a nonentrepreneur. It requires more of a person, but it gives back more self-satisfaction.

Change masters journey through three stages. First they formulate and sell a vision. Next they find the power to advance their idea. Finally they must maintain the momentum. I discovered the skills of change masters by researching hundreds of managers across more than a half-dozen industries. I put change-master skills in two categories: first, the personal or individual skills and second, the interpersonal ones, how the person manages others.

Kaleidoscope Thinking

The first essential skill is a style of thinking, or a way of approaching the world, that I have come to call "kaleidoscope thinking." The metaphor of a kaleidoscope is a good way of capturing exactly what innovators, or leaders of change, do. A kaleidoscope is a device for seeing patterns. It takes a set of fragments and it forms them into a pattern. But when the kaleidoscope is twisted, shaken, or approached from a new angle, the exact same fragments form an entirely different pattern. Kaleidoscope thinking, then, involves taking an existing array of data, phenomena, or assumptions and being able to twist them, shake them, look at them upside down or from another angle or from a new direction—thus permitting an entirely new pattern and consequent set of actions to take place.

Change masters, or the makers of change, are not necessarily more creative than other people, but they are more willing to move beyond received wisdom to approach problems from new angles. This is a classic finding in the history of any kind of innovation—that it takes challenges to beliefs to achieve a breakthrough. A large proportion of important innovations are brought about by people who step outside of conventional categories or traditional assumptions. They are often *not* the experts or the specialists. Rather they are "boundary crossers" or "generalists" who move across fields or among sectors, who bypass what everybody else is looking at to find possibilities for change.

Kaleidoscope thinking begins with experience not associated with one's own field or department. Moving outside for broadened perspectives was the common foundation of every innovation I studied. A woman change master at a computer company began an important project this way. She got her assignment, and the first thing she did was leave her area and roam around the rest of the organization, talking it over with nearly everyone she could find, regardless of field, looking for new directions, new perspectives, new ways to approach it—so what she could bring back would be new and creative. She did not start with what she already knew. She started with what other people could bring her: she crossed boundaries to do that.

This is how many important changes have been seeded. For example, frozen vegetables were invented by Clarence Birdseye, owner of a produce business at the turn of the century. The conventional wisdom of his time, like that of our time, held that the best way to run a business (or a department) was to "mind the store"—managing one's field and only one's field, watching it like a microscope image, getting better and better at knowing and doing just one thing. But Birdseye was an adventurer, and so, like many change masters, he wandered away from his store and his scope; he passed beyond his territory, quite literally, and went on expeditions. On one of his adventure trips, fur-trapping in Labrador, he discovered that fish caught in ice could be eaten much later with no ill effects. He brought that idea back and transformed his business from a local produce store to the beginnings of national distribution.

Organizations that seek innovation ought to learn from this kind of experience: allow people to move outside of the orthodoxy of an area, to mix and match, to shake up assumptions. One chief executive believed that such thinking was so important to his organization's success in a high-tech field that he staged a highly imaginative top management meeting. He took his top fifty officers to a resort to hold their annual financial planning meeting. Though it started out just like their usual meetings, he wanted this year to be different. He was concerned that they were getting stuck in a rut and that he was not getting much creative thinking, though his company needed innovation for survival. He made the point symbolically. Halfway through his talk, the meeting was suddenly interrupted by a cadre of men dressed as prison guards; these rather realistic toughs burst into the room, grabbed everybody there, and took them out to a set of waiting helicopters, which flew the bewildered executives off to a second meeting site. "Now we'll begin again," said the CEO, "and we will bury all the thinking we were doing in the last meeting and approach everything from a new angle. I want new thinking out of you." He continued to punctuate the meeting with sets of surprises, like a parade of elephants on the beach. First there was a small elephant and it had the natural financial goal painted on its side, then along came a bigger elephant with a bigger number, and then a huge elephant with a huge number, and he said, "Go for it! Stretch your thinking! " The symbolism of the whole meeting was to stretch, move outside, challenge assumptions, twist that kaleidoscope.

Communicating Visions

The second conclusion I drew about change masters' individual skills was their ability to articulate and communicate *visions.* New and creative ideas and better ways to do things come not from *systems* but from *people.* People leading other people in untried directions are the true shapers of change. So behind every change, every innovation, every development project, there must be somebody with a vision who has been able to communicate and sell that vision to somebody else (even when the change begins with an assignment, not a self-directed initiative).

Though innovation is a very positive term, it is important to remember that any *particular* innovation is only positive in retrospect, *after* it has worked. Before that, because change by definition is something no one has seen yet (despite models that may exist elsewhere), it has to be taken at least partially on faith. For example, why a continuing education program now? Why use funds to develop a new product when there are so many already on the market? Why take the risk of decentralizing the accounting office? In short, unless there is somebody behind the idea willing to take the risk of speaking up for it, the idea will evaporate and disappear. One reason there is so little change in most traditional bureaucratic organizations, I argue, is that they have conditioned out of people the willingness to stand up for a new idea. Instead, people learn to back off at the first sign that somebody might disapprove.

This second change-master skill can be called "leadership." Martin Luther King's famous speech in the March on Washington personified this as "I have a dream." He didn't say, "I have a few ideas; there seem to be some problems out there. Maybe if we set up a few *committees*, something will happen." But when I see managers present their ideas in just this sort of well-if-you-don't-like-it-that's-all-right way, I can understand why so many are so ineffective in getting new things done. Each innovation, shift, or novel project—even the noncontroversial and apparently desirable ones—requires somebody getting behind it and pushing, especially when things get difficult, as they always do when change is involved. This kind of leadership involves communication plus conviction, both energized by commitment.

Persistence

Leaders of innovation persist in an idea; they keep at it. When I examined the difference between success and failure in change projects or development efforts, I found that one major difference was simply *time*—staying with it long enough to make it work.

To some extent, *everything* looks like a failure in the middle. There is a point or points in the history of every new project, every original effort, every fresh idea when discouragements mount, and the temptation to stop is great. But pulling out at that moment automatically yields failure. There is nothing to show just yet. The inevitable problems, roadblocks, and low spots when enthusiasm wanes are the critical hurdles in achieving a healthy return on the investment of time and resources. Without persistence, important changes never happen.

In large organizations, the number of roadblocks and low points can seem infinite, particularly when something new is being tried. There are not only all the technical details of how the new program is going to work, but there are also all the political difficulties of handling the critics. Naysayers are more likely to surface in the middle than at the beginning because now the project is more of a threat, more a challenge to their own perceived status. There is little incentive for critics to tie up political capital by confronting the project until it looks like it actually may happen. This is a reality of organizational life.

At one major consumer products company, this phenomenon was demonstrated all too well. Today, the company has a highly successful new product on every supermarket's shelves. But when this project was in the development stage, it was known as "Project Lazarus" because it "rose from the dead" so many times. Four times people at higher levels tried to kill it off, and four times the people working on it came back and fought for it, argued for it, provided justification and evidence for why it should continue: "Just give us a little more time; we know we can make it work."

Every organization has examples like this one. If the team had stopped, the effort would have been a total loss—confirming, in a circular way, the critics. But arguing for the additional time and money and confronting the critics transformed a potential failure into a ringing success.

Coalition Building

In addition to the personal skills of change masters, interpersonal and organizational skills are also required. The first of these is coalition building. At the point at which there is a creative idea, with someone with vision behind it willing to persist, it still has to be sold to other people in the organization in order to get implemented.

Though the literature on organizational politics has emphasized one-on-one relationship building, my research moves the emphasis to the coalition. What makes people effective in organizations is the ability to create a whole set of backers and supporters, specifically for projects of innovative activities, that helps lend the power necessary to vitalize those activities. In this sense entrepreneurs inside a corporation are just like entrepreneurs outside: They have to find bankers, people who will provide the funds; they have to find information sources; and they have to find legitimacy and support, people who will champion the project to other powerholders.

Multiple, rather than single, sponsors and backers make the difference. An attractive young woman who now holds one of the top six positions in an American corporation began as assistant to the chairman and was subjected to many innuendoes about their relationship. But she proved to be a highly effective change master in her organization, responsible for many successful new projects, because she is a superb coalition builder, drawing hardly at all on her relationship with the CEO. She brings others into projects; she works with peers and people below to make them feel included. She creates multiple relationships and teams around her by giving people "stakes" in each project, solidified by promised personal benefit. Because of her coalition-building skills, she led successful change projects that in turn brought her recognition and early promotions.

Coalitions are especially important when change is needed because innovation—new projects or developments—generally involve going outside of current sources of organizational power. My research found that managers who wanted to innovate, or try something new, almost invariably needed more resources, information, and support than they had. They often needed money above and beyond their budget (though sometimes not much)—because usually their budget was for the routine, things they were doing, and if they wanted to do something novel, they had to find extra funds. They also needed higher levels of support because innovations sometimes interfere with ongoing things in an organization. Change is often resisted because it can be a nuisance and an interference; it requires other people to stop what they are doing or redirect their thinking. And new efforts also tend to require special information, more data, new sources of knowledge. Thus, the change masters I studied *had* to build a coalition in order to find the backers or "power sources" to provide information, support, and resources for their projects.

Coalition building not only attracts needed power to a project, it also tends to help guarantee success. Once others are brought in and contribute their money or support to a project, they also have a stake in making it work. Their reputations (and egos) are now on the line. As a result, the innovator is not out there all by herself, trying to convince a reluctant organization to do something. There are now other people to serve as cheerleaders.

This process of coalition building is so well-known that some companies have invented their own language around it. They call the whole process one of getting "buy-in" or generating wider "ownership" of a project from key supporters. First is a low-key step of gathering intelligence and planting seeds—just finding out where people stand and leaving behind a germ of the idea to let it blossom. Then the serious business of coalition building begins in the process they call "tin-cupping." The manager, symbolically, takes his or her "tin cup" in hand and walks around the organization "begging" for involvement, seeing who has a little bit to chip in, who has a few spare budget dollars to invest, who has a staff member to lend, who will be on the advisory committee, or who has key data. In the process of tin-cupping, two vital organizational functions take place that guard against failures. First is the "horse trading" required. For everything that is dropped into the tin cup, people have to feel that they get something back. Thus, one person's project has to be translated into something of wider benefit around the organization—which helps ensure success because it has support. And, second, in the course of tin-cupping, an innovator also gets a "sanity check"—feedback from "older and wiser heads" helping reshape the idea to make it more workable. (The only failures at innovation that I saw in high-tech firms occurred when the manager thought he or she already had so much power that coalition building was unnecessary.)

Coalition building, therefore, provides not just personal or political advantage; it is also an important process for making sure that the ideas that do get developed have merit and broad support. It is a form of peer control, a way of screening out bad or nonimplementable proposals. For this reason, top management at one computer company is more likely to provide large allocations for ideas that come with a coalition already formed around them.

Working through Teams

Once a group of supporters has been generated, it is time to get down to the actual project work. Now the next interpersonal-organizational skill comes into play: the ability to build a working team to carry out the idea.

Very few ideas and very few projects of any significance are implemented by one person alone: Other people's effort makes it happen— "whether they are assistants, subordinates, a staff, a special project team, or a task force of peers assembled just for this effort. But regardless of who the people are, it is critical that they feel like a *team* in order to make any new idea work. My research documents the importance of participative management when change is involved even if it is not necessary for managing the routine. Full involvement turns out to be critical when the issue is change.

For a routine operation in which everybody knows what they are doing high involvement and high intensity are less critical. But change requires above-and-beyond effort on the part of everybody involved. It requires their creativity and their commitment. Without such general cooperation, those trying to make something significant happen in an organization run forever uphill. Help is hard to find. Peers find other priorities; reports are late. When dependent on other people to get the job done, one must engage them. Everybody in an organization has at least one form of power—the "pocket veto." Even without directly challenging an idea, all one has to do is sit on it for a while, put it in his or her pocket, not respond, find other projects more important—and the change effort will be stalled. Loss of momentum occurs when other people are not motivated to do their part.

The development of a new computer at Data General illustrates the process of team building. Tom West, the middle manager behind this development team, worked extraordinarily hard to create a self-conscious sense of *team*—team play, ownership, and identification. He led young engineers who were just out of school to perform engineering "miracles"—record-time achievements that no one predicted. Their intense sense of ownership came from a team identity, symbolized by names (the "microkids" and the "Hardy boys"). The team genuinely had a mission. They also had fun together. They were given full responsibility and were always informed. They had room to make mistakes. West, the manager, supported by two assistants, did not impose his ideas on the team. Indeed, when he had solutions to problems, he sometimes went to the lab late at night and left his ideas on slips of paper for people to find in the morning—without knowing how they got there. Thus, he created an atmosphere in which people felt autonomous and in control and consequently became incredibly dedicated and committed to the project.

Sharing the Credit

Finally, bringing innovation full circle, people who lead changes share credit and recognition—making everyone a "hero." Instead of simply taking individual credit, change masters make sure that everyone who works on their effort gets rewarded. This behavior brings back benefit to the change master. I saw this dramatically illustrated in an insurance company. A manager had led a series of employee involvement projects that improved productivity in his region and boosted the firm's overall profits. At bonus time, his superiors were going to reward him with a fat check. He asked if he could also have bonus money for the people below who had also contributed to his efforts. Management, unfortunately, turned him down. So he took several thousand dollars from his own pocket, collected contributions from peers, and made up his own bonus pool for everyone down to the clerks who had contributed. That made people feel that their least effort was rewarded and they looked forward to participating in the next organizational improvement. Change became an opportunity rather than a threat.

For many people, projects of change and innovation become the most significant things they have ever done in their work lives. I have interviewed people who had spent 30 years in a big bureaucracy who said that the 6-month development task force was the only thing they were excited by and the only thing they would be remembered for— change was their mark on the organization.

Change, the development of something new, unleashes people's creative energy. It is exhilarating, stimulating personnel in a way that routine work cannot do. Giving people the opportunity for innovation and recognizing them for it fulfills both organizational and individual needs.

Rosabeth Moss Kanter, Class of 1960 Professor of Business Administration, Harvard University

A PLACE FOR CREATIVITY:
THE HALLMARK INNOVATION CENTER

Charles W. Hucker

"I began to write short pieces when I was living in a room too small to write a novel in."

Angela Cartwright, American Writer

Environments *are* important to creativity. Some inhibit creativity by being too dark, too loud, or too cramped. It is hard to be creative if you are uncomfortable. The myth of the starving artist in the garret producing great works of art is just that—a myth. When great works of art are produced under such conditions, it is usually *in spite* of the environment, not *because* of it. On the other hand, creativity flourishes when tools, support, and inspiration abound. An environment can inspire creativity by being beautiful or unusual. It can foster creativity by allowing freedom or feedback. "Places don't create, people do," is an oft-said aphorism. True. But it is also true that a place can *help* a person to be more creative.

Creativity is of great importance to Hallmark. That's why in 1984 we decided to build a place for nurturing ideas, a structure for stimulating creativity, a center for innovation. That idea place, the Hallmark Innovation Center, was designed to foster creativity and innovation by providing a stimulating environment in which different groups of employees could easily exchange ideas. The two-story, 170,000-square-foot center houses Hallmark staff from Advanced Technical Research, Equipment Engineering, Product Innovation, and the Creative Workshop. The building is adjacent to the main Hallmark facility at corporate headquarters. It is accessible from the main building, but still, it is a separate structure—a place set apart. About 180 employees are housed in the Innovation Center permanently; others rotate through, staying for several months at a time to explore technologies and expand vision.

Mixing Ideas

Society's shorthand for the birth of an idea is a light bulb going off above a lone person's head. Often, though, the real process is neither sudden nor solitary. It involves people talking together—sometimes in an office, sometimes in a lab, sometimes over a cup of coffee. Such creative brainstorming is what the Innovation Center is all about. People from one discipline—say, engineering—work with people from another, quite different area—maybe design. They come up with new ideas. (Whether these ideas become new products depends on needs and demands of the marketplace.) Consultants who help corporations and individuals foster creativity say collaboration is necessary for innovation. "It's important to cross-relate the senses," says one creativity specialist. "When groups of people with diverse training work on a project, they mix their vocabularies as well as their ideas."

I like wandering through the Center. The last time, I met a project engineer who was experimenting with enamel glazes. We talked about an informal workshop he had led the day before to teach a group of artists how to use enameling. Then our conversation turned to creativity and how it is aided by such exchanges of ideas. "Creativity is basically finding the best solution to a problem," the engineer told me:

> Here, you can walk one way and find a chemist or another way and find an artist or down the hall to find a press operator. With two or three spheres of knowledge, instead of just your own, you can find many fresh ideas to solve your problem. The more options you have, the better decisions you make. The more options you have, the more creative you can be. You hear a lot of "What about this?" "What about that?" around here. You've got no excuses when you're in this place. If you have energy to seek a solution, you can find it.

Designed for Communication and Inspiration

The whole atmosphere of this idea center has been to encourage collaboration—not only in formal sessions, but in labs, lounges, and lunch rooms. In designing the Innovation Center, we went to an architectural company known for creating structures that serve the function of the building. "We set out to design a building in which people mix as well as match," said Lewis Davis, one of the partners. "The Center is much like a very small town in which everyone understands what the other person does for a living. That sort of familiarity, mutual respect, and cohesiveness leads to more bright ideas and enhanced productivity."

The building encourages a free flow of information; communication is key to the design. That design is a constant, subtle reminder that the function of the building is the exchange of ideas. Conversation lounges and a small food service area promote employee interaction. The lower and larger floor consists of an open area the size of two football fields, adjoined by laboratories for traditional processes such as gravure, lithography, die cutting, and silk-screening, as well as electronics, lasers, ceramics, and plastics. Glass-walled conference rooms and work areas allow the Center's staff to see what others are doing. Doors—when they exist—are often open; many times they are literally holes in the walls. The Center's office walls are chest-high to encourage informal exchanges and drop-in meetings.

I once noticed three people sitting at a table in a glass conference room. Their coats were off; the meeting was informal. They were discussing jigsaw puzzles. How did I know? Through the glass I watched their gestures; through the open doors I heard their conversation. Then a fourth Hallmarker walked by and glanced in. One participant called to him. "You might know the answer," she said. A few minutes later, the meeting was over. Together, they had solved their puzzle problem.

"Too frequently a research facility looks like an ordinary factory. Little or no attempt has been made to produce an environment for innovation—to stimulate creativity or productivity of the R&D staff through design and setting." So states a call for entries in a laboratory design contest. Not so with this structure. The way things look is very important to Hallmark. After all, part of what we sell is beautiful design. It is essential that the structure of the Innovation Center support the function of its inhabitants. Light and color are critical ingredients in the

211

development of our products. The Center reflects that importance with its teal-and-burgundy color scheme and its unique lighting system, which combines natural and artificial light. To achieve this, a corridor around the main work space allows all employees access to windows. In addition, ninety pyramid-shaped skylights provide even, indirect lighting throughout. At dusk, photoelectric cells trigger fluorescent lighting to give the illusion of daylight. "There's something about the atmosphere here," said an artist working on new products. "It's more than just the physical atmosphere, although the physical dictates the mental. You feel really free here. You feel that it's okay to do something that's never been done before."

Creativity Comes in Many Packages

The Innovation Center has evolved from years of searching, testing, and evaluating new ways to encourage the free exchange of ideas with the purpose of developing new products. Our Humor Workshop is a good example. Here, ten cartoonists work on projects of their own choosing in an office outside the main building. In a sense, the workshop operates like a freelance studio in which the cartoonists develop product ideas to "sell" to the company's product management staff. The workshop is filled with visual humor designed to stimulate the cartoonists' creativity. Take Earnestine, the workshop's receptionist. Earnestine is a life-sized soft-sculpture dressed as a 1940s telephone operator who sits in the anteroom by a welcoming sign that says "Go Home." Inside the workshop, cartoonists work on a variety of work surfaces ranging from roll-top desks to workbenches and wooden doors. An occasional stained-glass window, rubber chicken, or gorilla mask adorns the ceiling and walls. "In the workshop, it is creativity through inspiration, not requisition," said the Humor Workshop founder. "It makes a difference."

We have experimented with other methods for stimulating creativity through environment. For example, we occasionally send a group of creative writers to a hotel room to eat pizza and brainstorm for writing ideas. We also send creative staff members to cultural centers—such as Paris, London, Milan, New York, and Los Angeles—to soak up ideas that might lead to products down the road. And we offer stimulating "get-away" places right in the building—libraries, lounges, and fine art displays—in which people can talk about projects and exchange ideas.

The Hallmark Creative Workshop, which is now housed in the Innovation Center, has been around for almost 20 years. Many of the idea-place concepts from the Creative Workshop have been expanded and applied to the Center. Thirty-five permanent staff members work in the Workshop's Model Shop, Plastics Lab, Process Development Shop, and Design Staff. Their job is to develop new products and new ways to use the company's manufacturing equipment. The workshop is an idea place, a locus in which innovation is part of the job. It's a good example of how the Innovation Center works.

Three times a year, a "rotation group" of nine or ten artists enters the workshop. They spend 4 months there, working with permanent staff and experimenting with novel production techniques and product ideas. The workshop is *not* a pot in which artists and press operators are boiled together to make some sort of social expression stew. It is a mixture rather than a melding, in which each participant remains individual and identifiable, but in which all add their own flavoring to the whole.

With the average tenure of permanent workshop employees at 27 years, you might expect some job burnout. "The operators still look at the workshop with inquisitive eyes," said the shop section manager. "Being fascinated, being interested in new ways to do things, that's written into the job description." " 'No' is not a word we use here," added the workshop director. "If an artist asks, 'Can you run this wrench through the press?' the press operator will say, 'Yes, but if I do, the press will break.' Trying to see if something works is the best way to learn."

The right attitude aids innovation. There was an artist in the Plastics Shop who had a reputation for poking through workshop trash cans. She would take "ruined" projects and experiment with them, viewing them in different ways. Cracked plastic might look like trash to most people, but to this artist it was treasure: a new technique that could give a card a brittle, ancient look. That vitality, that sense of wonder, is part of the history of the workshop, where they say "a mistake is only a mistake if you throw it away."

Working with the technical staff in this compressed, miniature manufacturing department, artists expand their vision—seeing what they rarely see while hunched over drawing boards. And that's a two-way street. Technicians often develop a method or material for which there seems no use. But the artist will look at it from a strange angle and suggest possible applications. Suddenly, a new product idea emerges. A press operator and design supervisor, working together to produce a new kind of ornament, chatted about their "creative combustion" theory. "Two or three people will be thinking about a project," the press operator said. "We all build on each other's ideas. We stand around saying, 'This sounds crazy, but . . .' Somehow, out of all the craziness, we figure out how to turn an idea into a product." The design supervisor agreed: "These fellows have lots of ideas. We artists have lots of ideas. When we get together, interesting things happen."

In Virginia Woolf's essay *A Room of One's Own,* the writer asserts that people cannot write unless they have a place to write. Place. It is often so ignored and always so important. We want our people to have a place in which just looking around stimulates ideas and encourages pursuit. We want our people to have a place big enough to write novels as well as short stories.

Charles W. Hucker, Divisional Vice President, Public Affairs and Communication, Hallmark Cards